Acclaim for Dav

IN NEVADA

"In this witty account—the polished notes of Thomson's personal inspection of the state—tourists, prospectors, gamblers, and native Nevadans come and go, meeting now and again as though they were random characters encountering one another in the Black Rock Desert."   —*The New Yorker*

"An unusual and unusually erudite book that is surely one of the best recent studies of America and the West."   —*The Oregonian*

"Mr. Thomson is one part John McPhee and three parts Don DeLillo. . . . His triumph is that he situates the wonderful accident of Las Vegas within the larger context of Nevada, and reveals the city's slot machines to be just one manifestation of a greater American phantasmagoria."

—*The New York Observer*

"Thomson finds Nevada both beautiful and terrible, and he does it justice in his surreal and scary book."   —*The Observer* (London)

"Thomson's take on Nevada is learned and wry. You can't help but feel his fondness for the audacity of the place, which comes across as a vast, running social experiment: often appalling, sometimes noble, forever fascinating."

—*The Denver Post*

"Thomson builds a brilliant portrait of this surprising place."

—*The Sunday Times* (London)

"Thomson is the perfect arbiter of the strange wondrous absurdity of Nevada. Thomson is a highly gifted stylist and one who treats Nevada like a smashed mosaic."   —*The Independent* (London)

DAVID THOMSON

IN NEVADA

David Thomson is the author of *A Biographical Dictionary of Film* (three editions); *Beneath Mulholland: Thoughts on Hollywood and Its Ghosts*; *Showman: The Life of David O. Selznick*; *Rosebud: The Story of Orson Welles*; and three works of fiction: *Suspects, Silver Light,* and *Warren Beatty and Desert Eyes*. His writing has appeared in *Film Comment, Movieline, Vanity Fair, The New Republic, Esquire,* and *The New York Times.* Thomson lives in San Francisco with his wife and their two sons.

Douglas—
A Nevada memento,
Happy Birthday dear friend
and Happy Trails,
always,
Sally

ALSO BY DAVID THOMSON

The Alien Quartet

Beneath Mulholland: Thoughts on Hollywood and Its Ghosts

Rosebud: The Story of Orson Welles

4-2

Showman: The Life of David O. Selznick

Silver Light

Warrren Beatty and Desert Eyes

Suspects

Overexposure

Scott's Men

America in the Dark

A Biographical Dictionary of Film (three editions)

Wild Excursions: The Life and Fiction of Laurence Sterne

Hungry as Hunters

A Bowl of Eggs

Movie Man

IN NEVADA

It is a desert kingdom, with many monuments and ruins, and lights in the sky.

IN NEVADA

The Land, the People, God, and Chance

DAVID THOMSON

Original photographs by Lucy Gray

VINTAGE DEPARTURES
Vintage Books
A Division of Random House, Inc.
New York

FIRST VINTAGE DEPARTURES EDITION, OCTOBER 2000

Copyright © 1999 David Thomson

Grateful acknowledgment is made to the following for permission to reprint previously published material:

Raybird Music: Excerpt from "Twisted," music by Wardel Gray and lyric by Annie Ross. Copyright secured by Raybird Music. Reprinted by permission of Raybird Music.

The Walter Van Tilburg Clark Estate: Excerpt from Nevada poem from *City of Trembling Leaves* by Walter Van Tilburg Clark (New York: Random House, Inc., 1945). Reprinted by permission of the Walter Van Tilburg Clark Estate.

The Library of Congress has cataloged the Knopf edition as:
Thomson, David, [date]
In Nevada : the land, the people, God, and chance / by David Thomson. 1st ed.
p.   cm.
Includes bibliographical references and index.
1. Nevada—Description and travel.   2. Nevada—history.
3. Nevada—Social life and customs.   4. Thomson, David, [date]—Journeys—Nevada.
I. Title.
F845.148 1999
979.3—dc21
99-15605
CIP

Vintage ISBN: 0-679-77758-X

Author photograph © Penni Gladstone
Book design by Virginia Tan
Map by David Lindroth

www.vintagebooks.com

Printed in The United States of America
10 9 8 7 6 5 4 3 2 1

for Jim Toback

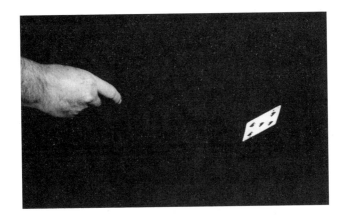

People living east of the Sierra Nevada Mountains and west of Salt Lake lose contact with the outside world as winter snows cut off all communications. The greatest cry from the people is for mail. Congress passed a bill August 18 1856 providing for a post route from Placerville, Calif. to Genoa, Utah Territory. So far no one has come to accept the mail-carrying job this year.

—Notice in the *Sacramento Union* that inspired
John "Snowshoe" Thompson to be the
first mailman in Nevada

Insert key into lock. Light will turn green. Pull door handle toward you slightly. Turn key toward hinge side of the door. Please engage privacy lock while in your room. Upon exiting your room, please confirm that your door is securely closed.

—Instructions on use of room key for residents
at Bellagio Hotel, 1999

CONTENTS

ACKNOWLEDGMENTS

I WAS READING BOOKS ABOUT NEVADA BEFORE I'D GONE VERY far in the state itself, and I thank their authors and the people who proposed the books: *Learning from Las Vegas*, by Robert Venturi, Denise Scott Brown, and Steven Izenour (MIT Press, 1972), mentioned by Fred Stout (it was also Fred and Lisa Ryan who first uttered the code words to the night, "Art Bell"); *Basin and Range*, by John McPhee (Farrar, Straus and Giroux, 1981), suggested by Amy Nathan; and *The Big Room*, an extraordinary evocation in text and drawings by Michael Herr and Guy Peellaert (Pan, 1986), given to me by Lee Goerner. I also thank Erwin and Marianne Jaffe, who recommended the books of Walter Van Tilburg Clark.

Then I need to thank Tom Luddy, who first showed me Las Vegas and drove me from there to Telluride, Colorado, and back. This was to attend the film festival, and I hope he has forgiven me for finding the landscape he unfolded even more impressive than the films. After that, I remember attending an antiquarian book fair in Manhattan with Sonny Mehta. We found a map of old Nevada, and as I talked about it he seemed interested—I think it was interest, though Sonny seldom makes such things unequivocally clear. Anyway, years later, he commissioned this book—and it turned out that he had published *The Big Room* in London.

In Nevada itself, nearly everyone helps you. This is not just a way of flattering the subjects of this book. Rather, it is an observation to be made about strangers encountered in the West, and one that I like to put up against the legend (current in the East and beyond) that they likely will kill you. On the contrary, the people at filling stations and motels, the guys sitting down at the other end of the bar, the valet parking men at the

Mirage or the cops from Winnemucca who cannot quite credit the speed you were doing, the people encountered at otherwise empty crossroads and those sitting next to you at the rodeo are nearly always amiable, helpful, generous, decent, and dry storytellers once you get past the shyness of those who disagree with you about 90 percent or so of history, fate, and fun. I thank them all, and trust that they will abide. It has required special qualities of faith, courage, and hoping for the best to live and stay in Nevada.

More particularly, in Nevada, I want to thank the staff, management, and ownership of the Mirage, the Bellagio, and New York, New York; Jim Allison of the Tahoe Regional Planning Agency; LaTomya Glass and Derek Scammell at the Nevada office of the Department of Energy; the staff of the Liberace Museum; the staff at the Nevada State Museum, especially Denise Sins for her drawing of the Spirit Cave Man; Kathy Wan, at Special Collections, in the University of Nevada, Las Vegas, Library; Marc Ratner at the Nevada State Athletic Commission; Suzie Cochran at the Nevada Department of Prisons; Richard Wade at the Electoral Division of Clark County; Lee Brumbaugh, the curator of photography, and Lee Mortensen, the librarian, at the Nevada Historical Society; the staff (especially Marice) at the library of the *Las Vegas Sun*; everyone involved in a trip to the Nevada Test Site; Paul and Jenn Sherer for offering their house in Truckee as a base; Julie Shafer and Phil Halperin for helping me with the Tahoe experience.

I have friends who talked about Nevada, sent me newspaper stories, and tapes of music to play on the long drives: Ken Conner and Mark Feeney were notable in their number (and the best tapes, I found, were Mahler, John Coltrane, and the recorded talks of Alistair Cooke).

At publishing offices, Jon Segal treated the book with his customary care and insight, and breathed deeply over all my thoughts of unusual illustration; Alan Samson gave very thoughtful comments on the text, and I hope I was smart enough to benefit from them. Otherwise, I would just say that the staff of Alfred A. Knopf as a whole (though few of them have spent time in Nevada) are as amiable and reliable as the state's citizens. Those thanks extend to Ida Giragossian, Virginia Tan, Kathleen Fridella, and Laura Goldin. Though not a member of my publishing houses, Jenny Turner (my editor at the *Independent on Sunday*) was kind enough to read the text and apply to it her sense of prose and my failings therein. Lorraine Latorraca turned untidy pages into disks with her usual expertise.

Finally, I thank two people: Jim Toback, a friend of twenty years now, a marvelous talker on any subject, but truly someone who has had ups and downs in Nevada, and who has responded by writing *The Gambler* and *Bugsy*, two of the best films about Nevada; and my wife, Lucy Gray, who took the photographs in such a way that I was able to find evidence of all my mysterious feelings about the place. It has been a pleasure to supply a text for her.

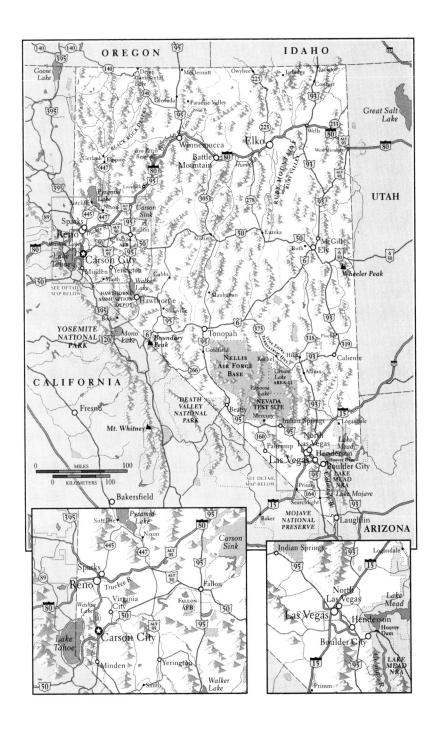

PART ONE

Prospects

It reads like a wild fancy sketch, but the evidence of many witnesses, and likewise that of the official records of Esmeralda District, is easily obtainable in proof that it is a true history. I can always have it to say that I was absolutely and unquestionably worth a million dollars, once, for ten days.

— Mark Twain, *Roughing It*, 1872

*More or less the heart of Nevada, at Austin on "the loneliest road
in America," where you meet Highway 376 and make a choice between
Ely (148 miles) and Tonopah (118)*

1. Setting Out

I'M NOT SURE WHY I FEEL COMPELLED TO TELL YOU THIS straightaway, for it was a plan I abandoned thoroughly long ago. Still, it did occur to me once to make my book about Nevada the journal narrative of some kind of investigator—he was maybe a simple-enough researcher, a lone and altruistic inquirer after truth, equipped with his own eyes, his mind, and a fairly reliable vehicle. Then at other times, I had a notion that he was grant-aided and burdened with a camera, a sophisticated video camera, one that could even operate on its own, panning and zooming at random. So the researcher might sit nearby, sipping a cold beer while the camera observed, recorded, and took in the beautiful emptiness and the just as tranquil, patient uneventfulness of Nevada.

But then, somehow, he was to begin to believe that he was being followed, and that his investigation—as it were—was being tracked by others (readers? or one of those "theys" we dread?). Had his witless camera seen some stray gem or germ of story, or minable intrigue, that his eye had never noticed? Had his inquiry stumbled on a secret? Or was the sense of secrecy just a measure of the odd loneliness, and its fever, that sets in as you drive through those places? After all, while some have said that, sooner or later, all the paranoids and conspiratorialists go to Nevada, others believe that it is the deep and ultimate vacancy of the place that stimulates storytelling. It is a great state for the kinds of belief that challenge reason, judicious observation, and the general reluctance to be carried away.

On the other hand, the sublime distances prompt thoughts of nothing more sweet or beguiling than being transported, carried off, of being in a state of traveling, as in a car at 80 miles per hour, or on a moving camera tracking over the speckled desert. These distances are all scientifically measurable: You can make notes from the odometer; you could, with surveying instruments, turn the haze and the vista into mathematics. You can work out the distances, the square mileage, the meager rainfall, or even the specific density of Nevada. You could map it all, and tell yourself that every page or portion of the state was available as an inch-to-the-mile diagram, or whatever. But put the map beside a photograph—more or less any photograph—and you cannot really avoid the indicators that the distance, the space, is more than the numbers. It is a romance and an idea—like "over there" or "once upon a time."

Well, it was the end of the decade, the end of the century. It was the millennium up ahead, and few could disown or deny the nervousness that was creeping in. On the great radio show that comes out of Nevada, Art Bell (a hero I pray not to meet, for distance is his enchantment) was talking of "the quickening."* He meant by that the rash of extreme weathers affecting the Earth, and the mounting scale of "incidents" in and around Nevada—the sighting of UFOs, or lights in the sky; the calm reports by ordinary people of how they had been taken away and examined by aliens; and so on. And the quickening was something that had the need of some great crisis ahead—Y2K, 2000, the collapse of economies; the sudden draining away of hope and human nature; a month in which no casino jackpot paid off (or every one did, breaking the bank), the necessary reprisal of some god or other. You never know—God save us, and let us never know.

And my thoughts—my interest in the real history, and even my urge to make a book—turned to Nevada. I wasn't quite sure why, and I used to enjoy being bland and helpless when people asked why. "I don't really know," I'd say. "It's this urge I feel." As if the whole thing were a love affair, or some kind of magnetic attraction. I began traveling in the state, driving, following the empty roads and the off roads, stopping here and there. This developed over a period of years, and I picked up history and anecdote as I progressed. But the idea of a book set in when I realized how much I was moved by the desolation, and its stories, and how much I wanted to explain or explore that feeling.

So the book begins with journeys, or traveling—for space here is history, time and again. The journeys are not unduly "organized"; they do not follow on or link up; but the driver, the eye, and the wonderings are all the same. Of course, you might analyze the drives I report here, and see a pattern—as if my car were really a UFO making certain mathemati-

---

* Art Bell is discussed more fully later. But, for those who don't know, he runs a nocturnal talk show out of the town of Pahrump.

cally aligned "passes." The alien looks at Nevada? Looking for a retirement place, like so many others? No, I am too young by far for that. And surely if I were an alien, I'd have been told. Wouldn't I?

Yes, that's right, I haven't really mentioned Las Vegas yet—and some believe that Nevada is nothing but that unique international city, not just the fastest-growing metropolis in the United States but an abiding El Dorado, or Hell, for the rest of the world. Have no fear: We do get to Las Vegas eventually; we will play its games and run its stories. But Nevada is much more—and was, for ages, before Vegas was ever thought of. And may be again. For the desert and desertedness are the true character of the state, and there is no proper getting to Vegas without crossing the desert first. That is how you can see its glow reflected in the sky, so that you wonder if it is burning already. And, as we shall see, in Nevada, there is burning for a moment, like a struck match, and being on fire for eternity.

All that is a way of saying that this book begins with travels in empty places and then moves south to consider Las Vegas and those other experimental places close to Vegas. So, be patient, for everything I describe has been here a long time already, and will see us off without stirring.

2. Burning Man

It is three days before Labor Day, 1997, and I have elected to drive north from Lake Tahoe. On the face of things, this is an error, or absurd; yet it has that hint of the perverse — or the blind hunch — that recurs in many things Nevadan. In this last week of August, in the flawless light, the waters of Tahoe are alive with every blue and green they are known for. The crowd at the lake is gathering for summer's last weekend. Every tee time at the Incline golf courses is taken. At Sand Harbor, families are staking out their bit of beach with umbrellas, barbecue equipment, ice chests of beer and soda, rubbery playthings for the kids, the Jet Skis and the water skis, and the wet suits that, even in late August, most people prefer in or on the riot of gorgeous fauve blues in the cold, cold lake. It always seems like a strange godly mistake that such blues are not warm or gentle. But gentleness is seldom in Nevada's nature.

I am driving north to a tiny town called Gerlach, some 120 miles from the northern shores of Tahoe. This road goes by way of Reno and Sparks and then into a kind of desert where there is very little in the way of "society." That escapist mood has often led me to Gerlach, which is, by many standards, an insignificant, wretched place, not worth going to. But I respond to the speeding emptiness of the road there, and the added feeling that Gerlach is the entrance to, or the last outpost before, the bleakest, least inhabited, or known, part of Nevada.

That northwest quarter goes another sixty miles or so to the border with Oregon. It has few paved roads, nothing like a township, and, in the ordinary way of things, as you drive there, you see very few vehicles. Anyone wanting to sense the landscape, the history, and the dangerous appeal of Nevada needs to go to that lonesome northwest quarter, which is another world from Tahoe's loveliness or the stunning, packed solitude of

Las Vegas. After all, Las Vegas and Gerlach are more than five hundred miles apart; in that many miles, you could go from the middle of Manhattan to the desolation of Appalachia. But on that journey, you would have markers to let you feel the transition. Going from Las Vegas to Gerlach, you are only passing from one desert town to another in a place where pride and vanity have to cling to the arid ground, praying for survival or dreams of destruction.

Going to Gerlach, one is countering the route taken by John Charles Frémont in 1843–1844, and that famous "pathfinder" had one of his most difficult times there. This was Frémont's second expedition, one in which he had gone across the south of modern Idaho and into Oregon, before turning south. Just after Christmas 1843, he and his party descended beneath the line of Oregon's southern border; by doing so, they were entering Spanish America, Mexican territory, illegally. Quite quickly, they came into the rolling sage flats, the mountains, the playa, and the black volcanic ground that are northwestern Nevada. There were twenty-five men, and a diminishing herd of pack animals—the mules were perishing, being eaten, or stolen, by the Paiute Indians. Frémont's men had a cannon with them, a howitzer. There was some snow during the daytime, and great cold at night, and they had eaten the last of their beef cattle. That famous scout Kit Carson was with them, but they admitted to themselves that they were lost and in dire need of some haven. Whereupon, on January 10, 1844, they came upon "a sheet of green water, some 20 miles broad." At first, they thought it was Mary's Lake (a phantom, reported by earlier explorers). But this lake fit no other description, and as they fed on the trout that were so easy to catch, they saw that curious upthrust of rock in the lake—just like the pyramid of Cheops, Frémont thought—and called it Pyramid Lake.

The lake remains, of course, longer than Tahoe, if never as wide. It has some of the same cobalt blues, but Pyramid has nothing like the riches of mountains and trees that surround Tahoe. Pyramid is a lake in a desert; it is warmer than Tahoe, and the mineral-rich water is more buoyant. You can fish and boat there, and some do, but it is by permission of the Paiutes, for the lake is part of an Indian reservation. In other words, it was left to the native peoples, while Tahoe was appropriated for modern America in all things except its name.

You can imagine today the relief that Frémont and Carson felt when they found Pyramid Lake. Still, there is something a little unearthly or lunar about the place. Put it this way: Tahoe is alpine, thronged with settlements and activities; it is an intense attraction. Pyramid, fifty miles away, seems deserted or neglected—it seems lost nearly, and a harbinger of the country to the north.

I press on. This is August, and the temperature will get into the nineties. I have a phone in the car for safety's sake. I loop around the lake to the south, go through the little town of Nixon, and then due north to Gerlach. This, on most days of the year, is a road where drivers might dream or doze. It is the kind of fatuous Nevadan road that goes fifty or sixty miles without much of a waver or bend. There are playa flats to the east—shimmering salt-colored dry lake beds, often firm enough to drive on, but sometimes slippery and fragile and so muddy that a car can become trapped. There are mountains to the left, graveled slopes that spill down to the road, and just the occasional sign to some ranch that may still be buried in those hills, or abandoned years ago. This is the land where Frémont became anxious coming south, not so very long ago—154 years is a blink in Nevada, like a lizard moving its eye to make sure it's alive.

There is some traffic this day. I come up behind a wildly painted bus, lumbering along because it is old and because it seems to carry a lifetime of camping gear as well as mountain bikes tied onto its roof. It has a slogan on its front that I have to decipher in my rearview mirror: EVEN FURTHER. Is that psychedelic bus just dragging itself northward until it collapses? Would people go farther into such a desert, just to see the fires of glory? Was that what Frémont and the other pathfinders were looking for? Did they mean to find a new world fit to be turned into Southern California suburbia, or did they aspire to a desert that caught fire and sometimes merged with Heaven's radiance? The American frontier has turned out so practical, so banal, but do not doubt the great urge to transcendence those things mask. Or the speed with which the mask can burn off, like morning mist.

Going north on the road (it is 447), you see the top of Granite Peak rising up ahead of you, and then you see the town of Empire on a ridge ahead, six miles short of Gerlach. Empire has a store and a one-pump gas station by the roadside, and there are signs out today encouraging passersby to fill up *now*. What a name for a town here—Empire!—it would fit some circle of hovels deep in the jungle in a Conrad story, where man's hubris has gotten out of hand. Yet this Empire is not a mockery. It is the base for a large factory, the U.S. Gypsum works. The houses in the town must accommodate the factory workers, and there is even a perfunctory, tatty golf course between the factory and the houses—pitch and putting, I think of it—called the Burning Sands Golf Course.

From Empire, the road drops into a bright white valley, flat and polished, a playa table, beyond which, at the foot of Granite Peak, one can see Gerlach. From afar, going across the playa, it could be a ghost town—a ghost town lost in all the white gypsum. But just before the town, one comes to the railroad: I once waited there at the crossing for a Union Pacific freight train of fifty-one cars (it is the line coming west from Winnemucca). As it enters Gerlach (population 350), the road curves to the left and so runs east-west between the railroad and the buildings of the town: a motel, a few bars, a civic center. In thirty seconds, you are out of the town and heading north. You can stop in Gerlach for a beer. Legend has it that one of the bars serves a good ravioli if the owner is around. In one bar, I saw a letter from Craig Breedlove, the high-speed driver, asking locals to keep the playa in good shape to aid his forthcoming attempt upon the world's land-speed record.

It's clear where such a driving "track" might be found, for the Black Rock Desert begins at Gerlach, stretching to the northeast and into its own infinity. That desert goes for over fifty miles, and after fifty miles, there is nothing but mountains and canyons until you come to towns like Denio or McDermitt on the Oregon border. This is one of the emptier quarters in the continental United States. But today, the traffic is building. On the road ahead, I might see five or six vehicles in a row on stretches where I would normally meet nothing.

But this is a few days before Labor Day, and by recent tradition, somewhere or other in or on the edges of the Black Rock Desert, there occurs what is known as the Burning Man Festival. About twenty miles farther up the road, north from Gerlach, just before it becomes a dirt road, in Hualapai Flats, there will be an event that comes to a climax after dark on Labor Day when the assembled people enter into the ritual burning of the figure of a man that stands maybe twenty-five feet above the playa. This year, it is reckoned, somewhere between fifteen and twenty thousand people will be there.

The camp is clearly visible from the road—tents, cars, camping RVs, all stretched out in rows on the playa. It is a great campsite, but there are no facilities. Every bit of food and water, every sound system, every piece of performing art, every grain of mind-altering substances—all have to be driven in to this place where the temperature will reach ninety degrees at least and then fall precipitously at night. And maybe twenty thousand people—hippies, if you like, crazy kids, freaks, pagans, ravers, and not many of them Nevadans—will be there for three, four, five days and nights, going naked, fucking like bunnies, stoned out of their minds. And maybe having the kind of intense experience that can never be ruled out in desert places.

There will be more to say about the Burning Man, but I mention it so early on because it relies upon a remote place and the extremism or way-wardness of going there. Only when these things are granted can one begin to grasp the power of Nevada as a place and as an idea. Or the significance of fire. Let us just say that whereas the use of cremation in the United States as a whole is just under 20 percent, in Nevada it is an ecstatic 55.

3. Frémont
and the Howitzer

JOHN CHARLES FRÉMONT SHOULD NOT BE PASSED OVER quickly. This crucial explorer, soldier, and politician was a burning man, if you like, a perilous mixture of courage and recklessness, of outward show and introspection. Few were cool about him: He made great friends and fierce enemies; he was admired and deplored; he had a long list of coups, and disasters. It is the pattern of a gambler, not so much professional as innate. As one of his biographers, Allan Nevins, puts it: "Frémont's habits and impulses were essentially restless and kinetic." He has to be regarded as one of the first Nevadans, someone profoundly American and inspiringly devoted to the idea of America, yet headstrong and imperious and so sure that *he* knew what America was and what it might become. The frontiersman was always someone looking to act on his own opinions—and then ratify the boldness with some seal of state.

Frémont was born in Savannah in 1813, the son of a woman who had left her husband and run off with a romantic but impoverished Frenchman, Charles Fremon (it tells us something about John Charles that he adapted his surname in two rather clashing ways—adding an American *t and* a French accent). He was expelled from Charleston College, largely because he had forsaken school to pursue a young woman. He reckoned that the punishment was "sweet as a perfumed breeze."

Handsome, flamboyant, and the proud bearer of his own scandal, he early gained the company of rich, powerful people like Joel Poinsett, a traveler and diplomat who would become secretary of war. Poinsett also helped form the Army Corps of Topographical Engineers and gave Frémont a position on an expedition to explore parts of the West, led by the Frenchman Joseph Nicollet. That journey, made in 1838, in the area of what would become North and South Dakota and Minnesota, was a training ground for surveying, geology, botany, mapmaking, and the crucial business of report making. For there was an enormous appetite in the eastern United States (and in Europe) for reports on the immense scale, spatial emptiness, natural beauty, and opportunities of the West—as great a place as it was an idea.*

When Frémont returned with Nicollet, he was twenty-six and an adventurer, with great tales to tell and the dark tan of experience. This was the young man who won the affections of the fifteen-year-old Jessie Benton, the daughter of Senator Thomas Hart Benton of Missouri. Jessie was more than just a kid and a beauty; she was the more intensely attractive for her wit, her acumen, and her practical ambition. (We must not be surprised if Americans continue to believe in astonishing, inspired, and inspiring teenage women—Jessie Benton was one of those who helped give credence to the myth.) Thomas Hart Benton (1782–1858) had been a newspaperman before he got into government, and he was a leading advocate of the theory of manifest destiny, which held that the United States of America had a natural, unstoppable right and duty to claim and develop all of its landmass, "to overspread the continent allotted by Providence for the free development of our yearly multiplying millions." Of course, in the early 1840s, Oregon was still a territory held jointly by the United States and Britain, while everything south of that was owned by Mexico.

Frémont wooed Jessie Benton in the face of her father's disapproval—and this father was a man of ugly temper. But in October 1841, with Jessie only seventeen, the two were married. The father, when he learned of it, ordered his son-in-law out of the house, insisting that Jessie stay. But Jessie—like a heroine in a D. W. Griffith film—held her husband's arms and quoted the book of Ruth: "Whither thou goest I will go; and where thou lodgest, I will lodge; thy people shall be my people, and thy God my God!" Benton had the sense to know he was in a melodrama, and to divine his role in it. He relented, and straightaway snapped up Frémont as the ideal man for manifest destiny.

In 1842, therefore, Frémont was off on the first of his famous expeditions: a survey of the routes to Oregon, which called for accurate mapmaking. It was a venture of exploration and topography, to be sure, but for Benton, its sponsor (he got $30,000 out of Congress for it), the intent was to bring back an advertisement for western expansion.

---

* This had begun with Lewis and Clark. They made their exploration of the Northwest in the years 1804–1806. But Lewis's death prevented the publication of his journals for nearly one hundred years.

Statue of Kit Carson (by Buckeye Blake, 1989)
on the lawn outside the Nevada State Supreme Court
in Carson City

With Kit Carson and a German mapmaker, Charles Preuss (who secretly scorned Frémont as a show-off and an inept leader), the party ventured deep into the Colorado Rockies. It was Frémont's plan to ascend the highest peak there. He got it wrong. There are more than fifty higher peaks than Frémont's Peak in the same Wyoming Rockies. Never mind— there was enough of the publicist in Frémont to know it would do if he took a bottle of brandy and an American flag to someplace and then brought the story home.

He was back in Washington by late October 1842. A few days later, Jessie gave birth to their daughter. Despite this distraction, she took his dictation—and listened to his tales—and composed the official account of the journey. Congress was so enthusiastic over this wondrous amalgam of scientific report and adventure story that it printed ten thousand copies. As such, it had an enormous role in establishing Frémont as an American hero, and in making the West a desirable place. Jessie was a real writer, and Frémont had been there. The two of them, and Benton senior, had a vision of what might be. Their collaboration was a lovely version of the American dream, and you can see and feel it in Albert Bierstadt's huge landscape paintings and John Ford's movie views of Monument Valley. Here is the report on seeing a herd of buffalo:

> In the sight of such a mass of life, the traveler feels a strange emotion of grandeur. We had heard from the distance a dull and confused murmuring. And, when we came in view of their dark masses, there was not one among us who did not feel his heart beat quicker. It was the early part of the day, when the herds were feeding; and everywhere they were in motion. Here and there a huge old bull was rolling in the grass, and clouds of dust rose in the air from various parts of the backs, each the scene of some obstinate fight. Indians and buffalo were the poetry and life of the prairie, and our camp is full of their exhilaration.

Yes, it read like a brochure, and neither Jessie Benton nor her father had been there. Yet I feel a reverence for that writing and for that perception of the West. Never doubt the way in which men and women have been and are still moved by the space, the light, the landscape, and the prospect of the West.

I am writing this book out of the same romance, and I hope I may leave you wanting to go there, to be there, to see and feel it for yourself. At the same time, the romance of America has always had one hand on its own pulse and one eye on the movie rights. It is Wordsworth's *Prelude*— and the pantheistic recollection of the boy in Cumbria—as told by Mickey Rooney. Be offended, if you must be; but do not think that any American can shrug off that intricate load of playing himself.

Does this seem difficult to follow, too tricky, or too close to self-deception for comfort? Well, let me add this story, one that brings Frémont back to Nevada. There were immediate plans for a second expedition, with Benton and the Corps of Topographical Engineers as sponsors again. Its ostensible purpose was to map out harbors in the northwest. By May 1843, Frémont was gathering equipment at Kaw Landing, the staging area of St. Louis. It was there that he acquired his cannon— actually a howitzer that fired twelve-pound balls. Why a cannon? To overawe Indians, maybe; to serve as some insurance against any confrontation with the British or the Mexicans—if, by chance, the party wandered south; and just to have a cannon—in the way boys like toy guns. The howitzer was never fired in anger, and some argued that the same weight in beans would have been more useful.

But that is not the story. Word of the howitzer reached Washington and raised alarm. Would a skirmishing incident spur war with Britain or Mexico? The head of the Topographical Corps, Colonel Abert, immediately wrote to Frémont demanding an explanation or the abandonment of the journey. The letter was opened by Jessie (by then in St. Louis), and stifled. That is the story: that Jessie took it upon herself to smother the official question, and instead sent her husband a simple imperative—set forth now: "Only trust me and Go." In fact, her letter arrived late. Frémont had already departed. It was the Frémonts' subsequent self-dramatizing (and surely this is the scenarist's "improvement" of the facts) that added the suppressed letter and the urgent note.

And so, with Broken Hand Fitzpatrick, Joe Walker, and Kit Carson as scouts, Frémont set out on that second expedition, the one that led him, against official orders, south of the Oregon line, down by way of Gerlach to Pyramid Lake—the howitzer always being drawn along on its carriage. That second journey was filled with dangers, errors, and signs of Frémont's recklessness—indeed, he may have been saved from starvation and being stranded in the snowy Sierra only by the mildness of the 1843–1844 winter. (Three years later, the Donner Party, only a few miles from where Frémont had been, paid the price of variable winter.)

Frémont came south from Gerlach to Pyramid Lake, and from there close to the site of Reno. He had a weary band of men; nevertheless, at this point, mid-January, he elected to go up into the snowy Sierra. He wanted to find a way into California. And so they left the safety and agricultural plenty of the Truckee Valley in search of a pass. The climbing was arduous, the animals suffered badly, and the food was running low. The howitzer was useless and heavy. On February 14, from the south, they saw the expanse of Lake Tahoe—they were the first "white" men to see it. Not far from there, they were compelled to abandon the clumsy cannon, and so at last, in early March, the desperate men found a way down the mountain slopes and into the Sacramento Valley.

It was a triumph, and nearly a famous tragedy. They had found not just Tahoe but also the essence of northern Nevada (the Spanish word means "snowfall"). In blissful ignorance, they had nearly trudged over the site of what would be immense gold and silver mines. The report of this second trip was once more the work of husband and wife. It sold another ten thousand copies, and it was as inspiring as the first. It was also filled with errors, so that the Mormon trips west, encouraged onward by the report, made Brigham Young one of Frémont's sourest critics. But Young had another romance in his head.

4. Mormon Stories

ALWAYS STORIES. MYSELF, I BELIEVE IN VERY LITTLE EXCEPT those who believe in stories. It is enough, and story is an arc of hope that can contain gold in the ground, beating the house in Las Vegas, and God, wherever He may be. Here is a story:

Joseph Smith was born in Sharon, Vermont, in 1805, two days before Christmas. He was raised in Palmyra, New York, by a mother who believed that he had taken on the power of mystical insights. When Joseph was seventeen, he reported that the angel Moroni had visited him in a dream, or some moment of heightened being. Moroni told Joseph to dig in a place not far from his home, and when he did so, Joseph found a set of pages, or tablets, made of pure gold. The pages bore writing—hieroglyphics, or what Joseph called a "Reformed Egyptian" text. He could make nothing of them, but the same hole contained a pair of spectacles that magically converted the hieroglyphics to English. Moroni told Joseph that no one else was to see these tablets or pages. So Joseph put up a large sheet of cloth to block the sight, and he then dictated the English text to his wife, Emma.* Once that was done, the tablets were to be destroyed, quickly, and Joseph, undoubtedly, believed every word of what he uttered, which helps account for the special American difficulty in distinguishing among confidence men, geniuses, and prophets. The dictated work was called the Book of Mormon, because the hieroglyphic text was the work of Moroni's father, Mormon. It told of how, some six hundred years before the coming of Christ, God had sent some of the faithful from Israel to America. That band split into two

---

* Is this a pattern? The man recounting the story; the woman writing it down—and improving it?

tribes: the fair-skinned, who were "delightsome," and those with red-brown skin, who were "wild and ferocious." These burning men won the war between the two, and the tablets were buried by Moroni, the last of the fair, after the final battle. Joseph's assignment (if he accepted, I suppose) was to reestablish the true Church. The Book of Mormon was published in 1829, and within a year, the Church had a thousand members. By 1832, Brigham Young, a painter and carpenter in upstate New York, had joined up.

As quickly as the Church grew, so it became the object of fierce opposition and physical attack. There were those free, critical spirits who loathed theocracy and Smith's assertion that he knew all the answers, including the guaranteed salvation of his flock if they obeyed and handed over a suitable tithe of their earnings. Then there was the business about Mormons believing in polygamy, a practice that might have killed that God-fearing American pursuit, infidelity. The Mormons were persecuted wherever they tried to come to rest. The Book of Mormon was burned; a settlement in Independence, Missouri, was broken up. Some dissenting Mormons had found the courage to oppose Smith: They disapproved of polygamy and his authoritarian ways. They set up a newspaper to voice their feelings, and Smith had it destroyed. Thus, he and his brother were jailed for a constitutional violation—abusing the freedom of the press. Illinois militiamen killed him in jail in Carthage in June 1844.

Brigham Young carried the Mormon Church through this turbulence and proposed that the entire faith be removed to that empty land, the West. He himself led a pilgrimage, or a wagon train of 150 people, from the Mormon city of Nauvoo, in Illinois, on the banks of the Mississippi. In July 1847, from a height in the Wasatch Range, Young saw the Great Salt Lake and what was the beginning of the Great Basin and declared, "This is the right place."

Young was an inspiring leader, a very practical, hardworking man, and he founded not just a strong Church but a city and a powerful moral force in the history of the West. Salt Lake City grew fast; it was a center of agriculture and industry, and a model city. By 1849, the Mormons applied for statehood. They were turned down, in part because of the ugly talk of polygamy, but also because what Young proposed as the State of Deseret (named after the honeybee, the ideal worker in the Book of Mormon) was to include not just what we now call Utah but also most of Nevada and Arizona, along with some of California, Oregon, and Colorado. Still, in

1850, Congress did confirm the new Utah Territory, which included all but the southern tip of what is now Nevada.*

It was in the spirit of that settlement that in 1855 Governor Young sent thirty men to establish a colony at Las Vegas. At that time, Las Vegas had no people other than Paiute Indians, though it owed its name—"the Meadows"—to exploring Spanish priests who had found springs and a welcoming campsite on travels from Santa Fe to California in the last quarter of the eighteenth century. Also, in 1829, Antonio Armijo, leader of a Mexican wagon train, had used the site of Las Vegas to discover a pass through the mountains to Southern California (what we now call Route 15).

In other words, Las Vegas was always something of a haven in the arid desert, a place with its own water (three natural springs), with trees and flowers. Led by William Bringhurst, the Mormons made camp, held services, and (with the help of Paiutes) built a fort, 150 feet square, with walls 14 feet high. A fragment of that fort may still be seen in Las Vegas; it stands in juxtaposition to the thriving business role that Mormons play in the city and the state.

Even if there were springs, and some shade there, building an adobe fort in Las Vegas in summer would have involved labor in temperatures over one hundred degrees. Set that achievement beside the pampered state of visitors now in the air-conditioned churches of fantasy and transformation known as the Mirage, the Grand, the Luxor, Excalibur, or Treasure Island. When people ask me, as they have, "Why a book about Nevada?" (which some think means simply Las Vegas), I like to pose the transition of 140 years, say, in which the proud fort at Las Vegas becomes the Strip of today. That "story" isn't really that much more far-fetched than the one Joseph Smith told.

Put it another way: The great state of Nevada—and you must read the name with a short second syllable, so that it echoes not *larder* or *harder*, but *sadder, madder,* or *badder*—occupies an area of 110,540 square miles; the area of Great Britain, from whence I came (without any vision or dream, except for the movies), is 88,745 square miles. The population of Great Britain is close to 60 million. The combined population of New York State and the New England States is approximately 31 million; and

---

* Nevertheless, there are western travelers who still use the name Deseret and honor its unity—and sometimes this book goes beyond the strict borders of Nevada (into Deseret) to talk of things that are relevant and of the same broad locality.

the landmass of this area—New York, Maine, New Hampshire, Vermont, Connecticut, Rhode Island, and Massachusetts—is only about 5,000 square miles larger than that of Nevada.

Yet the population of Nevada in the 1990 census was 1,201,833. That was a subject for marveling and speculation, for ten years earlier, the state had a population of only 800,493. In other words, it had grown by 50 percent. That was a record, but only just; in 1970, the figure had stood at 488,738. For over twenty years now, Nevada has been the most rapidly expanding state in the union. There are many reasons for the state's government and business to be cheerful about that: It means more building and increased property prices, more jobs and prosperity—it means "progress." But there are still Nevadans who lament the leaping growth, for they treasure a place that is capable of desolation, solitude, emptiness, and that stirring notion, desert. There were citizens of Gerlach in August 1997 who bemoaned the influx of the Burning Man Festival, no matter that they might be able to sell gasoline, water, beer, a bed for the night, new tires, ravioli, and a map of the empty places. They liked Gerlach to keep that godforsaken air. Indeed, for some there is even godliness or religion in the absence of society and other people's lives.

Let's face it. As of 1990, every Nevadan was down to a statistical living space of less than a tenth of a square mile. And the crowding will only increase. By 2020, the U.S. Census Bureau expects that Nevada could have a population of almost 4 million.

Such games with numbers are facile, of course, but they can quickly reveal how faulty our perspective is. Nevada is rampant with growth—if you like to think of it that way—and steady development will accomplish all the Census Bureau anticipates. But the history of Nevada has little to do with steadiness. Its population has been principally affected by the absolute suddenness of discovering wealth in the ground, by the vagaries of war, and the revelation of what gaming (the state's word) can offer. That enormous expanse of land was granted its own status as a territory (separate from that of Utah) in 1861. The census taken that year reported almost sixteen thousand residents—there were probably another few thousand not quite resident but in the process of moving in. That represented a 100 percent increase in a year, and something like a 1,500 percent increase in the space of three years. In other words, in 1858, there were about one thousand people living in what was set to become the state of Nevada.

What caused that prodigious increase? I'm sure you have good guesses and hunches, and so you may easily wonder how radically and dramatically the population of today—around 1.4 million, let's say—could be augmented if people discovered gold again, or God again, or some new system of blackjack out in the Black Rock Desert or the Big Smoky Valley. Alternatively, things might go the other way, just as fast, or faster, if the water dried up, if the state's geological history of ice and volcano returned, if the various toxicities put in the air over the Nevada Test Site began to pay dividends, or if God got the funds to invest elsewhere. That's a reference to a remark made by a great and important Nevadan, Steve Wynn,* who, when asked what he wanted to do with Las Vegas, said he intended to produce the kind of marvel that God might have made — "if He'd had the money."

---

* Wynn (born in 1942), chairman and chief executive of Mirage Resorts, has been a decisive figure in Las Vegas in the last fifteen years and the visionary for a new type of hotel-casino. He is a superb showman, an entertaining character, and an inspiring talker. However, "if God had had the money" is a line with some history, going back at least as far as the theatrical impresario Moss Hart.

5. Empty Places

GOD KNOWS WHAT IS BURIED THERE—AND LIKELY HE HAS forgotten, He has so much to do. So kick the ground. Who knows what you'll find? We all recognize the slouch of the sulky kid who walks away, kicking at the dust for a few steps until, diverted, he sees a glint in the ground—some bone, some treasure, or is it the promise of a hole to Australia that he might make a start on before bedtime? There is something ancient and innate about digging holes in the ground; it is an activity that can convert sulkiness and the brooding air of outcasts into fresh hope and the zeal of visionaries. Then think that, among many other things, this Nevada is more than 110,000 square miles of ground, where sometimes you can see colors never seen before and where you can smell that thing—mineral—rising out of the ground. Nevada is a mine, and not done yet. For all we know, hardly begun. Doesn't the natural prospector know to look in the harshest and most difficult places?

The personality of the prospector is a large part of this story. He is a loner, even if he seems to be with others; he does not trust the others. He cannot. For it is not just that they might talk too much, too soon, and give it all away. Far more, it is that true hunches have to be conceived, developed, and protected in solitude. Groups cannot gamble—with groups, the whole thing becomes a stock market. When individuals gamble, they pit themselves against the weight of others, and of history. They also mean to redesign the future.

The history of the West is crowded with prospectors, and it is surely true that, sooner or later, most of the lucky ones sold out to corporations and took on partners who could raise the money for proper building of the mine, the hiring of labor, and the building of roads to get the stuff out. That is the way of business. And even the luckiest prospector has a dream of making his killing and going off somewhere to sit in the splendor of his wealth, alone again. If and when that ease wears off, he might start again in some fresh, arid field. It is a pursuit so close to gambling and the profound refusal to be satisfied.

Prospectors are also like immigrants in that, very often, they have left such things as home, family, and ordinary life to sniff new ground. They justify that on the basis that the new, searching life will be so rugged and demanding—they will live in tents, with snakes, bears, cougars, and human savages to watch out for. They will be in remote places where there are no schools, no churches, no plumbing. Of course, my dears, I'd love for you to come, and how I will miss you, but stay here and I will send for you, by and by, when we are rich. When I learn to write.

Gone away—to America, to Colorado, to California, to Nevada, to places unknown. The populating of America was always a model for the fracturing of families, and so even if there is peace and bliss in the loneliness of prospectors, there may be guilt, horror, and madness, too, for those abandoned.

I was in what is called a ghost town once. It is off the road from Tonopah to Hawthorne, to the west. You get there by going ten or so miles on a paved road, and then another ten on a dirt road that leads into a broad, flat valley. You can see the "town" miles away, just as the town could see your dust coming—if there was anyone there. It is a dozen or so ruined buildings, good stone constructions that have lapsed in the heat and the wind and the cold. There was some mineral or other found there in the 1870s, but then the diggings failed and the crowd moved on. There are such places all over Nevada; indeed, its failed cities outnumber those that are still going concerns.

Anyway, I had heard a story on the main road that there might be an old man still living in these ruins. Sometimes he was there, it was said. He was over seventy, and presumably he had some instinct that there was something worth looking for and waiting for in the ruins still. No one was sure how he lived. I wondered if he might be . . . prickly, someone who regarded the town as his. But I was assured that he was harmless, not so much gentle as so shy and elusive that I would likely not see him.

Well, I drove to the ghost town, watched the dust of my coming settle slowly, got out of the car, and walked around. All the buildings were broken-down. There was no sign that any one of them could be, or had been, used as shelter recently. But in that light and weather, things fade and age so fast, it is not always easy to tell the ancient and the dead from something still functional. I did see dried animal droppings — almost certainly from a burro. But there are wild burros in these parts, the descendants of animals used by the old prospectors and left in the desert.

I saw no sign of life, but I felt that there might be someone there, in some recess in one of those shattered buildings, or even in a hole in the ground, waiting patiently for me to go away. There was little that seemed sinister or even perilous in the feeling, but it added to the natural loneliness of the place. Maybe I imagined it all; maybe I was primed by a tall tale. But there are prospectors still, all over Nevada. And they are people without an address or a Social Security number. They may be mad, unclean, waiting to become dry bones in the sun. They are, by our standards, lost souls. But they are expecting a great find.

Take Henry Comstock. That is a famous name in northern Nevada; a name that many people in commerce in San Francisco bless every day. But not very much is known about Henry, and little that is known is creditable. He was a man of contradictions: For instance, he was from Canada, yet he was a big talker and a boaster; he was also, allegedly, a prospector, but one reluctant to get his hands dirty.

You know, more or less, that in 1849, gold was found on the western slopes of the Sierra Nevada, in California. There was a momentous rush that brought many prospectors to the state; California's wealth, population, and reputation have so much to do with that gold strike. In the rush to get there, many of the newcomers came by way of Nevada, over the few passes on the Sierra that a man and a mule carrying the necessary basics for mining could traverse. On that long journey, it was natural for prospectors, most of them new in the game, to kick at the ground as they camped. Carson City began its life as one of those camps, and gradually in the 1850s as prospectors paused in the Carson River Valley, they found traces of gold. Not a lot, but enough to encourage the name of Gold Canyon, an area where a creek came down Mount Davidson and into the Carson River. In 1859, for instance, the gross mineral yield of all Nevada was only $257,000.

Henry Comstock had a little of that, and it was his habit to throw away the sludgy blue-black sand that often got in the way of serious gold mining. But in January 1859, a few prospectors had found respectable gold in the nearby Six Mile Canyon. One of those men was James Finney, also known as James Fennimore or "Old Virginny." The Fennimore in him had killed a man in California, necessitating his move. By June, Finney and two Irishmen—Patrick McLaughlin and Peter O'Riley—moved a little farther afield. They found gold, if only one could get the dark blue muck free of it.

At that point, Comstock came on the scene, looked at the find, and asked the others if they realized they were panning on his land. The laying and securing of claims was a sketchy business. Comstock was a talker and a man of bolder mettle than the others. There was muttering and grumbling—maybe violence was considered—but finally it was agreed by Finney and the Irishmen that Henry should be their partner. They went on digging that summer and got a modest amount of gold for their pains, tossing aside the infuriating dark blue sand.

It was a busy life, until someone thought to send some of the blue muck to Nevada City, in Grass Valley in California, where there was an assayer's office. The assayers' names were Ott and Atwood, and it was an accepted marker in their trade that if a sample produced $100 of ore per ton of material, then it was reckoned to be economically workable. The Nevada City assay report had to be double-checked, for it recorded $876 of gold and $3,000 of silver found in that blue muck.

Word got out. A Grass Valley judge, James Walsh, headed for Six Mile Canyon. The jubilant Comstock and his partners named their mine the Ophir (that was where Solomon, in the Bible, had found gold). It became apparent that the Ophir had touched upon a vast shelf, or lode, of silver. Very rapidly, it became known as the Comstock Lode, largely because Henry, instead of digging, walked around proclaiming the name and his part in finding it. He sold his share to Judge Walsh for $11,000, and for a while he ran a store in the area. But he slipped back into the life of wandering and failure that had preceded his find. Some say he went mad. Whatever, in 1870, broke, he shot himself in Montana. Only one of the partners did better, O'Riley. He got $45,000, but then he heard voices telling him to dig elsewhere. He dug, and dug, and eventually he had to be led out of the large empty hole and put in an asylum, where he died.

Walsh was the first of many shrewd developers of the Comstock Lode and what became Virginia City, which grew over it. George Hearst was about forty then, and he came from Missouri. He bought McLaughlin's share for $3,000, and within months he had made $90,000. He went on to find more mines, not least the Anaconda copper mine in 1881. His sons included William Randolph Hearst, the newspaper tycoon, who inherited the *San Francisco Examiner* and a ranch at San Simeon, in California, from his father.

By the early 1860s, Virginia City had more than twenty thousand residents, most of whom lived and worked in conditions of astonishing hardship, and glory. For over the next twenty years, about $400 million was taken out of the ground.

6. Spirit Cave Man

IF YOU'RE DOING MUCH SERIOUS TRAVELING IN NEVADA, FALlon is somewhere you keep coming back to. For a start, it is a useful junction, sitting on Highway 50, which goes all the way across the state from Carson City to Ely, and so into Utah—and way beyond: Highway 50 is one of those roads—less than a freeway—that stays true across most of the country. And Fallon is on Route 95, the road that drops south off Interstate 80 and goes all the way by Hawthorne, Tonopah, and Beatty (and Mercury) to Las Vegas itself.

There are more profound reasons for a significant town being where Fallon is. Once upon a time, a large part of central western Nevada (over 8,000 square miles) was covered by Lake Lahontan. It has dried up, apart from such remnants as Pyramid and Walker lakes. But it has left a vast dry lake bed centered on the so-called Carson Desert and the Carson Sink, and Fallon is at the center of that depression. Indeed, Fallon is less than four thousand feet above sea level, something out of the ordinary in northern Nevada: The Great Basin is what it claims to be, a sunken area surrounded by mountains, but at its lower points, it still has a height that keeps the air dry in summer, and clear for most of the year.

So Fallon dates back a bit: In 1896, just as movies were invented, the year after Freud published *Studies in Hysteria*, and as Utah became the forty-fifth state in the union (having agreed to abandon polygamy), one Mike Fallon had a ranch there that accommodated a post office. In another ten years, the area came into its own as an agricultural region with the Newlands Irrigation Project (a harnessing of the Carson and Truckee rivers).* That made thousands of acres in the Carson Desert

---

* Francis Newlands (1848–1917), though born in Mississippi, was one of the great figures of early Nevada. He stood for the state in the U.S. House of Representatives from

sweet and arable, and ever since, the Fallon area has produced quantities of alfalfa, very good melons, honeybees, and turkeys, as well as cattle. Even so, by 1940, the population of Fallon was still a little under two thousand. Today, it stands at 7,800. That is part of a general statewide increase, of course, but it owes a great deal to the decision, in 1942, to build a naval air station. That field closed for a few years in the late forties, but it has been open for business ever since the Korean War. Named Van Voorhees at first, after a local hero, it is now the U.S. Naval Air Station Fallon, with a runway of fourteen thousand feet, the home of those elite fighter pilots popularly known as the Top Gun boys.

Much of this we can come back to, but it is some setting for the warm, bright May day, with fighter aircraft landing and taking off a few miles away, when I went to Grimes Point. Grimes is about a dozen miles east of Fallon, which is, in turn, about sixty miles east of Reno. The old Lahontan lake bed is apparent there in expanses of salty playa and the low hills of shale that build toward modest boulder-strewn crags. It is not a spectacular place by any means, but Grimes Point is the entranceway to a collection of petroglyphic paintings on boulders and to what is called Hidden Cave (actually a set of quite small caves in those crags).

On August 11, 1940—before any air station—when it would have been hot, though bearable, two archaeologists, husband and wife, Sidney and Georgia Wheeler, were working in those caves on behalf of the Nevada Parks Commission. They had been alerted by locals who mined guano (bat droppings) there for fertilizer. These men had uncovered what they called "a few Indian remains." The Wheelers searched and found a cave within a cave, one that the guano diggers had not noticed. This was not a deep cave or a large one, but it contained a burial mound. Within that, they found the figure of a man, five feet two inches tall. The body was carefully wrapped in a material made of bulrushes and hemp, some of which was like a hood over the man's head. The conditions of wrapping and the atmosphere of the cave had had a most curious effect: From the feet to the chest, the man was a skeleton, but above that, he was so mummified that much of his skin and long black hair had survived intact.

Spirit Cave Man, as he was called, was taken to Carson City, where the handsome U.S. Mint building on Main Street was in the process of being converted into a state museum. The Wheelers published a short scientific report in 1944, but by then, apparently, the figure was in a box,

---

1893 to 1903, and in the U.S. Senate from 1903 until his death. His name was given to the Truckee-Carson irrigation project.

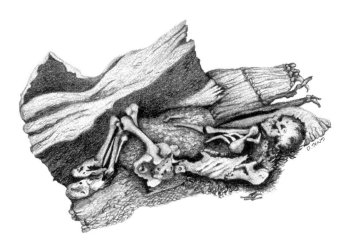

Spirit Cave Man
(drawing from life, by Denise Sins of the Nevada State Museum, courtesy of Ms. Sins)

screwed shut and being preserved as carefully as possible as far as temperature and air pressure were concerned. The Wheelers thought that Spirit Cave Man might be as much as two thousand years old. No other mummies that old had survived. But still, apparently, the Wheelers and the new museum were not overly impressed.

The box remained in Carson City, shut, for more than fifty years, so we have to conceive of this extra oblivion, with Spirit Cave Man interred and utterly unaware of the atom bomb, rock 'n' roll, television, the end of communism, or the rise of Las Vegas. If that seems unduly ironic, let me stress the weird congruency of "great" events and a greater unknowingness. The story told now by the serious and estimable anthropologists attached to the Nevada State Museum (which has become an exemplary institution over the ensuing decades) is that scientists were waiting for more advanced methodology to be developed. In other words, Spirit Cave Man was kept as stable as possible until carbon dating could reveal—as it did in 1994 and 1995—that the figure was between 9,460 and 9,350 years old.

That is another kind of assaying, with the result nearly as shocking as the one reached in Nevada City in 1859 (one of those many moments when no one had any idea of Spirit Cave Man's existence). For as is now known, this is the oldest human figure found yet in North America.

Another record for Nevada, but one of the least expected, surely, in a place renowned for desolation, absence, and that echoing idea that just as once there was nothing, so it may come again.

The anthropologists in 1994 were as excited as they were surprised, for the mummified remains offered great potential for DNA analyses that might reveal so much more about this man. But a discovery that might have been easily digested in 1940 proved more challenging now. Some of Nevada's Indians claimed the man as theirs. Maurice Eben, a member of the tribal council for the Northern Paiutes, said, "They don't need to do any further scientific studies. They should return the remains now."

He was referring to the Native American Graves Protection and Repatriation Act of 1990, which requires that any museum or entity working with federal funds should catalog archaeological findings and then promptly return them to "closely affiliated tribes." But nearly all authorities believe that the present-day tribes of Nevada came to the area far more recently than 9,500 years ago, and some observers feel that Spirit Cave Man has a more Asiatic cast to his face, suggesting some migration across what was once a Bering Strait's bridge into North America.

The matter is still in dispute, and no one is much inclined to volunteer information on where the man is. We are left to hope that he is being properly taken care of. It is a delicate issue in a society that now feels guilt about how it treated the Indian tribes but which cannot abandon the principles of scientific evidence or honor every profound, sentimental narrative that places the Native Americans as founders, and wronged owners, of this country.

It was easier once upon a time. As the Comstock Lode discovery sucked men into the area of Carson City, so the life of the Paiutes was disrupted. Their food was taken by hungry prospectors. The pine trees were chopped down for buildings in Virginia City. The hallowed Paiute space was infringed upon. This was a western pattern that affected far larger tribes than the Paiutes. When Custer and his men were wiped out at the Battle of the Little Bighorn in June 1876, that land was not Sioux or Cheyenne land. It was simply a place, in Montana Territory, to which those peoples had been driven as their own land fell prey to white invaders who had found gold in Sioux territory and who mindlessly killed and ate the buffalo that supported Indian life.

A similar thing befell the Paiutes, who had been friendly enough to Frémont and Kit Carson in 1844. In May 1860, the leaders of the Paiutes and the Bannocks gathered at Pyramid Lake to consider a response to the white intrusion. As they talked, word reached them that three whites had

7. Statehood

THE DAY AFTER THE NOVEMBER 1996 GENERAL ELECTION, I happened to be driving around within range of the Reno radio station KOH, and its young afternoon talk-show host, Brian Maloney, a vigorous conservative voice. He was asking the question, in view of the election results, whether Nevada had changed and become a "liberal" state. For the second election in a row, Nevada had decided on a Democratic president, though the margin of victory was far narrower than in most of the rest of the nation. Bill Clinton had received 44 percent of the votes, Bob Dole 43 percent, and Ross Perot 9 percent.

Maloney and his listeners lamented together that the sturdy conservatism that is Nevada's tradition might be a thing of the past. One listener said that that interpretation missed the point, that Nevada was (and should be) unlike other states, that it has always been, above all, "independent." That seemed to mean that Nevada, constitutionally, defiantly went against every grain, as if America and its electoral choices made that possible. Then another listener said that it was all a matter of two states. The final result was to be blamed on those "down there," in Las Vegas and Clark County. In Reno, and in the north of the state generally, Las Vegas is regarded as a place of youth, irresponsibility, and instability, even to the dread point of liberalism. Though someone on the radio might be wary of saying as much, the definition of "down there" also includes broken families, homosexuals, people of other than the white race, people in "entertainment," and those whose livelihood depends on gambling. That's right, said someone else, that's an "urban" population. Everyone fastened on that, because "urban" in most of Nevada is universally recognized as a harmful, and even depraved, condition. There is a drastic split in the state now: as witness these figures in presidential voting in four counties—

been killed by Bannocks at Williams Station (between Pyramid and the site of Fallon). They believed, probably correctly, that this action was a retaliation against some white man who had kidnapped two Indian women. As a result, the settlers and prospectors quickly put together a vengeful body of men who would punish the Indians. It was a group of 105 volunteers, led by William Ormsby of Carson City (there is a hotel in that town now named after him). The whites marched on the lake and, rather like Custer, went on too valiantly or with too much confidence. Just south of the lake (near what is now Nixon), they were ambushed and badly beaten. Ormsby was among the seventy-six men killed.

The response was paranoid and massive. Over 750 men, including soldiers, were now sent to rebuke the Indians who had been attacked, and a second battle was fought, in which the Paiutes were slaughtered and dispersed. Shortly thereafter, a fort was set up—Fort Churchill (between Carson City and the site of Fallon; its ruins still stand)—to safeguard the area. The Indian tribes had been subdued to make Nevada safe for progress. Indeed, the battles of Pyramid Lake—sometimes described back east as a war—were vital in Nevada's advance toward statehood. Ironically, the Paiutes were left with Pyramid as their reservation area—as bare a place as Tahoe is sylvan and developed. With its rock formations, and its shore empty of all but the pelican, Pyramid Lake has a slightly prehistoric air; it is a place where Spirit Cave Man might have fished for cutthroat trout and wondered if there was anyone else on Earth. Perhaps he and a few companions played a very early form of dice to guess which of them would be eternally famous. The gaming may have led to a dispute and violence, for Spirit Cave Man has a fractured skull. The history of Nevadan violence began early.

Clark, Washoe (Reno), Douglas (the area south of Carson City), and Carson City itself:

	Carson	Douglas	Washoe	Clark
Dole	9,168	8,828	47,855	103,431
Clinton	7,269	5,109	43,839	127,963
Perot	1,591	1,486	9,697	23,177

The split in these figures is not simply between liberalism and conservatism. Far more, it shows how Clark County and all it represents (Clark includes not just Las Vegas but also the cities of Laughlin, Boulder City, and Henderson) has outstripped the rest of the state. Reno is a true city, in the north, and it virtually joins Sparks now; their joint population is very close to 220,000, but since 1926 it has loved to call itself "the Biggest Little City" in America, or the world, which presumably keeps it clear of the dread urbanization. Still, within a very short space of time (the last fifty years), there has been such a shift in the state's balance that some Nevadans have trouble in knowing how to regard themselves. For the lively history of Nevada's statehood has nothing to do with the south, and everything to do with the new turmoil that linked Carson City and Virginia City in the 1860s. (Not even Reno figured then. Some reckoned that one person lived there in 1860, C. W. Fuller, who had a log cabin on the Truckee. The town, as such, only began after 1868 as a point on the new Central Pacific Railroad, and it was named Reno after a general in the Union army.)

That man on the Brian Maloney show who spoke of Nevada as "independent" probably regrets statehood. There are Nevadans, and not only the prospectors holed up at the ends of remote box canyons, who would prefer no government at all. In the early years, Nevada was so empty, arid, and inhospitable, it attracted those people who were willing to live apart from all semblance of order. I sat in a diner in Fallon once, eating my lunch and listening to two men at another table who were on a steady matter-of-fact rant against all government and all "theys" who sought to impose regulations of any kind. It was a wonder that they were ready to abide by the institution of the diner, its agenda (the menu), or the white lines on the tarmac of the diner's parking lot.

Had it not been for the Comstock Lode, it's an open question how long Nevada would have lingered on as untended space, at best the far edge of Utah Territory, at worst an authentic no-man's-land, where no law reached and brute possession was everything. Of course, in some senses, Nevada has turned out that way. Despite the tally of progress—the dramatic increase in population, the suburban sprawl of Reno as well as Las Vegas—there are enormous tracts of the state where no one lives, or wants to have their car break down. And considerable parts of these tracts are owned by the federal government and rigorously fenced off against intrusion. The government has always regarded Nevada as a place unlike others, fit for tests, experiments, and ventures it would sometimes rather not talk about. And so the state that has had a special appeal to loners, libertarians, and anarchists is also a playground of the federal government. State control and absolute liberty come very close together; sometimes it is hard to tell one from the other.

The discovery of treasure in the ground brought the threat and the pomp of organization. There were, all of a sudden, so many people—an increase of 1,500 percent in a few years. Many of the newcomers, driven by greed and enormous hope, were not naturally scrupulous or well behaved. And there was such plunder to be had, it made some people uneasy. Never forget that one of the first actions of the new Nevada Territory was to build a prison—to this day, visitors to the state wonder how a place so uncrowded supports so many jails.*

The Utah Territory did what it could to hold on to Nevada. It shifted the county seat from Genoa (the old Mormon Station, and still a pretty place clinging to Genoa Park) to Carson City, and it gave status to Virginia City. But the new wealth of the area cried out for local authority, and a proper sense of identity. If that had not been enough in itself, the nation needed a Nevada, for the United States was close to a war in which states' rights were a vital issue. Nevada became a territory on March 2, 1861, only months after South Carolina had launched the series of Southern secessions from the Union.

James Nye was appointed to be governor of the territory and Orion Clemens was made territorial secretary. These and many other jobs were given out as rewards by Lincoln's Republican party in thanks for work and favors done in the 1860 election. These officers were not Nevadans. They had to journey to the new territory, and so Nye was not welcomed until July 1861. He enjoyed several banquets in Carson City and Virginia City,

---

* Nevada has seven state prisons for men (Ely, Lovelock, two in Carson City, Indian Springs, Jean, Warm Springs), one privatized prison for women (Las Vegas), and ten prison camps. As of January 1999, the total prison population was 9,617.

and seeing little except a thriving disorder at all levels of business and law-making, he simply proclaimed that the territory was now organized.

We have a wonderful, ironic account of Nevada at that moment in that Secretary Clemens was accompanied west by his brother, Samuel, a man who would soon take the name Mark Twain. He is supposed to have exaggerated what he found for comic effect. Perhaps; I suspect this is pretty reliable stuff:

> We found the state palace of the Governor of Nevada Territory to consist of a white frame one-story house with two small rooms in it and a stanchion supported shed in front—for grandeur—it compelled the respect of the citizen and inspired the Indian with awe. The newly arrived Chief and Associate Justices of the Territory, and other machinery of the government were domiciled with less splendor. They were boarding around privately, and had their offices in their bedrooms.

It was not long before Sam Clemens found a newspaper job in Virginia City on the *Territorial Enterprise*—though only after he had failed as a silver miner—and it was in February 1863, in that paper, that he used the name Mark Twain for the first time. He was a delighted observer of the territory. He reported the pitiless Washoe Wind that set in every afternoon, the inescapable alkali dust that got everywhere, the regular feeling in Virginia City of the ground shaking beneath one's office as it was mined and blasted, and the importance of murder as a status symbol.

Clemens even remarked once, as Nevadans grappled with the question of how to tax the mines (one of the chief impediments to statehood itself), that it might be more sensible to tax murder. There were judges now in the territory, but not many of them for a community where disputes over holdings, liquor, possession, games of chance, women, and so forth were very frequent, and where—according to Clemens—a real man was expected to have committed a murder or so. The first twenty-six graves in the Virginia City Cemetery, he wrote, were all those of murdered men, adding this sotto voce tribute to faith: "So everybody said, so everybody believed, and so they will always say and believe."

Governor Nye did a lot in a few years. There were elections to send members to Congress. There was a new census carried out in 1861; it reported about 15,500 people, an increase of well over 100 percent in the space of a year. English common law was adopted as the basis for Nevadan law. Gambling was forbidden—"it captivates and ensnares the young," warned Nye, "blunts all the moral sensibilities and ends in utter ruin." There's government for you, always trying to save you and your money. But most significant of all, there developed a serious argument as to whether the essential taxes—no one, once governed, can ever quite question the philosophy of taxation—should be on the mines as valued property, on their gross income, or on their net profits. And there was no point in taxing anything except the mines.

But a flat tax on mines—including claims that were not yet producing—seemed grossly interfering and stifling to the prospector community. Moreover, the early years of the territory produced public outrage at the ineptness of the courts, and especially the corruption of juries. Twain was a noted satirist of the latter—"the jury system," he said, "puts a ban upon intelligence and honesty, and a premium upon ignorance, stupidity and perjury." There was also a feeling that the move toward statehood was being directed by Californian business interests, and that they—especially William Stewart, one of their leaders—would end up in charge of the state, and so the "small" voters, many miners, the farmers, and those who were waiting for something to turn up, ganged up against statehood.

There was a constitutional convention (full of Californian people but short on mining interests) that proposed a setup that depended on tough taxation of the mining industry. In January 1864, it was defeated by about four to one (just over eleven thousand people voted). But Lincoln would not, could not, be denied. He needed Nevada, not just so that its money could help pay for the war but as a vote in measures against slavery and even as a safeguard if the 1864 presidential election went to the House of Representatives.

Within a month of the reversal in Nevada, an Enabling Act passed both houses of the U.S. Congress and was signed by Lincoln. Governor Nye was bound to order a second constitutional convention. This group met, overcame early doubts, devised a tax scheme based on the proceeds from mines, and urged that only statehood could properly reform the judiciary. The new state constitution went to the people on September 7, 1864, and was passed by 10,375 votes to 1,284. (In all of this, Nevada had far less than the minimum population required by Congress for a member in the House of Representatives. The deficiency was simply ignored.) The earlier state constitution was then wired to Washington—that cost $3,417. On October 31, 1864, just a few days before the presidential election, Nevada was declared a state. It voted solidly Republican. As a few complained back home in Nevada—those who wanted to be left alone—the state had been used. A tradition was shaping up.

8. Pugilism

THERE WAS A NOTICE POSTED IN THE HOTEL WHEN WE
arrived, a placard on an easel by the elevator, that said Henry Akinwande
would be training every morning in the ballroom. Everyone was invited
to attend. This was the July Fourth weekend of 1997, and I was at the
Ormsby House in Carson City with my family. In a week's time, Akinwande—a British heavyweight boxer, though born in Nigeria—was
scheduled to fight Lennox Lewis. We were eager to see him training. My
two sons—seven and two—began to spar in anticipation (boxing will take
a lot of killing or legislating away so long as there are boys around).

We heard from people in the hotel that Akinwande was a sight to
behold, an authentic spectacle: black, of course, his head shaved, over six
and a half feet, and weighing about 230 pounds. He had won thirty-two
fights so far, lost one, and drawn one, and he had nineteen knockouts. We
planned which morning we would be at the Ormsby House ballroom.

At the appointed hour, nine in the morning, we were in the lobby of
the hotel, just one flight up from the casino floor. Another version of the
placard was outside the ballroom doors, but Akinwande and his entourage
had not yet arrived. We peeped through a crack between the double doors
and could see a boxing ring—immense and empty—set up in the ballroom. Time passed, and no one arrived. Since the ballroom doors were
not locked, we went in and studied the ring.

Whatever you think of boxing, a real ring is a wondrous construction—raised on a platform, built with stanchions and guy ropes as thick as
a girl's wrist, it has a stretched canvas floor laid upon some matting that
allows a true spring beneath the feet (to decrease the likelihood that a
felled boxer will suffer a concussion). These ropes were gnarled and solid,
oddly like the umbilical cord on a newborn baby. Tiny strands of loose
cotton hung down from the ropes, wavering in the draft of the hotel's air

conditioning. Steps led up to two of the corners; there were stools and half-full bottles of mineral water; there were towels dropped on the floor, with one hanging over the ropes. There were even dark blots and specks on the stretched canvas flooring—natural flaws, the imprint of squashed flies stepped on by heavyweights, or bloodstains gathered over the years? There can't be that many full-size canvas floors in existence, and it's hard to see how you could launder them.

The ring nearly filled the ballroom, an oppressively tawdry room with trashy mock velour and fake portraits on the wall. It was a room of cut-rate 1980s design, attempting to imitate the 1880s. It seems very likely that one of the solemn faces in those drab portraits was even the Major Ormsby killed at the first battle of Pyramid Lake. If it seemed unlikely that a heavy-

The boxing ring at the Ormsby House Hotel, Carson City,
set up for Henry Akinwande

weight fighter, a real contender, might be training here in this ballroom, it seemed just as far-fetched that there should ever be anything like a ball in this forlorn room. There were ornate factory-built chandeliers, cursory versions of the real thing. Nevada's history is not so distant, but here in the state capital, and in what is reported to be its best hotel, there was not a vestige of the ability to remake that past properly. In my mind, I prepared for the surrealism of a Nigerian with a rough London accent going through the motions in front of these ersatz portraits, beneath the queasy chandeliers. So enormous, so noble, so thoroughly constructed, the ring seemed as poised and sinister as a Magritte painting in the lackluster ballroom. My wife could not help but take photographs of it, though we were a little nervous to think that the enormous Akinwande might enter and find us capturing, or spooking, *his* place.

He never showed. Henry Akinwande did not train that day. We heard that he was thought to be in the hotel somewhere, but not yet ready, or willing. We talked to the hotel chef, who said that Akinwande was so zealous about fitness that he disdained the hotel food—this was wisdom, or even taste—and had special dietary materials flown in from somewhere. We could not wait forever, so we moved on sadly, prepared to cross the Sierra.

But we were very attentive, a week later, when Akinwande actually fought Lewis at Caesars Tahoe, in Stateline, at the southeastern corner of the lake. Akinwande was a 3–2 underdog, but still there were some commentators who reckoned that he might be more than anyone anticipated. At ringside, however, reporters felt he looked nervous, and as the fight began, he started to hold his opponent, rather than fight. In the second round, he was warned by the referee, Mills Lane, and had a point deducted from his score. Then the referee gave an official warning to Akinwande's trainer, Don Turner. There was another warning in the third round. By the start of the fifth, the bitter crowd was chanting, "Fight! Fight!" The holding went on. Lane gave a last warning. Turner told his fighter that he risked disqualification. And before the end of the round, Lane stopped the fight and gave the win to Lennox Lewis. "I did the best I could to let the fight go on," said the baffled referee, "but the time comes when enough is enough and that was enough."

This was gruesome timing, for on June 28, at the M-G-M Grand in Las Vegas, in a bigger fight—promoter Don King had called it "the biggest event of all time," which does away with "fight of the century" bravado— Mike Tyson had been disqualified (by the same Mills Lane) for twice biting the ear of heavyweight champion Evander Holyfield.

Once again, the art, business, and flimflam of boxing had been brought into disrepute. Journalists asserted that Tyson was deranged, or too cunning to suffer the normal defeat he foresaw. Some said that, yet again, Don King had made a fortune out of a grisly farce—the Pay-Per-View fee for watching the fight at home was $49.95; Tyson had earned $30 million and Holyfield $35 million (let us pray there was something left for Don, for he came in for much scorn and abuse).

The Nevada State Athletic Commission was moved to take action.

It punished to the limit of its abilities. Tyson was fined $3 million, and his license to fight (in Nevada) was revoked for twelve months. The five members of the commission were unanimous: Elias Ghanem, a doctor; Jim Nave, a veterinarian; Lorenzo Fertihe, an investor; Nat Carasali, a Las Vegas casino owner; and Luther Mack, the owner of fast-food franchises in Reno. They let it be known that Tyson could not expect to have his license renewed until he pursued personal therapy and detached himself from the bad influence in his entourage (Don King was mentioned most specifically). Of course, with $27 million, Tyson could afford a lot of therapy and many new friends.*

But the State Athletic Commission and the state itself were stunned by public criticism of the fight and of the state's regularly profiting from such events. So a day before the Akinwande-Lewis fight, Governor Bob Miller signed into state law a measure that permitted the commission to withhold *all* of a fighter's purse after a questionable performance, not just 10 percent. One commissioner proposed that Akinwande's purse be withheld, pending a hearing.

But one week later, he was paid in full. The commission's executive director, Marc Ratner, told me that while Akinwande had been properly disqualified, he had done no worse than other boxers who had come to the state.

These days, we think of Nevada as being inseparable from boxing. So many championship fights in the last twenty years have been held there, either at the M-G-M Grand or at the open-air arena that used to stand behind Caesars Palace (until the needs of parking grew greater). A big fight brings not just visitors to the hotels but also action to the casinos. Even now, if there are commissioners and others horrified at Tyson's loss of control in the ring, there are yet others who wonder how much control was lost. For if in 1998 or 1999 or 2000 ("Millennium Rumble"?) Tyson

---

* Nevada has now reinstated Tyson. But by 1999, he had been jailed in Maryland, an action likely to jeopardize his probationary status in Indiana.

can regain his license, and if Evander Holyfield has not settled by then for a life of ministry or contemplation, and if the battered, abused Don King can be persuaded to offer his services again, then there are those who suspect that Holyfield versus Tyson III would be not just the biggest event of all time but a mother lode.

In fact, the modern history of prizefighting in Nevada began in the early 1960s. For several decades previously, the center of the fight game had been in New York, at Madison Square Garden. Joe Louis did serve time after his retirement as an official "sight," or "greeter," at Caesars Palace, but he never fought in Las Vegas. Neither did Rocky Marciano, Jake La Motta, Willie Pep, or Sandy Saddler. But in March 1961, Sugar Ray Robinson fought Gene Fullmer there, and in July 1963 in Las Vegas, Floyd Patterson lost his heavyweight title to Sonny Liston. In November 1965, Muhammad Ali beat Patterson there, and in February 1978, long after he should have stopped fighting, Ali lost there to Leon Spinks.

But it is not just a modern story. Late in the nineteenth century, Nevada was in a depressed condition. The Comstock Lode had run its course. The population of Virginia City was falling steadily: It was nearly two thousand, and it dropped close to five hundred in the next forty years. Mineral production in the state had fallen from a gross yield of $46.6 million dollars (in 1877) to $2.7 million dollars in 1899. There were some who feared that the state was slipping back into its desert condition, and in the years from 1890 to 1900, the total population of the state *fell* from 47,355 to 42,335.

Boxing then was in a precarious condition, trying to make the transition from bare-knuckle fights of uncertain rules to what is known as Marquis of Queensberry contests with padded gloves. Fights were reckoned to be an attraction to the criminal element; there was said to be racketeering in the promotion, and even dishonesty in the bouts themselves. Gambling, drinking, and other sordid traits were associated with boxing. And so it was outlawed in many states. To avoid the authorities, in 1896 there had even been a contest staged on an island in the Rio Grande, opposite Langtry, Texas, the town presided over by Judge Roy Bean.

Nevada stepped into that available opportunity. In January 1897, Governor Reinhold Sadler signed an act allowing fights in Nevada. This was so that Carson City could stage the heavyweight championship meeting of James J. Corbett and his challenger, Bob Fitzsimmons. It occurred on St. Patrick's Day, March 17, in a specially built ring and stadium in the open air beneath the snowcapped mountains. Tickets ranged from $5 to $40 for what was called the "battle of the century." The fight began at noon, the best time of day to get not just an audience but also the best possible light—one side of the ring was dominated by a hut with small windows that rather resembled a World War I tank, but that was actually a booth from which the fight was filmed. There was the future. Only seven thousand people came to see Fitzsimmons win—and the promoters lost money.

In 1906 at the mining town of Goldfield, for promoter Tex Rickard, Battling Nelson fought Joe Gans. Nelson was disqualified after forty-two rounds for hitting Gans low. (Then and now, the interpretation of the rules was at issue.) Then in 1910, in Reno, the great Jack Johnson nearly killed Jim Jeffries on July 4. That fight earned promoter Rickard $270,775, and it put Nevada on the map. A few years later, the young Jack Dempsey (a Colorado kid) fought some of his early fights in Reno, Tonopah, Goldfield, and Ely (the new mining towns). Then boxing moved away, in large part because the eastern cities had bigger arenas, but also because the new medium, radio, required East Coast starting times.

No matter, Pay-Per-View would have its day, along with the great casino battles of our time and the Socratic judgment of the Nevada State Athletic Commission, which inspired fusion of law and liberty, so fully in the Nevada tradition.

9. Black Rock Desert

TO GO OFF INTO THE DESERT ALONE, TO BE THERE IN THE silence and light, may make for a profound experience. It may form you, save you, or leave you unfit for much else. But the effort to speak of that solitary exaltation, to convey it, is gambling with your own privilege. For if you are any good at the speaking, if your pen rises to the lugubrious charm of emptiness like water to the wand, then you risk drawing others in behind you. And then, maybe, the desert is gone. In its place, there is just a stamping ground of restless people vexed at seeing one another.

There is something of the fate of Nevada in this fable. For just as it is natural (yet perverse) of man to want to make a society out of the desert, so there are forces in that desolation that are ready to disown the attempt, like sinners longing to discard their sin. There is no long-term interference with the desert. And so, when those brilliant pictures came in from Mars during the summer of 1997, showing a seemingly unlimited expanse of geological rubble—the poised abandonment of real rocks, brown, ocher, gold, and black, reaching out to the horizon like water lapping to the edge of a table—Nevadans were not surprised. They know that landscape, and what it means for human history.

The Burning Man Festival came and went in 1997. It got more attention than ever before. And perhaps it faced its own limits. There's only so much organization a thing like that can take.

The festival began in 1985 on Baker Beach in San Francisco as an impromptu affair—just a few people camping out for a weekend and finding a spontaneous celebration of nothing they could articulate, and which therefore came to be called "primitive" or "mystical" or "spiritual" or some weird hippie thing. Someone must have said, "Let's do it again next year"—a perilous quest if no one was quite sure what had been done in the first place. And maybe out of the urge to put off passersby and sight-

seers, locals unwilling to be involved, the event shifted to the Black Rock
Desert in northwestern Nevada, a place where there are no passersby.

There was a leader for the festival, Larry Harvey. Some said that the
first burned effigy on Baker Beach had represented a relationship in Harvey's life. By 1991, he had moved the affair to public lands in the Black
Rock Desert, and in the nineties, more or less, the event grew, building in
attendance every year. By 1993, for its few days of existence, the festival
published a newspaper, the *Black Rock Gazette*, that included this self-
description:

> Welcome to Nowhere.
>
> There are no spectators here, only participants. No audience, only
> players. Here on this sere and desolate plain, our community
> springs from the desert floor like a strange and beautiful mush-
> room, a post-modern Brigadoon in an ancient wasteland. Its name
> is whatever you name it. Its wealth is whatever you bring. Next
> week it will be gone, but next week might as well be never. You are
> here now.

It was the Creation, if God had come from Haight-Ashbury. There
were naked, painted humans; there were versions of theater, happenings,
and dances; there were statues built—not just the ever-larger effigy, waiting to be burned, but sculptures constructed from desert debris; there was
golf on the desert floor; windsurfing; races for bizarre self-made vehicles;
there were drugs, drink, and what is still called "free love" in some
stretches of society. No one got hurt apparently, and Harvey spoke of the
"fun" as an attempt "to invent a vision to fill the vacant heart of the Wild
West, the great empty quarter."

By 1996, there were ten thousand people there. There was an entrance
fee of $40 a vehicle to pay for organization and overhead: not least, the
provision of portable bathrooms. There was some tension. Although guns
were forbidden at the festival, there were armed people and some shoot-
ing after dark. One reporter described a naked young woman blatantly
offering herself to a cowboy from a nearby ranch; there was a sort of provo-
cation in the meeting of natural conservatism and Bay Area libertarians.
Three people were injured when a vehicle drove into a tent, and a motor-
cyclist was killed when he hit a van.

The attention mounted. *Burning Man*, a large coffee-table book filled
with color photographs of the event, was published in the spring of 1997.
But Pershing County, Nevada, voted to ban any future festival on its pub-

lic land, referring to the expense of police supervision and "incompatible values." But then Harvey found a private property—Fly Ranch, on the Hualapai Playa—that would put on the festival. Harvey said it would still be the same: "We needed to create a skin that would let in some things, keep others out, like any community . . . if the majority of people are creatively participating, decency will prevail. Freedom and order are not allergic to each other."

But order now meant the construction of fences (it had been easy to gate-crash in earlier years), a system of marshaling, an adequate down payment to cover the police presence for Washoe County (the move had shifted from one county to another), and insurance. The organizers were required to have forty-two firefighters on the site. Washoe County was set to take the first $320,000 of the proceeds. As a result, entrance prices were put up to $65 for advanced tickets bought on the Web, and $75 at the gate. Still, Harvey reckoned to attract between twelve and fifteen thousand people without detracting from the nature of the event.

Late in August, *Time* magazine ran an article on the festival by Kevin Kelly, executive editor of *Wired*, a participant for many years, and someone involved in the publication of the coffee-table book. This was rather more advocacy than journalism. Kelly blithely predicted a crowd of twenty thousand, including himself and his two young daughters. He stressed that it wasn't just an event for hippies; it also attracted the computer workers of Silicon Valley:

> Anything lacking meaning will be assigned one. My bet is that Burning Man will be the holiday for desk-bound, no-collar workers. Not only does it offer the usual American past-times—fast cars, parades, costume balls, picnics and all-night music—but it also provides the more contemporary attractions of survival camping, neon lights, nudity, performance art and staged extravaganzas. It's got the sun-dried culture of postmodern road warriors: deep ritual without religion, community without commitment, art without history, technology without boundaries.

You can't put all the blame on that garbage. The prices were nearly doubled. The talk of that large a crowd deterred many purists. And there had been danger in the air in 1996. As it turned out, the 1997 festival had a crowd of ten thousand again, perhaps a little less. The sad word came out that proceeds had not even covered the required payment to Washoe County.

*One of the tableaux at the Burning Man Festival? The Luxor Hotel on
Las Vegas Boulevard? Or some other vision of rapture or quickening?*

But fans remained loyal. The *San Francisco Chronicle* ran a letter
from a participant who said, "The Festival represents more than just
nudity and hedonistic depravity. Burning Man is the timeless celebration
of humanity in all its creativity and variety."

Time magazine now turned on the festival. It ran letters that came in
the main from Nevadans. They were far less charitable. A man in Reno
wrote that "Burning Man is a boil on the butt of the desert. We locals wish
they would go away before serious damage occurs to the land and the
social fabric of near-by communities."

Now, a person from Gerlach might smile to think that anyone from
Reno shared his land or his community. But the point is well taken. The
withdrawal from Burning Man is a traffic jam, and some Gerlach people
do reckon to get out of town for the weekend. More important, the tenuous idealism of the festival itself is surely threatened as it becomes larger
and an annual habit.

I turn to Raymond M. Smith, the author of *Nevada's Northwest Corner*, a fine book on that area of Nevada. This book is not only a fund of
research on life in the empty quarter; it is also quietly certain of its beauty
and spiritual power. Smith was an early friend to Burning Man—"a

strange event, but no one is hurting anything and all seem to be having a good time. What is wrong with that?"

Nothing. But Burning Man is . . . a cult, a festival, a moment in Nevada. It may resemble others: the flaring up of the Comstock Lode; the explosions at the Nevada Test Site; and even the culture of Las Vegas. But for a few people—it has to be a few—to go north of Gerlach, say, is to partake of Smith's grave sense of silence, and even extinction:

> Some may try to tell you that there is no additional pleasure to being alone in the back country. But this is not true. For being in solitary accompaniment to the music and magic of the hills is an exclusive pleasure, real in quality and with an inner intensity. And the solitary rapture must not be sullied with material or other purposeful intents such as a carefully predetermined plan to get from A to B. It is enough to seek the high desert country for its own sake. Any more can desecrate the solitude and somehow blow the enchantment.

10. The Shape

WHEN A STRANGER, OR SOMEONE FROM THE EAST, LOOKS AT the map of the United States, and at the West, Nevada is the odd-shaped state. My children have a wooden jigsaw puzzle of the USA, and whenever they work at it, Nevada comes late in the solution. It is like a wild card thrust in there to hold the West together. After all, Wyoming is an exact rectangle. California is bound by the coast and the run of the Sierra. Utah, Colorado, Arizona, and New Mexico are not quite rectangles (well, no, look again—Colorado *is*), but they do meet at their famous Four Corners point. Oregon and Washington are pretty regular, wavering only with the line of rivers. Idaho fits into Montana, the two of them making a thick, blocky **L** shape. Whereas Nevada is like a spike, a jamb, or a wedge—it does seem modeled on some useful bit of carpentry for the mines—a shape that must have been hammered in, with two angled corners, one of them so sharp that a man could have one foot in California and one in Arizona, while peeing in Nevada. Or he could if he were giant enough to bestride the Colorado River.

This is not an accurate rendering of history. In the brief span of its territorial status, and in the first years of statehood, Nevada was pressed to get its boundaries in order. In the process, it managed to eat up a good deal of what was then still an apparently available West.

Yet contested. Here and there along the border of California (a state since September 1850) and the Nevada Territory, there had been disputes. When the Nevada Territory came into being, Nevadans were not inclined to abide by the California line. Rather, in the terms of the Nevada Organic Act, they argued that the true line ought to be the distinction between the place where water either ran down to the Carson Valley or westward toward the Pacific. That vagueness aspired to a border that followed the highest ridge of the Sierra.

Nowhere was the argument fiercer than in Aurora. It was in 1860 that large shelves of gold were found there. The town was classically named, and it drew prospectors from east and west. Indeed, close to 7,500 feet high in the range of mountains that are plainly east of the Sierra, Aurora was only twenty miles or so by rough road from Bodie, one of the most notorious mining towns in the West. For a heady period in the early 1860s, Aurora had close to ten thousand people (one of them was Sam Clemens, trying to get so lucky that it might have erased his need for irony) and it produced about $30 million worth of gold. Its wealth was displayed in the quantity of brick buildings, and surely the bricks were shipped in from California—a dollar a brick, it was said. Equally, they must have passed through Bodie, which remains an essentially wood-built city. So bricks here were a mark of extra class and privilege.

In those early 1860s, Aurora was claimed by both Mono County, California, and Esmeralda County, Nevada Territory. The bustling town had dual elections and cheerfully sent representatives to both capitals. In some cases, though, the situation prompted scuffles that were duly described as a "war" for newspaper readers far away.

By 1863, California and Nevada agreed to a joint boundary survey. It largely adhered to the old California line; thus the state line runs well east of the Sierra and assures that the present Route 395 runs for the most part in California. The border from north to south followed the line of 120 degrees longitude; thus the Honey Lake area, also argued over, fell into California. That line reached into Lake Tahoe itself, and turned at an angle toward the east about three-quarters of the way into the lake. There is surely something lovely and poetic in a frontier that is lapped over by the lake's indifferent waters, and the decision has forever afterward involved both states in matters that affect Lake Tahoe. But at a point in the lake, the boundary line does shift, and it is possible from a boat on the lake to see the boldly cleared line going up the mountainside on the southeast shore—what is now Stateline. Unfortunately, an error was made by the men who did this, and the true line is thus some two-thirds of a mile farther south, well clear of the hotels and casinos of Stateline (the place where Henry Akinwande didn't want to fight).

That ongoing line ensured that Aurora was in Nevada. But that could not save the boomtown. By 1865, the population had fallen by half; by 1870, the best estimate was that Aurora had been used up. No matter the splendor and wind resistance of its brick buildings (this is an area of fearsome winds and blizzards), many people left for Bodie, the wealth of which lasted longer. But Bodie was disreputable. The Aurora newspaper painted a sentimental picture of a little girl leaving with her family. The child was heard to say, "Good-bye, God. We're going to Bodie." In retaliation, the Bodie newspaper (all those upstart towns had their papers) said, no, her line had been misheard in the wind. What she (was her name Aurora?) had really said was, "Good, by God! We're going to Bodie."

Hardly a trace of Aurora remains now—the ghost town was stripped for its bricks in 1946—whereas Bodie is one of the great monuments of America, just a few miles away on a rough road that goes between Beauty and Brawly Peaks.

Let it be known here and now that I claim Bodie as Nevadan. This is not to dispute the state line again, but atmosphere cannot be denied, and there are millions of Californians who have never heard of Bodie, let alone been there. Bodie may be the largest ghost town in the country, a city of shacks—all tilting with the wind—beneath the great hill and its mine.

The diagonal line slanting southeast extended originally as far as the line of 37 degrees latitude. That is where Nevada ended for a few years, thus excluding the sites of Beatty, Mercury, Las Vegas, Henderson, Boulder City, and Laughlin from the state. This is the most arid and desert part of the state, the hottest and the lowest. An attempt to annex the land failed in 1865, but the next year the very large triangle was ceded to Nevada, thus ensuring its sharp southern point, and the ragged southeastern border with Arizona along the Colorado River and Lake Mead. In fact, the line itself was deemed to run down the center of the river, a decision that ensured the future Hoover Dam as belonging to both Nevada and Arizona. In addition, a fair amount of Lake Mead would be granted to Nevada.

Arizona was unhappy, but that territory did not become a state until 1912. (Nevada preceded into the union not just Arizona but also New Mexico, Oklahoma, Utah, Wyoming, Idaho, Montana, both Dakotas, and Colorado.) In the same period, the eastern border of the state was moved east by two entire degrees of longitude, from 116 degrees to 114 degrees—one degree in 1862, and another in 1866—at the mortified expense of Utah. That appropriation included what we now know as Elko, Wells, Ely, and Pioche. It is an enormous piece of land, and one where there were already prospects of mineral wealth. Indeed, the lunging extensions to the east and the south were both made on the assumption that Nevada had already acquired such expertise in mining that it deserved these fresh opportunities.

And so, whatever the haggling, bullying, and chicanery, we have the present state of Nevada. Several paradoxical points may be made straightaway. It is, as the somewhat larger descriptive name implies, a Great Basin state, placed between the Sierra Nevada and the Rockies. Yet Nevada regularly surprises the visitor with the heights it maintains. Throughout the north and well into the south of the state, it is high enough for considerable winter snows: Reno is, at 4,491 feet, an important winter sports area; Gerlach, though it feels as if it is in a desert valley, is at 3,933 feet; Elko is at over 5,000 feet; Austin and Ely are over 6,000 feet, and so is Tonopah.

Though the state declines as it reaches south, Las Vegas itself is at over 2,000 feet; its summer temperatures of over 110 degrees are actually alleviated by the altitude. The site of Hoover Dam is at 1,232 feet, despite the temptation to reckon that a river runs at sea level. The desert town of Beatty, between the Test Site and the Amargosa Valley, and proud to announce itself as the entranceway to Death Valley, is at 3,392 feet. Thus imagine the drop to Death Valley itself, where some spots are below sea level and where the temperature can reach 130 degrees, with smothering humidity. Las Vegas can sometimes seem painful and burning in July or August, but it seldom has any damp air.

Within the basin, Nevada is rippled by mountain ranges that run north-south and the wide valleys that separate them. The truth of this can easily be perceived by driving Route 50—the road that crosses the state east-west at about its midpoint. Some of these ranges are very impressive: In the Toiyabe, Toquima, Monitor, Creek, and Ruby ranges, there are many peaks over ten thousand feet. Wheeler Peak, in the Snake Range, near the Utah border, is over thirteen thousand feet—and about one hundred feet lower than Boundary Peak, in the west, in the Sierra really, the highest point in the state. There are rugged mountains in the northeast corner of the state and something like a mountain plateau in the northwest. There are even the Spring Mountains to the northwest of Las Vegas, where Charleston Peak is 11,918 feet high.

There is the "depression" of Carson Sink and the "lowlands" that surround Las Vegas and Henderson. There is a great quantity of desert or playa on both sides of Gerlach, where the Smoke Creek Desert joins the Black Rock Desert. But Nevada is lofty, clear, and fragrant in nearly all places. It is a very healthy environment. If you doubt that quality, then try the least common way of entering the state. I am thinking of the road from the northwest, Route 140, which comes out of Oregon, by way of Lakeview. Shortly before it crosses the Nevada border, there is an immense climb, from the top of which you look down on a battered plain. There you are on the edge of the Charles Sheldon Antelope Ranch at six thousand or so feet. The ground consists of brown and gray rocks, and there are mountains that are silver and mauve. If you are lucky, you will meet very few cars on that road. You are more than fifty miles from anything resembling a town. In winter, you cannot make the climb without chains. In summer, there is a warm wind on top of the plateau, and probably few days when the temperature climbs past ninety degrees. You could walk into the hills and go for days and days, if you were lucky or unless something happened to you. And if it did, why, in another ten thousand years or so, you might amount to something in history if someone found you.

11. Heaven's Gate

THE TOWNS ARE STILL SO FEW AND SCATTERED IN NEVADA— and so many of them are no longer living towns, but shells, ghosts—that I'm not sure the nature of the state is really a network of vital places so much as an intermittently and briefly interrupted nullity. But, no, not quite nullity, for this is something more than nothing. This is the endless variety and bare beauty of the slopes, the half-hidden valleys, the dry washes going nowhere. Such forms and colors are hardly nullity. Yet there is an absence of culture, civilization, man, or progress there to warn or guide you. Time and again in Nevada, you feel the human thing has hardly got a hold, and so whenever you get to Las Vegas—and you can't really resist going there, the sediment sinking down to the bottom of the state, hoping to get away on the Colorado—you can't help but notice that this city, so boisterously expansive, is desperate, frenzied, hysterical, and shaky. It hangs on like a girl's dress on a hot, windy day. Make a killing, you say to yourself, and get out of town.

Walter Van Tilburg Clark (1909–1971) was a Nevada man for much of his life, and he wrote at least one book—*The Track of the Cat*—that anyone interested ought to read, because it suggests how the few people who abided, and did what we call "live," in those remote and tenuous places were sometimes nearly deformed by it. It's a book about people shaped by loneliness, the siege of winter, the remorseless simplicity of life, and the notion (part dread, part expectation) that there was a wild cougar out there in the snow and the mountains waiting to destroy them. The novel is actually set in the California Sierra, but it could be the Nevada Clark knew, for it has an ingrowing solitude, not tranquil or nourishing, but the walking separateness that almost guarantees there is no society. You can see the same mood sometimes, macabre and haunting, on the packed casino floors of Vegas, where every player is alone with his or her chips and the script that Fate is working on. Whatever happens in the game, no matter the cries of other emotions here or there, *you* know the numbers work out just for you. And if you lose—and eventually you will lose; everyone loses—you have to see that the losing suits you. You are a loser, which is a loner gone soft.

Anyway, Walter Van Tilburg Clark wrote a poem once, a piece of whimsy, in which God took the first five and a half days to make the rest of the world, then kept the remainder of His time for Nevada. Because that was the real challenge. But it wasn't time enough. So God left the job unfinished—which is a way of saying that anything we do is doomed or futile:

> *So the hills are in rows and they're piled up too high;*
> *They are colder than death and they trouble the sky.*
> *Though at night you may freeze, yet at noon you will fry*
> *In the unfinished land of Nevada.*

By that lulling rhyme scheme, of course, the last line should end with "Nevadie" or "never die." You have to have some of the patience and sangfroid of a ghost to get along there—you need to be not quite what you were, not quite alive to this world, but breathing history and with time in your veins.

When Arthur Miller wrote *The Misfits*—which is set in and was filmed in Nevada—he wrote it as a kind of novella. And it has a passage where Roslyn (the Marilyn Monroe character) is driving along a straight, endless highway:

On both sides the bare Nevada hills are spread out, range beyond range. An occasional dirt trail winding into them raises the surprising thought that one could follow it and arrive at a human place in the interior. No house shows; only an occasional line of fence indicates that cattle range here sometimes. The hills front the highways like great giants' chests; to the eye speeding past, their undulating crests rise and fall as though the Earth were silently breathing. The noon sun is lighting up red, wound-like stains on their surfaces, a sudden blush of purple on one, the next faintly pink, another buff. Despite the hum of the engines, the land seems undisturbed in its silence, a silence that grows in the mind until it becomes a wordless voice.

Am I being followed? the writer wonders. It is a recurring question on these straight roads that swoon, the mountain ranges lined up like the clashes of manic depression.

On a Sunday, driving east out of Reno toward Elko, there is no sign of winter. It is sixty degrees or so, and most of the way, there is a thin, pale sunshine, like beer, enough to begin to pick out the mineral staining in the ground. But there is a wind going all the while, tugging at the car and sending dry wheels of tumbleweed skittering over the highway. If you hit them just right, you can see the dusty shrapnel in your rearview mirror. But the clumps of tumbleweed keep coming and, like illegals, many of them make it all the way across the highway. There is a stupid urge in driving to miss them, to play tag with them—all at the open-highway speed limit of seventy-five—which is not really decent. And somewhere along I-80, there comes an accident in the distance. The Highway Patrol is there and candy-colored cones send us off I-80, down an exit ramp, and then back up the other side. The accident has occurred on an overpass. There is a car pushed, or smudged, into the barrier and one of those artic- ulated vehicles that transport cars—it was going to Salt Lake, or Omaha, say—broken-backed and askew. The whirl of the tumbleweed carries on regardless, trusting that ceaseless, nagging wind (the prevailing wind) that sets in on Nevada's high northern plateau and leaves the arms of truckers hard and cramped from holding their rigs against the steady urging. The balls of tumbleweed seem like furies if you have seen enough bad smashups on windswept I-80, when it is often hard enough to stay awake, let alone think.

Monday morning, in Elko, at seven o'clock, there is that silent white light pressing at the window—as weak and patient as the Living Dead. Snow has fallen on this last day of March, and a dense mist has settled at a distance of a couple of hundred yards. The weather people will call it "a chill-down," with temperatures ten or more degrees below normal. It's only a light snowfall, but it is there still, specks hesitating in the air. There is traffic. The roads are just rain and slush. We are at over five thousand feet in Elko, and no matter that you could walk around yesterday evening at nine without a jacket, this is still winter.

I take a leisurely breakfast, giving the weather a chance to improve. The snow stops, and for maybe half an hour, one can see the first hills out- side town. Then the mist inhales more deeply and it is as close as the shopping mall across the way, hovering above Payless Drugs and JCPen- ney. The snow begins to fall again, coming in aslant, for the wind is still there. I notice that the flakes have a stubborn life like the sage had, carried by the air, reluctant to land or hold a place on the ground. This is the Sagebrush State, after all, and sage isn't just the clumps of pale green thriving in the desert. It is these bindles of dryness that tumble on forever until they persuade a car to blow them to bits.

It will take a little longer before there is any use in going out. It's time to look at USA Today and go through the channels—surfing, or saging—on the Holiday Inn's cable system. I begin to see a forlorn inner calm or entropy in being stranded on I-80—it comes on like a depression, and surely it is a mood most people in America, or USA Today, would recognize. But in Nevada, as with so many other things, depression is a kind of gaming—toss a coin for going back to bed or going to the casino.

The paper that has become the ubiquitous American newspaper, and which is important not just for that reason but because of all the things that it ignores, has a double-page spread of potted biographies of the thirty-nine who killed themselves the other day in Rancho Sante Fe, near San Diego—the Heaven's Gate people.

There are postage stamp–size photographs of most of them and captioned careers: the woman from Mesa, Arizona, who had told her coworkers at an osteopath's office that she was a nun and lived in a monastery, but who actually had a base in a trailer park in Scottsdale; the parents of five, the mother a postal worker, who found Heaven's Gate on the Internet, and who left the five children with a grandparent, saying, "Here, they're yours"; the nurse whose world collapsed when her father died and was never seen again; the University of Washington graduate whose brother now says that he didn't feel alarmed by the cult, "but when we received a video from Peggy that had Applewhite declaring himself the second coming of Christ and that he intended to lead his flock to redemption, I got a real bad feeling then. . . ."

These lives are not extraordinary or vicious. They are, in the pictures, bland, pretty faces, faces from yearbook situations and so on, putting on a chipper look for the camera. They are people from all over the United States and our recent todays who moved on or began to lead double lives, and who, quite evidently, felt at a loss, dissatisfied, otherwise empty or unfulfilled, miserable maybe, or cheerfully hoping for something better somewhere else. They are very much the sort of people USA Today is aimed at, and people who might easily gravitate toward the beckoning of Nevada, or Heaven's Gate, or Hale-Bopp's arc, or 2000—don't forget 2000, that heady turning point, and the terrible vulnerability of this crowded, empty country, and its hunches about numbers. So many of us are going to be betting 2,000.

After all, *USA Today* today—apart from its immediate news (its main headline is SECURITY HIGH AS OKLA BOMB TRIAL OPENS and that is next to a kind of Internet image of the Heaven's Gate logo, some of the postage-stamp faces, and the heading EARTHLY WOES LEAD MANY TO SPACE CULT)—has a big feature on Dave Thomas, the founder of the Wendy's chain. DAVE'S BACK, the sixty-four-year-old's T-shirt says (*USA Today* is a T-shirt kind of paper), referring to his heart bypass surgery, and inside there is the boxed life—how he was born in Atlantic City to parents he never knew; how he was adopted by people in Kalamazoo, Michigan; how, as a boy, he dreamed of owning the best restaurant in the world; how he dropped out of school at fifteen, married a waitress, got into the Kentucky Fried Chicken business, sold his KFC franchises, and formed Wendy's in 1969, and now there are five thousand of them and he is famous for more than five hundred TV commercials he has done.

Dave is some kind of American idol—the foundling millionaire—the would-be gourmet who found himself in fast foods indistinguishable from all the others. And Dave's postage stamp could be on the other page so easily. And there's his boxed story along with the regular feature "How in the World." (Today's question is: "On average, how long does a U.S. dollar bill stay in circulation?" The answer, printed in small type, vertically, at the side of the box, is "Eighteen months.") There is also a piece on how, in Amarillo, Texas, you can play the game of eating the big steak dinner— a seventy-two-ounce sirloin, with baked potato, shrimp cocktail, and salad—in one hour. Make it, and the dinner's free; dawdle, and it's $50. Since the early 1960s, forty thousand people have tried, and only seven thousand have succeeded. I wonder whether any of the Heaven's Gate people had tried, and failed, and taken that as the last straw, the sign to follow that frozen-faced, unblinking Marshall Herff Applewhite.

I do not mean to condescend to such people, or make them into crazies. Indeed, I think they are only half an inch or so from being very ordinary Americans—and it is an ordinary American dream, anyway, to get your picture in the papers. These are no more than men and women who acknowledge a slightly out-of-the-way respect for pursuing happiness. And I-80 is a road made for that pursuit; it is the quick, sure way of getting people out of the Midwest—out of Chicago, Iowa, Nebraska—and nearer to Reno, California, Hawaii, Las Vegas, all those places that are alleged to offer a better chance and are probably yellow and orange, if not red, in the

USA Today weather map, where other places (the places they have come from) are blue and green with cold.

And it doesn't seem far-fetched that someone less than happy or secure, say, might be paused on I-80, in this late snow, and looking out at the drab mall facing the Holiday Inn—at Baskin-Robbins, Albertson's, the tax-service office (April 15 is coming round again), Payless, Burger King, JCPenney, and Pizza Hut (all of them to be found in Iowa or Nebraska)— or remoting his way through the TV channels: talk shows, game shows, weather forecasts, Whitney Houston forever climaxing in the same music video, an instructional cooking program, a clergyman speaking directly, earnestly, to us in close-up, a C-Span debate, in long shot, on policy issues, a Nickelodeon cartoon, the Home Shopping Network with a hand holding a necklace, Shirley Temple in *Heidi,* college basketball players trying to find the words to say how it will go tonight (it's the Kentucky Wildcats versus the Arizona Wildcats—are the duplicate nicknames an omen?), a segment on how to install a shower, and the program schedules. No, it's not out of the question that that traveler might go next door to the Red Lion Inn and Casino and lose it all, or drive to San Diego or wherever some fresh hope is broadcasting on the Internet. You go with your hunches and put the spin on the results and the play in your mind.

By the way, did you know that the Heaven's Gate people went to Las Vegas for a few days before they did what they did? Were they just trying it out, as entrance or exit? Suppose one of them had had a big win there— would they have lived awhile longer? Then wonder how many Vegas players also have suicide in mind as an option.

12. The Experiment

ON ONE OF MY TRIPS TO NEVADA, I FOUND MYSELF IN FALLON with time for a late lunch before getting the plane out of Reno back to San Francisco. There are places to eat in a town like Fallon, arranged along the road like filling stations. It doesn't make a lot of difference which one you choose, and so gradually, I suppose, you might come to think of yourself as a vehicle. I had the club sandwich and coffee, and it was a club sandwich I have eaten so many times before, with toothpicks and little colored cellophane twirls on their ends, holding the three layers of toast together. Then there is the turkey, as white as an inner thigh, cool still from the refrigerator, and impeccably tasteless. Can this really come from a fowl, irritable and odd, that has stepped on actual ground and dabbed its head to get the corn in the gravel? Or is there some likely refrigerator roll of "turkey" sandwich filling that stretches from Fresno to Hoboken, endlessly sliced, always renewed, a national grid?

What I mean to say is that, much as I want to offer Nevada to you, no one here is going to lie to you and tell you the food is anything but terrible. There are big hotels in Reno and Vegas, of course, and there are some good name restaurants in the Forum at Caesar's Palace in Vegas and at the Bellagio. There are a few places around Lake Tahoe where the cuisine is as good and Californian as Mill Valley, say. But on the road in Nevada, you might be wise to eat breakfast three times a day: It is fresh, simple, extensive, and American—I don't think there is anywhere else in the world that takes a couple of eggs, sausage, hash browns, and toast for granted for breakfast.

Later in the day, you get the cheeseburgers and the club sandwiches, monotonously cloned. But worst of all are the dinner specials—the roast pork, the chicken Kiev, the fish and chips, or, of course, the turkey dinner. Have breakfast again, and don't think of going near the salad bar, the last abode for diced and shredded vegetables such as could easily be flown in from the "China" that seemingly has to manufacture any plastic toy nowadays that you buy for your children. And beware the coffee later in the day: This probably would corrode your car if presented, so why risk yourself?

Traveling in Nevada—watching, say, sad employees eating chocolate glop at the Nevada Test Site—you have to wonder about the place of food in the personality of a state. This is a topic to return to, but for the moment, just let me say that too many club sandwiches on the Nevadan road gives you an incentive to get out. In other words, the thought of living in Nevada would alarm me—and that may offend many good people in Nevada who will read this book, and who treasure their retirement there.

I was thinking along these lines as I made my way through a club sandwich in Fallon. This was in a diner attached to a small casino with some name like Nugget, Bonanza, or Lucky Strike, names that defy the listless air of the place and its hollow assurance of transformation.

There was a girl sitting at the counter, not eating or drinking, but left alone by the waitress. She wore scuffed sneakers and faded jeans with a sateen shirt the color of dried blood. Her lank brown hair was dyed so that it turned puce and then pink at its ends. She had vivid acne, but it seemed not to worry her. She was about thirteen.

For a while, she was on her own, idle and unoccupied, unamused by the clash between her startling colors and the drab, forlorn look of her face. Yet she brightened, or curled up a little in some slight, instinctive response when a boy appeared. He wore a Metallica T-shirt and had a dip of beard on his chin. He sat next to her and played Keno to a PA system that was calling the numbers. He was fifteen or sixteen, I guess.

Despite their blatant callowness, this couple had some air of elderly, and even sweet, marriage. But will they be content with that for fifty or sixty years? When we look at strangers like this, they become actors of a sort: We study their appearance for information, or story. It is not fair, but it is not human to be a blank spectator making no judgment. There are couples like this one all over America, alarming, sad, and quietly feral. They are in most respects underage, not that anything about them—not even her white ankle socks—promises innocence. They are on the margins of poverty, and likely below even this country's depressed norms of educational competence.* Are they the kids of military people at the Fallon base? I doubt it; they are too dowdy. Do they have a parent or an elder working in this diner/casino? Maybe. That would explain why no one takes their order or asks them to leave. But are they just hanging out in the slack certainty that no one cares enough about them to take the trouble of moving them on? They're not dangerous, are they? Or are they sustained in this lackluster place by some religion, some deep knowledge that the inconsequentiality here and now in Fallon is just necessary waiting? Was the girl sitting unoccupied, empty or bored, or simply patient? To answer that, you'd have to decide what kind of story she's in.

San Francisco is less than six hours away by car; no more than three if you drive and fly. It is an international city (no matter that it clings to a few marks of parochialism that remind you how, before the 1930s and the two bridges, it was a city somewhat marooned by water). There are great restaurants there, an opera, a symphony, a ballet, a stock exchange, many movie houses. There are law courts, universities, superb hospitals, and large, relatively unhindered minorities—the Chinese, the Latin Americans, the gays. To the south of the city is Silicon Valley, a center for the world's computer craze.

Fallon, and Nevada as a whole, are so close, yet they lack all those things. Being in Nevada, and seeing some of its young people, you have to wonder what mixture of fear, defiance, and distaste keeps them from going to the city. I think some of them would say they despise the city for its crowds, its corruptions, its unhindered minorities, and its removal from desert space and grim human nature. The city is a trick still, isn't it, through the great dull expanses of America? And in truth, the cities are not exactly rooted. You sometimes feel you could scrape away Los Angeles with a spatula, the way in this diner, every half hour or so, someone scrapes the hot plate free of egg crisp, onions, grease, and charred gunk. As for that San Francisco, well, it's just waiting, isn't it, for the Big One, the earthquake? You'd have to be an idiot to live there. And these two kids are damn sure they're not fools. After all, they might ask you with cocky grins, why do you think they chose to put the Top Gun boys in Fallon, and why have they got that whole setup waiting in Area 51? Doesn't anyone

---

* The Nevada Education Reform Act of 1997 imposed higher scores on candidates for high school diplomas (this because of widespread complaints in the state that graduates were lacking in basic skills). Failure rates jumped from 16.4 to 21.3 percent in reading, and from 17.9 to 33.2 percent in math. Nearly 40 percent failed to graduate.

with sense know that it's all coming back here, to the desert? Isn't that where the aliens are coming? That's where it'll be decided. And pretty damn soon, too.

I love America, I love Nevada—as if that makes either of them less alarming. Am I saying that Nevada is in some ways characteristic of the rest of America, that its threat or promise is the same as America's? No, not quite. Nevada is not typical, suburban, not mainstream or heartland, though we may find traces of all those things. It is wilder, more abstract or notional, less gentle, accommodating, or viable.

Nevada is on the edge, on the wire, off to one side, in the empty quarter, or even in the rest of the country's head as an idea, a possibility, an alternative. It is an experiment, or a kind of theater. Yes, that's somewhere nearer to the answer, for America has used Nevada as a testing ground, and not just for weapons and their destructiveness but also for new social ideas, and their explosiveness. What happens if you allow divorce, prostitution, gambling? Can there be community and purpose if you encourage things deep in human nature yet supposedly alien to order and togetherness? Don't we need to find out?

Does that make Nevada sound like a hellish game? Well, there are surely images of Hell here, some made for the tourists, and some hushed up. But there is a constitutional emptiness, a dullness, an availability, an absence of those things that are regular. And that is an openness Nevadans love, or adhere to, and it is beautiful beyond more accepted senses of that word. There is beauty, let us propose, in a city with an opera, great restaurants, and the busy conversation of society as a whole. Yet there is some other rapture inherent in the lack of those things. And the most sophisticated urbanites of America long, too, to get away from it all, to see nature, emptiness, however they think of it. And just because the wonder of built-up America is so new, so recent, and so sketchy, no one forgets the emptiness there was once before. And Nevada is that image and idea of an America "before time," or prehistory, and yet "after time," too, after we have accomplished the complete destruction of ourselves. For it is not just that something in the base form of Nevada promises survival. No, it is beyond that. It is endurance.

And so sometimes in Nevada there is nothing more reasonable to do than wait for some sort of ending. You cannot be eager, or greedy for it, but patient, abiding. So it is not simply a fear of change, or a loathing of modernity, that may make some kids stay in Fallon, or Nevada, where they have nothing much to do. Rather, it's the wry wondering whether it makes enough difference that is somewhere between nullity and philosophy. When we get to Las Vegas, be ready to see how far the "frenzy" of gaming, the artificial exhilaration, the willful loss of assets, is just a way of killing time.

There's no end of time in the desert, you see, and not quite the mad rush to fill it, stretch out, and let it fill you. Think of it as an experiment.

13. Frankly

Ladies and gentlemen, whether at magic hour with the baked shadows stretched like mad giants or in the pink blush of predawn while the guys are still out in the open spaces burying the bodies in the Cadillac headlights, the camera comes swooping in and down across the lone and level sands until we are at the lip of the Sands itself, with his high-gloss black wing tips adorning the silica gray sprinkle, and the camera looks up at his grin, his glee, his wolfish, insecure eyes, begging for our attention, but with the runt's charm that goes ring-a-ding-ding in all our secret sexual fantasy chambers . . . ladies and gentlemen, he's here!, and the town is on tonight, the greatest entertainer in the world, Mr. Las Vegas, the Chairman of the Board, the Lord High Rat of the Sands and his great pack, show time, post time, time to fuck the ladies and anyone else in sight, and watch out for his temper, for this may be the last real king on Earth, ready to have your insolence, dispute, or even a hard, staring scrutiny offed—ladies and gentlemen, Mr. Frank Sinatra.

And then it's the real thing, the dream, for an hour or so, cruising and soothing in and out of "I Get a Kick Out of You," "I Get Along Without You Very Well," "I'll Be Around," "I've Got You Under My Skin," "Mind If I Make Love to You?," "I Guess I'll Have to Change My Plan," "One for My Baby," "Willow Weep for Me," "Try a Little Tenderness," "All the Way," and doing "Chicago," once, quick and tough, for the boys at the table in front who are in town tonight (catch you later), but eschewing "My Way," because, after all, he never was much for that song, but just doing it his way, letting his own special arrangements, by Riddle, Stordahl, May, or Hefti, just issue forth like long narrative lines, telegraph lines in the desert, and letting the lyrics in on his very good voice on what is a very good night, so the hookers and the wives and the bimbos and the broads know that it's them alone he knows, and their guys, the hoods, the made men and the would-bes, the Corleones and the Brascos, and all the guys in from Jersey and the Midwest who dream of being gangsters can just swing along on the notion of this ugly little guy being so sweet when everyone knows he's tough, and thank God he sings for the next hour, so he doesn't have any reason to lose his temper for that while, unless the fucking second trumpet fluffs again.

"Sure," Tommy Dorsey, the bandleader, his onetime owner, had said, "he's the most fascinating man in the world, but don't stick your hand in the cage." And that ruined look, vengeful, thrown back over his shoulder at the dark of the audience, told you why. It was self-pity vindicated. For Frankie Sinatra was always playing a very nasty guy nursing that thing about respect.

He had so much: not just movie money, but record royalties from a six-decade career, appearance fees that were the highest in the world—and a little bit of the action. But then on top of that, he always wanted to be comped. He had everything he wanted: a loyal local Italian Catholic wife who gave him children; an astonishing beauty, Ava Gardner, whom he adored because she never sat there and took it from him; a child bride, a kid from the New Hollywood in the age of Lolita; and then someone solid to look after him in Palm Springs. And all the way he had taken more— starlets, socialites, blondes picked out of the crowd, hookers, not chasing dames like the lady who is irony's tramp, but big hair and big mouths who did as they were told and no talking about it afterward. And then he had within him some ultimate sad eloquence, a way with the best songs of this century—which may yet prove the jewels of our age—such as no one else matched. He had his voice, his instrument. And sometimes he never bothered with it. And even when he was on, and was something like a poet there at the Sands or Caesars, he was also the bully, the needler, the angry runt with bodyguards who would stay up all night looking for trouble, and who could sometimes attack people with the zeal of a rat. And never an ounce of natural humor in him, but a meanness of spirit, as if the real forlorn tenderness in his voice shamed him with the guys. So he could betray his great instrument and snarl at hatcheck girls, croupiers, or those passing visitors from Iowa or West Virginia who had just looked at him, because they loved him—and because his self-pity was somehow irked at having so much.

Sinatra is the split personality standing astride plenty and pain, never quite sure which is which. As such, he is a very important example of, and to, Nevadan men, poised like the ball over the wheel, ready to win or lose, but doomed in that fall to his own pitiful identity. The reason why he is and was so vital to the state and to Las Vegas for twenty years or so was not just that he spurred business with his presence, but also because in his attitude he was the little man, the loner, the hanger-on, who dreamed of winning but who went in dread of its discoveries. For winners must be like princes, or risk losing our respect. And Sinatra was never more than a goodfella, except when he sang. And a guy can't sing forever without being regarded as a sissy. He has to fuck around, get drunk, and talk like the gutter. He has to act as if he's above anything as slight as human nature, its great talent, or his extraordinary songs.

The split takes a mockingly physical form, like the dotted line along which we are expected to tear, separating the invoice from the receipt. It is the line called Cal-Neva, the frontier that hits the northern shore of Lake Tahoe, where the mass and mind-set of California and Nevada meet. There are traffic lights on Route 50 and a cluster of garish buildings, small casinos that promise to stay open twenty-four hours for you. And off to the right, on the very shore of the cold lake, there is the Cal-Neva Lodge, a low-slung fun spot, the apple of Frank's eye, a place where the boys could relax and the family gather.

Nancy Sinatra, his daughter, saw it this way:

> To say that he had worked hard to make Cal-Neva a success would not begin to approximate his efforts. But it was worth it—a dream come true—a Sinatraland with bright lights, music, gambling. It offered night life and razzle-dazzle juxtaposed with natural things: clear water, clean air, giant trees, outdoor sports, and the purple mountains.

Frank had been into the Nevada idea early on. Hadn't he and his side-kick Phil Silvers been big on the "Good evening, Mr. Siegel, and how are you?" act in Los Angeles around 1944 and 1945? Sinatra had a natural respect for Ben Siegel, the way kids get wide-eyed when big ballplayers pass by. Sinatra loved Siegel's reputation, his saturnine, smart look, and the way he seemed to be forever comped in life—the parking, the room, the table, the broads, the alarmed-looking guys who were all patient and attentive to his crazy eyes. And there were some who noted the deep impression left on Sinatra by the absolute ease with which Ben could go from the lady-killing grin to the psychotic temper that said, Hey, who did we kill today? Frank knew that shift from Jersey and New York and Chicago, his kind of towns, and the wise guys who would laugh all night until someone laughed too loudly back and they shot his toes off. That terrific mock-stylish change of tone and meaning, as if all you had to do was snap your fingers the way Frank did to count the band in.

And Frank had been going to Nevada from the late 1940s and the early 1950s. He became an institution at the Sands, not just a singer there but part owner, too, and hadn't he used the state for his divorces, first from Nancy Barbato and then from Ava Gardner? And he had liked Cal-Neva because it was quieter and more out of the way. At the Labor Day weekend in 1951, he and Ava had been there—the Nancy divorce pending—when they had had one of their rows, and she had stormed out, and Frankie had taken pills and nearly done himself in. In those bad years, he was screwed-up by Nancy and Ava, wanting them both; he hated desire because of the fool it makes of you.

So he was sentimental about Cal-Neva, and it got to be his place. Over the years, his ownership percentage crept up—by May 1962, he had half the place. Was it the Cal half or the Neva? he could joke in his act in the Celebrity Room. The dotted line, it was said, went right through the premises, so you could drink in California and gamble in Nevada, and hey, little girl, you were romanced so you didn't know which state your ass was in.

The short summer season ran June through Labor Day, and Cal-Neva got its boost from Frank and the friends he would hire in to the Celebrity Room and from the money that was drafted in to refurbish the place. Paul "Skinny" D'Amato was the manager there, and he was working for Sam Giancana, the Chicago boss—his kind of town—and Frank and Sam were like that.

Like what? Like you know what. Like a lot of mutual respect and shared dreams. Sam liked Cal-Neva because when the McGuire Sisters played there, he could be there, quietly, with Phyllis, without the glare of attention, inasmuch as Sam was one of those people, in the Black Book, forbidden to be on the premises of a Nevada casino. And sometimes Frank and Sam would hit a few golf balls together and take in the scenery for which Tahoe is so famous.

But then Ed Olsen, chairman of the Nevada Gaming Commission— we are talking the summer of 1963—chose to get himself into the imbroglio of whether the Cal-Neva was just a place for laundering mob money, not to mention Sam Giancana's R and R favorite. There were interviews and so on, fact-finding sessions, with talk building in the papers, and Olsen beginning to see dangers in a renewed license for

Frank to run a casino. There was subpoena talk, and Frank getting into the kind of dialogue he knew the rhythm and the line to as well as those of his own songs:

> You just try and find me, and if you do, you can look for a big, fat surprise . . . a big, fat, fucking surprise. You remember that. Now, listen to me, Ed . . . don't fuck with me. Don't fuck with me. Just don't fuck with me.

I mean, is that incriminating, or is that rhythm? Frank always had a big, bad mouth on him, and there's not a dame who hadn't heard him at the Sands, or wherever, who didn't *know* that he could do Larry Hart lines, or whatever, so you knew he was fucking you to the beat. And hadn't Ava Gardner said once that, sure, Frank was so skinny, he was only 110 pounds, but 100 pounds of that was cock? In other words, his talking to Ed Olsen that way was sui generis more than it was incriminating, and it was a crying shame how the misunderstanding got in the way of the whole Cal-Neva dream. Not that anyone but a romantic nut who loved the lake would even have thought there was real money to be made at Cal-Neva. After all, Tahoe in the summer is the kids and their mothers and fathers getting up there for the weekend. The thing about Tahoe that is never going to work—not work as far as real money is concerned—is that it's all nature. And Frank, that dreamer, he never worked that out.

So you had to see Frank's getting angry with Olsen as no more than the irrepressible little guy not knowing how to back down. Sam Giancana told him to shut up and cool it, and Jack Warner said the same. That is Jack as in Warner Bros., because at that very time Frank and Warners were in big negotiations, with Frank getting ready to trade his own record company, Reprise, for Warners stock and cash. And the casino stuff, said Jack, was soiling the deal. So Frank, because he never had wanted to make trouble for anyone, resigned his ownership at Cal-Neva—he even gave up the 9 percent of the Sands he had in Vegas—to make the Warners deal. And, of course, since Frank was giving up on his dream to have a little place on the shore, they had to make the deal sweet enough. That was 1963, and even Jack Kennedy had said once to Governor Grant Sawyer, "Aren't you people being a little hard on Frank out here?"

That was a classy thing to say, but, of course, Frank had put out for Jack, too, in the past, in Chicago—their kind of town—so it was water under the bridge. But ever afterward, Frank was just a little bitter—let's say wry—over Vegas and the casino business. And he did Vegas afterward for the fat fees, and the comped suites, and the list that had all his friends on it. And why not, he'd say, because look at the crowds—are they here for you, fuckhead, or are they here for me?

In the late 1950s and into the 1960s, the Rat Pack thing was the central part of the Vegas allure—with Frank and Dean and Sammy and all the others. And, above all, the attitude: Hey, this is a wide-open time, for swingers, and there are floors full of hookers after we go upstairs, but meanwhile let me do "One for My Baby," or would you like "The Tender Trap"? And Frank liked to gamble, too, and he expected comped chips for that, and he reckoned to win, because, hey, it was good for business if the people saw him win, and they won themselves, so there were times when Frank even took over as croupier and let whatever number he wanted win. These are only numbers, right, and this count is just shit that goes through the pipes? And Vegas was a place where you might see gangsters and hookers and Frank Sinatra. And don't you know that people with dumb, dull lives need that thrill?

Ladies and gentlemen, we are talking about a true son of Nevada, never mind where he was born or where he chose to live. We are talking about the dream that losers, jerks, flakes, broken-down guys can still get the broads, the comped room, and the *respect* they deserve. Hey—come fly with me. Show time. Post time. Ring-a-ding-ding time. That's Frank.

But don't put your hand in the cage.

14. Anthrax!

YOU NEVER KNOW WHAT THAT CAR UP AHEAD MIGHT BE carrying—and its driver is just as ignorant about what you've got in the trunk of yours. (After all, he has half a notion that you are following him.) But sometimes, all of a sudden, the buzz is on, and you realize that the slow-building unmarked "traffic" you've been experiencing coming into Las Vegas, from Henderson, is the loose outline of what can on the radioed word, the command password, close in as being a "phalanx" of FBI vehicles ready to isolate the suspect's car and guide it up onto the shoulder of the highway.

Not that that's exactly where you and your loved ones would want live anthrax to come to rest. Anthrax! That's a word you don't expect to hear on a dull winter's morning. Then again, in Nevada, you never quite rule out the kind of cry you didn't expect to hear, like "Eureka!" "Winner!" or even "Zero," of the kind that goes between 3-2-1 and the big bang, or like "Zero," the last word you'll ever hear.

Well, on the evening of February 18, 1998, FBI agents had "swooped down" on a medical clinic in Henderson, ten miles or so southeast of Las Vegas, and they had taken into custody not just a pale beige Mercedes sedan but also a cooler chest, several petri dishes, and two men who were believed to be in possession of deadly—or potentially deadly—anthrax bacteria. By the morning of the nineteenth, the two men had been charged and Bobby Siller, Special Agent in Charge of the Las Vegas FBI office—and of the swooping task force—was giving a live news conference, live on CNN, in which the very little that Mr. Siller knew and could say was being spread out pretty thin in the gray winter air. The conference was in the open air—somehow, with anthrax as a possibility, you want to have the high sky above you.

Suddenly, on some highway, the encounter with fire and trouble

The two men already in prison clothes and chains—you have to wonder if these things aren't just costume markers so the FBI guys won't forget which ones are in custody—Larry Wayne Harris and William Jobe Leavitt, Jr., and the newspaper descriptions of them give us all fair warning about what the turbulence, the joy, and the dismay of life can come down to.

Thus, Harris, of Lancaster, Ohio, was said to be a freelance water tester and a microbiologist, a former member of the "ultra-right-wing" Aryan Nations, the author and publisher of a book, *Bacteriological Warfare: A Major Threat to North America*, and a man who was on probation from a 1995 conviction for obtaining bubonic plague bacteria under false pretenses. Leavitt was a microbiologist who lived in Logandale, Nevada, a place too small for many maps, a devout Mormon, owner of a fire-safety business, a man with a hobby—that of looking into cures for the great diseases of our time.

Harris, forty-six, was large, fully bearded, and the wearer of heavy spectacles. Leavitt, a year older, was lean, gaunt, and with short, receding hair and rimless spectacles. They did not look like a match, and they did not really seem to know each other very well. But you could put them side by side, in jailhouse drabs and chains, and with the word *anthrax*, they looked pretty sinister. Of course, anyone can play sinister nowadays, and there's nothing more suggestively furtive than the lowered gaze that is just trying to mind its own business.

If Leavitt was as quiet as Logandale—there in the Moapa Valley, just north of Overton and between Lake Mead and Highway 93—Harris was colorful. Apart from his white supremacist ties, he alleged contacts with Iraqis who had warned him of that nation's plan to "unleash" a biological attack on the United States, and he had made it his business—both in his book and in a readiness to lecture around the country—to spread the word of that threat. No one quite knew why he had wanted bubonic plague bacteria, but he had sometimes said that a "globe" of that stuff set off in the New York subway system could kill as many as 100,000 people. He had also said, from time to time, that he had been attached to the CIA. The CIA denied that, and Harris would say, "Of course they do. What do you expect?"

What do we expect? Is that Mercedes up ahead actually CIA, or just a car driven by a middle-aged fantasist with a beard so foolish that it could be false, who likes to pretend he's a secret op? Are you just singing along with Sinatra on the tape deck, or smoothing away the miles in the day-dream that you are Frank, guiding the song lyrics into your bruised mem-ories of all the times Ava walked out on you? Why did she do that? Because she loved reunions, silly.

A day later, in apprehensive Las Vegas, the news broke: The seized material from the day before was *not* the deadly anthrax bacteria, but a "harmless veterinary vaccine" that was actually helpful in preventing anthrax. The two men, it seemed, had been looking to conduct some experiments at the Henderson laboratory, with a view to eliminating anthrax. However, the twelve-hour pursuit that led to their arrest had been set off by a Ronald G. Rockwell, who had been approached about helping with the tests. He had got the impression that they had "military-grade anthrax"—anthrax!—and "it scared me so bad."

Why Henderson? we have to ask. And very likely the answer is that Leavitt knew of the place, and maybe Harris had fancied a few days in Vegas. Just because a man knows the terrors of worldwide plague doesn't bar him from wanting to try his luck. But the "misunderstanding" had had some salutary effects, it was said. After all, Americans are all too inclined to believe they have the greatest and safest nation on earth, and anthrax was and remains one of the weapons, or words, that Saddam Hussein is said to have ready for use in and around his Iraq. All of which was, as they say, going on at the same time in another desert kingdom.

Come to that, the nation Iraq fears most of all had and has its own deposits of "military-grade" anthrax not that many miles from Las Vegas—

I'll say no more, because this information is classified and I haven't entirely given up on the schoolboy hope of being useful to the CIA someday.

The incident came and went. Leavitt is back in Logandale, chastened no doubt, and head down again in the fire-safety business. Harris was detained longer, and one hopes he is still under "surveillance." But America is not yet a country that has found ways to lock up every dangerous fantasist without due process. There are plenty of people in and around the Las Vegas casino whose heads are filled with wild dreams of a big break, or of what they are going to have to do if their number doesn't come up.

And, if it comes to the real nub of the matter, if you want to test anthrax — and see just how easily it could become anthrax! — then Nevada is your place. Yet again, not that many miles from Las Vegas there is a great tradition of using the empty places, patient livestock, and even the U.S. armed forces in tests and experiments to see just exactly what this or that will do under these conditions of wind or weather. There are folks to the northeast, way beyond Logandale, up as far as St. George, in Utah, in line with the prevailing winds that sweep the Nevada Test Site, who have had growths on their faces as large as Harris's beard. That could be by unhappy chance, of course; our government keeps an open mind on that one, to let time test the evidence and carry away the wounded.

But so much more has half-life in the wind and the space where toxins ebb and flow. Nevada can be looked at as an area where highways intersect, where beige Mercedeses or wine red Toyotas are coming in from the Midwest, doing as much as one thousand miles a day, to the point where the drivers are dangerously tired. And that is the liberty of America, that if your wheels can get you there, you can go, and good luck to you. There is a web of roadside diners and filling stations to sustain you, and there is the strange community of traffic. There's no road rage out on the interstates, but, rather, a kind of unspoken fraternity, with maybe the hand just lifting from the wheel in a small wave of acknowledgment. And the microbiologist never knows for sure who the murderers are. Never knows that he may be one himself.

And Las Vegas, say, is one of those places to which exhausted, depressed careerists go for solace, as well as outlaws who are merely seeking crowd cover. You can meet anyone there — no questions asked. And if you were to order a summary raid on the contents of all the cars parked at all the casino hotels, say, no one would be amazed if the haul included several cases stuffed with money, enough AK-47s for a military mission, the manuscripts of great novels, a few bodies, and enough military-strength Black Death (I pick it at random) to take out a moderate-sized South American republic. So spare us the raids, the inventory, and its embarrassment, and let the trunks pass by. We all of us carry luggage that we hardly know how to abandon, let alone explain.

15. Fast Numbers

THERE ARE SO MANY TIMES WHEN ONE IS "OUT THERE" IN
the open extensiveness of Nevada when it is not easy to gauge whether
one is looking at (or waiting for) the past or the future. The landscape
itself, of course, is so often prehistoric and futuristic at the same time—or,
at least, it quickly guides the innocent spirit or imagination into that kind
of thinking. By which I mean to say that one may look at certain panora-
mas—Pyramid Lake, say, and what lies to the north of it—and reason that
this may look very much as it did ten thousand years ago, or even more.
Equally, is there any real reason to think the view would be altered much
in another ten thousand years?

We face such conundrums in time and space, like a known contin-
uum that would take so many light-years to traverse. But as we draw up in
the lee of this millennium, the years A.D. 2000 and 2001—with so much
fuss and touristy anticipation—how do we begin to imagine the world ten
thousand years from now? It is far easier to construct the simple life that
existed on the shores of Pyramid Lake ten thousand years ago. Intricate,
scholarly examinations have been made of the dry fecal material associated with Spirit Cave Man, say, and so we have an inkling of the fish, the
vegetables, and the grains he depended on. We can muster an outline
awareness of the physicality of his life, even if we can hardly approach
what he thought, said, or imagined. Even if he believed that he was as up-
to-date as it was possible to be.

But look at the last one hundred years in our history. Reflect that there
are people alive still (or were very recently) who survived the San Francisco earthquake of 1906, or the *Titanic* disaster of 1912. These are people
who were raised without television, air conditioning, or the fear of nuclear
fallout. Go back another thirty years, and there was an age that knew
nothing of powered flight, the telephone, electric lighting, the auto-

mobile. And think of the progress made in all these areas by the year 2000. Weigh the dramatic increase in the rate of change: The common experience of men and women between 1770 and 1870, say, altered far less than it did in the next one hundred years. Then try to grasp the range of progress possible in another ten thousand years, granted that it is not easier to suppose that, somehow or other, we will have eliminated ourselves—by some great blast or the toxic aftermath of it, by overcrowding that brings on some terrible friction, by an ingenuity that lets us go somewhere else, or from sheer boredom, even. How many ghost towns would Nevada still have in ten thousand years? Or would the world of A.D. 12000 look very like the one of 8000 B.C.?

And on October 15, 1997, not so very far to the north of Pyramid Lake—actually about two and a half minutes away at the speed it was going—something we would have to call a vehicle, or even a car, exceeded the speed of sound (which on that day, in its conditions of weather and altitude, was estimated to be 748.111 mph).

We are back at Gerlach again, the headquarters not more than two months earlier for the Burning Man Festival—that weird, sentimental but heartfelt yearning to reach back to something like a simple, unfettered, primitive existence (with the best piped-in rock 'n' roll, of course). For Gerlach was the base for a very serious attempt upon the world's land-speed record.

For decades, the site for such ventures was the Bonneville Salt Flats, a once smooth and firm salt flat just over the Nevada border, within sight of Interstate 80 in Utah. Between the wars, several new records were set there in glorified racing cars. The speeds then were in the 100 to 200 mph range. But in the last fifty years, the Bonneville Flats have changed their nature and consistency. The salt flat has shrunk, and it has lost much of its salt, to be replaced with mud. No one is quite sure why, but some blame weather changes, the fact that I-80 is so close, and nearby mining operations that may have sucked away the salt. Utah is not taking this easily, by the way: It has plans to flood the area with brine, thus reinstating the smooth surface.

At any event, Bonneville's decline awakened the world's speed zealots to the claims of the Black Rock Desert—flat, hard (once the rains have stopped), and so extensive that the long approach runs required could be accommodated. It was at Black Rock, on October 4, 1983—October is the ideal season—that the Englishman Richard Noble set a new land-speed record of 633.468 mph in a Thrust jet car. That record had stood until 1997, although in October 1996, the American Craig Breedlove had achieved a speed of 675 mph and then crashed. He had not secured the record. To do that, a driver must make two measured-mile runs in opposite directions within the space of an hour. The average of those two speeds must then exceed the old mark. But Breedlove's car, the Spirit of America, had swerved, lost control, and suffered damage. It was reckoned that a wind gust between 15 and 20 mph had been enough to cause the accident, from which Breedlove walked away unhurt. Noble reckoned that, at the age of fifty-one, he was too old to drive (Breedlove had been fifty-nine when he crashed). So the next British attempt would employ an RAF test pilot, Andy Green, no more than thirty-five years old. The British party arrived at Gerlach with their car, the Thrust SSC (or supersonic car). Fifty-four feet long and weighing almost 1,500 pounds, the new Thrust resembled a jet aircraft without wings but with an extended dorsal fin at the rear of the craft. Black and silver, it had two Rolls-Royce Spey engines that could supply 110,000 hp and 50,000 pounds of thrust. It rode about ten inches off the ground, with aluminum wheels that worked well on the Black Rock's hard desert. The British party had support equipment that amounted to ten times the weight of the car, and Richard Noble was spending most of his time raising enough money from private corporate sponsors to help the team in the desert.

On September 25, Green broke the old record with two runs that averaged 714.144 mph. But the real target of the venture was to break the sound barrier—and the crucial date was October 14, which would be the fiftieth anniversary of when Chuck Yeager had broken that mark, in the air, over California's Edwards Air Force Base (about three hundred miles to the south).

In fact, on October 13, Green broke the barrier. On the thirteen-mile course, he set a mark of 749.687 mph on his first run, and then did runs of 764.168 and 760.135. To the plume of dust he left behind him, there was added that curious, palpable thudding noise that is the sound barrier collapsing. But those last two runs were made sixty-one or sixty-two minutes apart, and so they could not qualify as a record. On the next day, the fourteenth, Yeager's day, the wind was too much. But on the fifteenth, with five minutes to spare, Green did runs of 759.333 and 766.609 mph. The new record was established at 763.635.

So what, you may say, if the drive back from Gerlach to Reno still takes a couple of hours or so? To drive in our most advanced metropolises seems to take longer every year—so much of driving is in impacted, or crawling, states, which make a mockery of 700 mph. To say nothing of the cost of getting that speed, the enormous amount of fuel burned up, or even—one day—the likely impact on the flora and fauna of the Black Rock Desert. For now, Gerlach is a fairly rugged community, happy to have any bit of action in its desert, and pretty philosophical about risk. But there are already those who have begun to lament that the desolation of Gerlach is not what it was.

And there are great stretches of Nevada where no one can go—or should go—just because of what has been done there in the name of speed, power, and progress, not to mention numbers that are off the known chart. There are also crowded places where news of the new mark—763.635—would dictate the kind of bets people placed for the rest of the evening: "Know what I played? I said seven nines are sixty-three and zero, three, and five are eight. So I played nine and eight all I had. Seventeen came up. So I went to the phones and I called my cousin Harvey in Boston—617 area code, get it? I told him what I had done and he said he would front me as much as he had, $11,000. I went back in, to the same table, waited till seventeen minutes had passed, and I put it all on 17 again. We are in Acapulco!"

That may not seem the most sensible way of making yourself intact and secure tomorrow. But suppose your ambitions go beyond tomorrow or more security. The daily rate of interest at work in the economy enables you to plot a staircase for your future, and that plodding advancement is not for the transcendent. They need a way of changing the level of their enterprise dramatically, radically, and way beyond the stealth of interest or increment. They are looking for the big break—which means "break," not just as opportunity or stroke of fortune, nor even as in "break out," as in the sense of making an escape, but "to break," as in severing the previous known laws of continuity, logic, physics, or evidence. Remember, there are really only two kinds of people playing 17—those who hope it wins, and those who know it will. And 17 will win someday, so if you play with certainty, then surely a moment is going to come in which your play seems ordained, a given, a proof of some profound communion with fate. You have to know that you deserve 17—then anything can be accomplished.

Let me put it another way. Only a few weeks after Andy Green did his two runs inside an hour, at an ominously or auspiciously named place that is actually the next place down the road from Gerlach, there was a defiance of order, logic, and evidence so great that nothing but confidence would carry it. It is November 25, 1997, and we are in Nixon, close to the southern end of Pyramid Lake, and the old tribal headquarters of the Paiute Nation. A meeting occurred that day between five anthropologists, from the Nevada State Museum and the Bureau of Land Management, and twenty-six representatives of the Paiutes. The party of five visitors included Donald Tuohy and Amy Dansie, leading figures in the scholarly and scientific description of Spirit Cave Man and Wizard's Beach Man. It was their purpose to make the case in face of Paiute opposition to further study of those remains.

It was part of the anthropologists' plan to present a great deal of information about the Native American Graves and Repatriation Act of 1990, as well as spelling out the scientific evidence they had gathered. To that end, a form of questionnaire was given to the Paiutes to ascertain their understanding of NAGRPA and the implications of the scientific work.

One must admire the reasonable attempt; one can only concur with the scientific argument. The anthropologists' case is beyond refutation. Still, it can be ignored, especially by certainty. The Paiutes at the Nixon meeting simply held to their wisdom that the figures in question were theirs and that they should be returned for immediate reburial. At Nixon, and on the Paiute reservation as a whole, it is all too evident how little the Indians have—and thus it may be easier to understand the emotionalism in what they claim. Some of the visiting party felt their position was akin to that of Major Ormsby in 1860, about to be wiped out in the Pyramid Lake war.

The Nevada State Museum newsletter would describe the extraordinary standoff between two kinds of certainty:

> Amy [Dansie] wrote this handout to all Nevada tribes and she did not receive one answer to her question about sacred objects, cultural patrimony, consultation, repatriation, information and heritage, and political process; not one answer. We thought we would get some answers from the Numa [the Paiutes] on the 25th of November meeting. Instead what all three of us got from the meeting was a history of what the Anglo did to the Indians for the last 180 years (in both Paiute and English), at times bordering on pure rudeness! I did not think of this thought at the time, but eventually the United States soldiers conquered the northern Paiutes and won the war of 1860—or did we? And, so ended this inquisition by the Pyramid Lake Paiutes; their side coming out strongly in favor of the sacred nature of the whole Pyramid Lake Reservation against what we scientists know about the burials we found there (by using Paiute crews).

16. In the Cards

THOUGH THE LANDSCAPE OF NEVADA SOMETIMES SEEMS SO ancient and static, there can be a poised or primed air about it, some verging on extraordinary drama that makes us think of savage or comic shift, alteration, change. It was a May morning, the cloud cover pervasive and opaque, so that one seemed to be driving forever toward a receding cyclorama, some vast illumined shell or image meant to represent distance. And the road—straight enough and surely monotonous—might have been moving, rolling like a treadmill, so that it was only I in my car who was really still. Of course, I was getting there—I was in Las Vegas by the early afternoon—but sometimes on Highway 375, there was a sensation that maybe the world, the scene, the panorama were so arranged to delude me.

And something happened, some fluttering or unfurling overhead, so that the light was briefly intervened in—the steady, flat, nearly suffocating light somewhere between the colors of dust and pearl. I've no idea what it was, yet it seemed too large an alteration for, say, a flock of birds, or even the slow, swallowing roll of a Stealth bomber doing one of its solemn exercises above me. Maybe there was even some surge or ebb in my brain, and my eyes, so that I seemed to experience something like this stroke that diminished the light for a few seconds. We are not the steadiest or the least emotional of observation systems; we are hardly good enough to be trusted. And we are so helplessly prone to imagining what causes some brief physical episode that we do not understand.*

* On March 13, 1997, for instance, over Phoenix, Arizona, around 8:00 p.m., several people saw a winged formation of lights, moving as one; then at 10:00 p.m., other flarelike lights. There is a video of them, but no explanation. Governor Fife Symington ordered an inquiry—and then produced a man dressed up as an alien when the report was given. All comedy.

For that matter, who can drive on Highway 375—the bare, blank road that even the state of Nevada has agreed to call "the Extra-Terrestrial Highway"—without some mocking sense of readiness?

Even so, I looked at the steady ocher texture of the land around me—so rough, in fact, yet seeming so smooth from the car, like baize almost—and I supposed to myself that maybe some large playing card, a platform, yet as wafer-thin as a fresh card, had passed over me, like the 2 of spades dropped on the first three cards of a trick, a trump drifting in with the lovely slow motion of authority. And I supposed it had landed on the ground and on the earlier cards with no more sound than the skid or the sigh a card makes dropped on the green tabletop. Why shouldn't a spacecraft be like a playing card? And why not argue that the spots on the cards are the aliens? Straightaway, you'd have your case made that Las Vegas, Nevada, was their prime target on Earth, where such cards have been making fun or havoc—read it as you will—for over fifty years now.

Of course, my surmise could easily be explained. I am one of those people who on a long, lone automobile drive is likely to replay a few games in his head—Stiles to Ball going down the right wing, then across to Hurst, so quickly that he has time (always) to gather the ball, steady, and shoot on the turn, falling backward so that the ball hits the underside of the crossbar and bounces on or around the line. That was given as a goal—3–2. Or else some rare, perilous contract in 5 clubs brought home against an overconfident press.

More than that, I had read that morning in the paper how Las Vegas in its effortlessly democratic way—no questions ever asked, no cause deemed outcast—was playing host to the Cavendish Invitational Pairs, one of the most illustrious and glamorous competitions in the bridge world. So I was likely seeing the tilt and spin of cards not just politely put down but flighted onto the table, like stylish invaders, or so lightly flicked that they slid across the cards they had defeated.

Las Vegas is steadily in the convention business—Lord knows, it has the hotel rooms, the attractive rates, the accessible flights, and the machinery for putting the package together. So maybe Vegas—whether the Excalibur, the Luxor, or Bally's—isn't exactly the atmosphere where you'd expect to see bridge played. It's not a Connecticut country club or a graceful Charlottesville restaurant where a well-fed foursome can ask for a pack of fresh cards and while away the time until cocktail hour. It's not the first venue you would think of if you're so set in your mind that bridge is an upper-class game, played by the wives of retired stockbrokers and so on. Maybe those ladies do play for small side stakes, just as their husbands on the golf course have their own version of Skins going on. But those wagers are modest and discreet, and there's no pressure on when or how to settle. You wouldn't call it gambling, or even gaming; it's simply a little side action, or leverage, to make the afternoon interesting. And very likely over the course of the rest of their lives, with the luck of the cards, it all works out, so that no one's far ahead. A real player, someone better at bridge or golf than the gang, and taking advantage of it, isn't going to stay in the group for long. It's not like the steady forty years or so of professional gambling that the men put in on Wall Street in their prior lives, when the hunches were life or death, and there were days when you got the train home scarcely able to keep quiet about how much you'd made, or wondering if you wouldn't just go on to the end of the line and drink that extra drink your doctors warned about.

Safety, after all, even the security those people talk about, is a fragile thing.

The bridge players with a chance at winning the Cavendish—which has prize money of $1.2 million—are not the world's most reliable or steadfast citizens. They may well come from the Upper East Side of Manhattan or the better parts of Dallas; they may even have terrific addresses in Paris, Toronto, London, and Cairo. But they are world travelers, too, following the cards, and they are very much at home in a Vegas hotel, taking the comped room for granted and knowing the best restaurants in town, knowing even the number to ring for the most sophisticated entertainment. Those are people who may travel with two or three tuxedos, while having credit-card debt in some countries that keeps them away for the moment. They are often handsome, gracious people you could take anywhere—indeed, people who have entrée in many salons denied to you or me. They are well educated. They speak several languages. They know Proust, Mahler, Bonnard, and the laws of relativity. They are astonishing self-taught math masters. They can play the most complicated game of bridge in their heads. And some of them are hanging on by their manicured fingernails. For bridge can be a game where nothing matters except the absurd courage for making a play.

Take this hand, played, in fact, in the 1998 Cavendish. Never mind the names of the players; never mind whether they fit my possible description. North and South found themselves in 6 diamonds on this deal:

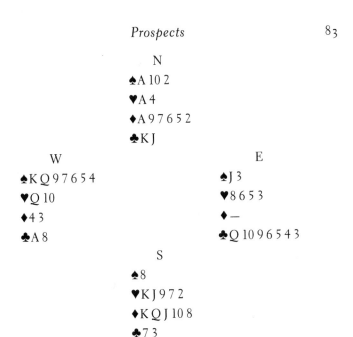

N

♠A 10 2
♥A 4
♦A 9 7 6 5 2
♣K J

W

♠K Q 9 7 6 5 4
♥Q 10
♦4 3
♣A 8

E

♠J 3
♥8 6 5 3
♦—
♣Q 10 9 6 5 4 3

S

♠8
♥K J 9 7 2
♦K Q J 10 8
♣7 3

Look at that layout a moment. Six diamonds is easy in nearly any circumstance. It is not really a contract that requires much playing from these players—unless West leads the ♣8. Why should he? you say. He might if he wonders whether East has the queen. For, if that is the case, then South, playing the hand, has to decide whether to play his king. Suppose he plays the king, only to find that the ace and the queen were in opposite hands. Then East wins with the ace and leads back the queen. Whereas, as things lie, if South has the nerve to call for the king—dummy will do no more than slide the card into the cockpit—then the contract is safe. Just as it is safe, too, if West makes the obvious play and cashes in his club ace first. So it goes. A lot of bridge is more elaborate, less pointed, and nerve-racking. But there is not a card game that doesn't sooner or later ask a player to make the call full of his life's experience and the precise current of nerves in his body. And it can be the difference between sober prosperity for the rest of your days, keeping the house and the wife, and selling arms to the Arabs—which isn't necessarily the road to ruin, but which could be uncertain. At least it is enough to make South watch closely the fluttering surface of whichever card East tosses into the tray.

And then suppose that after the evening's session is over, South, or whoever, gets up and strolls around the casino. He has his tuxedo on still, yet that gets little more attention than he offers to the guy sitting next to him in Bermuda shorts and a Michael Jordan 23 shirt. No one assumes that what you wear in Vegas is other than costume.

But South pauses to watch some of the action at blackjack. He has never really played the game before. But he feels good this evening, because he let that king ride, and because nearly every gambler there ever was depends on that slight ebb and flow of mania and depression. He has got it under control, he tells himself; it's nothing like a problem. But he has a mood on him and an energy that his own card game didn't exhaust. And he notices there is a pretty woman playing blackjack at this table. So he sits at the opposite end of the arc from her, where he can see her clearly without seeming obtrusive. And without really thinking about it, he wins six or seven hands in a row, until he's got the table's attention. There is even a little ring of people watching. And he realizes now that his tuxedo cannot help but look sinister, or professional. But the woman is watching him more than she is playing her own cards. He loses the next hand, deliberately, to let the tension ease. Then he wins three more in a row.

And the woman says to him and to the table as a whole, "Why, sweetheart, I do believe you're counting cards."

And South gazes at her with the serene smile of a winner—he could be a movie star tonight—and realizes he doesn't know how to play without counting. But he doesn't need to embarrass anyone, not in a tuxedo. So he gets up and invites the lady to dinner at Spago in the Forum at Caesars. And his life is never the same afterward. The wife was lost, the kids, the house, the horses, and the yacht—all gone within a year, and a year after that, the lady at the blackjack table was gone, too. She wasn't going to stand around and let him take shots at her, she said. She could read the signs.

17. Rachel

THIS IS HOW ONE OF THE STORIES GOES. THERE WAS A TOWN called Sodaville, which was on the way south to Tonopah (which we will come to in due course, but for the moment let us just say that Tonopah was important because of a great silver strike made there in 1900, and Sodaville was useful because it was on the way there, and was the place where the road became a dirt road, so that goods for Tonopah sent from Reno had to be taken from coaches and put on pack animals there). Anyway, Sodaville had some additional claim to hot mineral baths, where the dust of travel might be washed away, and it was a significant junction out there in the dun-colored veldt.

Early in the century, on a crowded Saturday night, a storekeeper discovered a Halloween mask en route to some child in Tonopah. In secret, he put it on to amuse his customers, and suddenly appeared behind his own counter, looking like some kind of devil. An Indian in the store was so terrified that he threw himself through the window to escape. He never came back, and he told other Indians not to go near that haunted place.

There are so many stories like that, and you can interpret them as a mark of loathing for the Indians; a sign of the cheerful chaos of early Nevada, and the sideswiping collision of so many cultures; or as a test of the Devil's ingenuity. Of course, it's also the kind of tale told over the wreckage of ghost towns. Sodaville scarcely exists now, and Tonopah's a shaky place where tourism tries to do what mining has given up on.

Mining towns sink their roots, their jaws, and their souls in the ground. Then the ground betrays them. The ore stops; the earth turns to dust or becomes so hard in the sun, the town is blown away in the next decade's wind, or is just swept into history's dumper by the fine edge of some playing card.

A row of mailboxes, waiting, Rachel, Nevada

This is an intriguing place, a very Nevadan place, on Highway 375, the road where I was imagining the overhead passage of a playing card in that thick pale pink and amber of an overcast day. And you can make a case for saying that the Devil has been there, if you're of a mind to.

One hundred and fifty years ago, for a certainty, there was nothing in this place except the rolling high desert and the daily show put on by the sun. Be careful of pausing to calculate how long that had been going on, for it will only lead you into the Nevadan impasse (or paradise — read it as you will) that nothing is as natural as emptiness.

Maybe a few Shoshone were going this way or that; maybe rustlers taking cattle and horses into California, though you have to marvel that any animals could survive that journey, let alone command a price after it; or even fierce settlers looking for some promised land. In the winter of 1848–1849, a party of pioneers — headed, they hoped, for California — passed across the desert a little to the south of this place. They ended up beleaguered in Death Valley, and it was from there that two men, William Lewis Manly and John Haney Rogers, hiked out to find and return with rescuing provisions. That party, generally known as the Manly Party, is the story of survival that balances the disaster of the Donner Party, farther north.

The pioneers often marveled and trembled at the desert they saw. It was the burden of their prayers just to pass through without mishap or accident. This is the Sand Springs Valley, the sparseness crossed by Highway 375, the empty quarter where you may now come upon the town, the settlement, or the gesture that is called Rachel.

That name seems biblical, but in fact it comes from Rachel Jones, perhaps the only child actually born in the town that was previously known as Tempiute Village (Mount Tempiute is a few miles to the northeast), Shady Grove, or Sand Springs, or even just Sandy. Rachel was born on February 15, 1978, and died, apparently, on May 24, 1980. I say "apparently" because there are stories that her family just moved to Alaska. But the gospel version is that the child died, and that she had respiratory problems caused by her being close to Mount Saint Helens when it erupted.

In the early 1970s, the Union Carbide Company opened a mine at Mount Tempiute. There was some silver, tungsten, lead, and mercury there, though none in large quantity. A small trailer town grew because of the mine. By 1974, it is said, the population was sixty. Four years later, power lines from Hoover Dam were hooked up, and in the early eighties there were over 150 people in Rachel. There was even a tiny school, though that broke up when the teacher left town (there were stories that he had persuaded young boys to dress up as women). After that, the kids were bused into school in Alamo, an old Mormon town, some fifty miles to the southeast. By 1988, Union Carbide had given up on the mine. In the regular Nevadan way of things, you would have expected the precarious settlement to vanish within a few years.

But that hasn't happened yet. And the chief reason for that is that Rachel sits off the northeast shoulder of the Nevada Test Site, and its notorious yet very secretive Area 51. The Test Site is a small matter of 1,350 square miles of unpromising desert, established by Harry Truman in December 1950 as the Nevada Proving Ground, a place where nuclear testing could be carried out. We will be going there, in due course, to see the results of some of the test explosions conducted there. The U.S. government lets you in for free—so long as you do as you're told.

The Test Site has numbered areas, from 1 to 30 (though a few numbers are missing). Its northeast corner reaches out to the area of Groom Lake (a dry lake); indeed, the Mercury Highway, which operates through the Test Site, goes off toward Groom Lake. And that is where Area 51 is supposed to be. Thus, Rachel is reckoned to be another twenty-seven miles to the north of the center of Area 51, the control tower, from which, apparently, the base uses the call sign "Dreamland."

It has been the steadfast policy of the U.S. government to allow as little acknowledgment of Dreamland and its works as possible. But there is no doubt that in the mid-1950s, and largely at CIA direction, airstrips, hangars, and other buildings were erected there, though there seems to have been early alarm that Area 51 was far too close to, and far too directly in the line of prevailing winds from, the Test Site. For it was there, in those same 1950s, that nuclear weapons were being blown up aboveground. Part of the rationale in locating the Test Site originally had been to ensure a fallout dispersal pattern that affected as few people as possible. (Though few was not none, as we will see later.) People in Las Vegas hotels—to the southeast of ground zero—could therefore enjoy the light show (it usually came at dawn) and even the blast without having to worry about the toxic airborne matter.

Area 51, it is now generally assumed, was the place where the U-2 reconnaissance aircraft was developed and tested. Very likely, it has also seen the nursing along of other sophisticated vehicles, the B-1 bomber, the Stealth bomber, and the SR-71, known as the Blackbird, and possibly several others that the broad, innocent, and unconcerned "we" don't know about because they pooped, collapsed, exploded, or entailed a degree of expense that not even the U.S. government could conceal. And then, possibly, ventures were undertaken there that we could hardly dream of—should hardly dream of—by which I mean things that the anxious, the paranoid, the fanciful, the modern could easily imagine.

Though unacknowledged, the Groom Lake base, or whatever, is very real. It has a paved main runway that is nearly six miles long, as well as a shorter second runway. It contains many large but "normal" hangars, as well as "Hangar 18," more than one hundred yards long and one hundred feet high. There are other hangars, a large control tower, oil tanks, radar installations, and many other buildings for housing personnel. There are daily flights transporting workers to and from Area 51, from McCarran Airport in Las Vegas, and a bus running workers in from the Alamo area. But it is thought that many of the most important personnel reside at the base. In which case, the U.S. government has likely laid on a full range of facilities for their leisure time.

There is another dry lake, Papoose Lake, ten or so miles to the south-southwest of Groom Lake, and there are more buildings there. Papoose Lake has the extra glamour of being unviewable from anywhere except the air. Groom Lake can be seen from Tikaboo Peak, twenty-five miles away. But the best photographs of Groom are from White Sides Mountain and Freedom Ridge, locations that were ruled out of bounds by the government as recently as 1995.

Now, and for several years, anyone attempting to penetrate the base at ground level runs the risk of arrest, confiscation of vehicle and equipment, heavy fines, and imprisonment. The warning signs even admit USE OF DEADLY FORCE AUTHORIZED. These security forces are not government personnel of any kind; instead, they are the employees of a private security organization. So no "outsider" has penetrated Area 51, or emerged to tell the tale. All of which is part of the legend that, beyond the testing of new aircraft obedient to no known laws of physics, Area 51 houses the headquarters for American research into what are generally known as aliens and UFOs.

Over the years—but, notably, in the years since the closing of the Union Carbide mine, as if to prolong the life of the township—many people have reported seeing and hearing strange things in the sky south of Rachel. These include bright hovering lights; illumined bodies that suddenly change direction and move at great speed; extraordinary noises, unlike any known form of machinery; and apparent flying objects that scrutinize the watching people. There are even those who say they have met aliens and been in their company. One of these is Merlyn Merlin (self-styled "ambassador"), who, about ten years ago, realized that he was himself an alien and who has subsequently reported contact with extraterrestrials in the area of Rachel. Others say that Merlin's real name is David Solomon, that he comes from Silver City, Nevada, and that he is "not an alien, but . . . a human with some profound personal problems."

The highest form of this religion, or mania, is that the aliens who landed near Roswell, New Mexico, in the summer of 1947, and their craft, are housed on Area 51. One alleged worker at the Test Site, Bob Lazar, found a kind of fame a few years ago by saying that he had actually seen the flying saucer, repaired and flying at Groom Lake. Lazar is the only person employed at Groom—if he was—who has ever broken the oath of silence required of the Test Site workers. There is much more to be said about all this, but let us conclude for the moment with noting that in April 1996, Governor Bob Miller of Nevada—probably born on Earth— conclusively voted for by the citizens of his state, and generally reckoned to be far more amiable than odd, officially renamed Highway 375 the Extra-Terrestrial Highway, no matter that the measure had been killed the year before in the state senate. Then, in February 1996, the Department of Transportation and Lieutenant Governor Lonnie Hammargren, chairman of the State Tourist Commission, simply declared it a done deal and gave orders for the erection of road signs.

For those of you determined to believe that Nevada can never escape the flagrant opportunism of nineteenth-century hucksterism, for those ill-disposed to recognize mysterious spiritual affinities, let me add this: At the very same time, apparently unbeknownst to Nevadans, Twentieth Century–Fox was making a movie, *Independence Day*, in which, under threat of hideous alien attack, a shattered U.S. government and its tousled president home in on Area 51 to make a last stand for the Earth. It was successful on-screen, and a box-office sensation.

Not for the first time, Nevada threw in its lot with show business and arranged for a dedication of the new highway that would also promote the upcoming movie (the key scenes of which, alas, had been shot at the Bonneville Salt Flats—in Utah!). Is this a silly mask on the face of the Devil? Well, who can decide yet? Meanwhile, Rachel has become not so much a giddy little town as a manifestation of philosophical debate, where you can walk a few hundred yards from skepticism to faith, just like someone at Greenwich, England, standing astride the mean-time line.

A geezer and Mrs. Geezer, sitting out under a canopy hooked onto their RV. In matching white plastic chairs. In their seventies, with Arkansas on their license plate.

"Come to see the sights?" I ask.

"Uh-huh," he says, and she puts on her dark glasses.

"Seen anything?" I wonder.

"We don't talk nothing about it," she tells me.

"Why not?" I ask.

"Out here," he says, "you don't know who you're talking to. You don't know where it'll go."

"Me?"

"Uh-huh."

"Think I might be FBI?"

"We don't know what you are," says the old man.

18. Directions

IF YOU COME IN TO RACHEL ON HIGHWAY 375, YOU HAVE driven from Tonopah, 110 miles to the west, or from Alamo, fifty miles southeast. And you're most likely on the road because something or other has persuaded you to take a look at Rachel. The only exception to this is if inhabitants of the Alamo area wanted to get to Tonopah. But if anyone in Tonopah wanted to go to Vegas, he would stay on Route 95 and save himself time. Locals reckon on no more than a dozen cars an hour on Highway 375 during the day, and one an hour late at night. It's a good road, though, and hardly wearing out from traffic. Some of the people of Rachel say, "Watch out or you'll miss us." But that is not really likely. The view from the west begins ten or twelve miles away, from where you see a smudge of dark on the south side of the road. And the downhill gradient from the east lets you see Rachel two or three miles early. That valley would be a lot more ominous or desolate without the town; it would leave Highway 375 as a steady straight scar in the wasteland, even if you could see aircraft to the south going through the swoops and rolls of military exercises. Indeed, if Rachel weren't there, you might wonder to yourself what the hell the road was for. I mean, it would verge on the suspicious, as if there was some secret purpose that the ordinary traveler was meant to enjoy but overlook. For this is far lonelier than the vaunted Highway 50, a sweet and lovely drive, with charming stopping places, a road that traffic might easily take to miss the clutter and noise and the sheer use of I-80; no, with Highway 375, you'd soon ask what the road was for, if it weren't for Rachel.

But it can matter a lot which way you approach Rachel, and the difference says everything about the recent flourishing of the town. It also reminds us of Nevada's helpless predilection for "story."

If you come in from the southeast, from Alamo and Las Vegas, then
the first significant stopping place (on your left) is a mobile home identified as the Area 51 Research Center. You enter a small space crowded with
desks, fax machines, a copying machine, books, files, papers, and shelves
of videotapes. Yes, you can buy a cap there and a few souvenirs, but the
best-selling item offered is the *Area 51 Viewer's Guide*, compiled by Glenn
Campbell, who runs the place. This is a ring-bound pamphlet of over one
hundred pages, scrupulously researched and generally well written—
cogent, amusing, but serious about the various factors and circumstances
that may persuade people they have seen, or been abducted by, aliens.

A couple of hundred yards down the highway, at the other end of
town, so that it is the first place you see coming from Tonopah, is the
Little A'Le'Inn, a freestanding building that functions as a bar, a restaurant, and the office for a motel arrangement—ten rooms in an adjacent
building. The main barroom is quite large. It has a blast of air condition-

The Area 51 Research Center

The Little A'Le'Inn

ing whenever needed, and it serves as a classic Nevada bar, where you can sit at the counter and drink while reading the brusque signs on the wall, shoot a little pool, order an Alien Burger—which turns out to be a conventional and decent hamburger—and look at the several photographs on the walls that supposedly show UFOs in the sky.

The Little A'Le'Inn is owned and run by Pat and Joe Travis, and Joe is available as a Nevadan "character" in the bar, and a general all-purpose aider and abettor of tall tales and alien rhetoric. You can rent a room for $25 a night, or hook up your RV for $8, and then study the night sky to fancy's content. This inn offers souvenirs, too, although they are generally a little more vulgar than the ones you get up the road. And it has its book, *The Area 51 & S-4 Handbook*, written by Chuck Clark. This is ring-bound, too, though only sixty-five pages, and it is open to just about every rumor and possibility of what is going on at Groom Lake and Papoose Lake.

Thus, in its odd way, Rachel is the best living example of a small western town divided by hostility and the famous split of ideology that sepa-

rated Hatfields and McCoys, or farmers and cowboys. Now it's the believers and the don'ts, and—depending upon the direction from which he
approaches—the innocent traveler runs the risk of being taken up by one
side or the other. You can make one stop at Rachel and come away oblivious to the fact that it's a hotbed of nuts or rationalists.

Of course, you can stop off at either end of town, sample the two
atmospheres, and buy both books. Yet the onetime traveler doesn't realize
that, and doesn't quickly grasp the intensity, the humor, or even the consequences of the feud in Rachel.

Its story goes as follows. Rachel's future seemed grim in 1988 when the
Union Carbide mine closed down. Ladell and Harold Singer had had a
place in town for a few years, the Rachel Bar & Grill. It had had previous
lives as the Oasis, the Watering Hole, and the Stage Stop Saloon, but at
every turn, it had failed. The Singers could hardly believe their good fortune when a couple from Las Vegas, Pat and Joe Travis—she a cook, he a
carpenter—seemed ready to buy the establishment. But the deal was
done in late 1988.

It was in May 1989 that Bob Lazar went on a Las Vegas television program and made his first claims about what he had seen and done at
Groom and Papoose. Not long after that, the Travises abandoned the
name Rachel Bar & Grill and came up with the Little A'Le'Inn instead.
That coup did nothing to alter the actual circumstances of Rachel: It was
still a scratch in the desert, at close to five thousand feet, which meant
winter night temperatures of minus ten degrees and summer highs over
one hundred degrees, albeit a dry heat. But at any time of year, fierce
winds were common, shifting the dust from one side of the road to the
other and sending coils of dry sage past the noses of bewildered cattle.
There was power in the town, and water in deep wells. The mail came
when it had to. But there was no law in Rachel, no government, no interference, which was pretty much what the Little A'Le'Inn culture wanted.
The mood was not just right-wing; it was steadily set against government
of any kind. All of this was ironic in view of the way the inn's claim to existence and income was founded on whatever skulduggery the government
might be up to a few miles to the south.

But a few people came, and they surely began to see things. No one
had ever denied how many planes you might see from Rachel in a day, or
bothered to analyze how they look at night. The planes had unusual lights
sometimes; they dropped flares for ground exercises, and who knows if
sometimes the wicked, bored flight crews didn't put on light shows for
groundlings ready to believe anything. Word got around—despite the evi-

dent closure of the Cold War, despite President Clinton's moratorium on even underground bomb tests at the Test Site—that there were weird things going on at Groom and Papoose, and that there were aliens held captive there, dead, alive, and in all in-between states that might be accessible to the breed.

Glenn Campbell only came to Rachel in 1992, driving there in his camper and parking at the Little A'Le'Inn. He was from Boston, a bright, inquiring, nonconformist guy who had been in and out of a lot of colleges, who had worked for the National Park Service and as a computer programmer, and who had found himself around the age of forty with some money and in need of a challenging idea to pursue.

As a kid, he had been fascinated by UFOs, but over the years he had come to be less interested in them themselves than in the people who believed in them. He had heard about Rachel and the tales of things seen there, so he made the trip. He stayed, started stargazing himself, and came to the conclusion that just about everything he saw could be explained. He was a natural explorer: He walked the land, and he hiked up to all the high places from which it was still possible to see Groom Lake. He began to gather information and, sitting in the bar at the Little A'Le'Inn, he started to complete his *Viewer's Guide*. Like the Travises, he enjoyed the place—the space, the freedom, the lack of clutter, the chance that they were all on the edge of something astonishing. But whereas the Travises were easy believers, Campbell was a skeptic. He told writer David Darlington:

> I'm not into UFOs, I'm into humanity and philosophy. I'm a philo-sophical warrior. I have the existential view that as soon as you're born you're faced with problems and the purpose of life is simply to solve them as efficiently as possible. In the process, I try to go about shooting down icons as best as I can.

Campbell kept a kind of office at the Little A'Le'Inn. He did his work on the *Viewer's Guide* there, and sold it from there. Apparently, he called the Travises "Ma" and "Pa" and they reveled in the extra trade that the *Guide* and Campbell's expertise brought to the area. There was even a UFO seminar at the inn—attended by Bob Lazar—on May 1, 1993, for which around two hundred people gathered.

But then Joe Travis began to grow envious of Campbell's eminence and the way his inn was being used. That summer of 1993 cooked the rivalry. At some point, Travis went off on a private spree, and soon after he came back, there was a crisis. He was drinking late into the night. He surveyed the walls of his own inn and noticed photographs of Groom Lake being offered for sale by Glenn Campbell. So he went out back to Campbell's camper, woke him, and told him to get the fuck out of there.

Campbell asked why; he sensed that Travis was armed (many people in Rachel had and carried guns).

"Because I hate you, you bald-faced fucker," said Travis.

So Campbell unhooked his camper and drove off to another site. It was the moment of parting, and the genesis of Campbell's research center at the other end of town. From there, he has gone from strength to strength, enlarging and improving his *Guide*, in which he points out how methodically he has mapped and walked the country, while the Travises stay put in their bar. The *Guide* is now a remarkable achievement: Indeed, apart from possible government reports held secret, I doubt whether any part of Nevada has been studied or described with such care and affection.

Campbell describes the history and topography of the area. He respects the real wilderness and the landscape so vulnerable to romantic and paranoid interpretation. He records strange lights seen—by himself and others—and then gives a lucid explanation for them. He guides explorers on how to handle the terrain and the security forces. And he always keeps his eye on the central issue—that official secrecy is bound to stimulate paranoid fantasy or madness.

Let me quote from the *Guide* to give some idea of Campbell's mind and prose:

If anyone knows what is going on at Area 51, it ought to be the people of Rachel, who have been living under bizarre aerial displays for years. Nearly everyone in town has seen unusual lights, but hardly anyone claims a full understanding of everything going on at the "test site." The only people who claim to know are the outsiders, the folks who come up from L.A. on Wednesday night and see exactly what they expect to see. The truth is, recognizing a flying saucer or exotic aircraft here can be immensely difficult amid the vast circus of routine military activity, the optical illusions of the desert and the confusing swamp of speculation brought here by believers. The majority of "UFOs" people see here can undoubtedly be explained by the testing of non-secret aircraft and weapons.

Most visitors have already made emotional investments and bear private grudges that they expect UFOs to support, and it takes very little evidence to confirm their views. Everything happens on a Wednesday night: UFO proponents expect to see flying saucers, and they do. Hardened skeptics expect to debunk the saucer stories, and they do. Spiritualists see spirits. Doomsdayers see the end of the world. Conspiracy buffs find just the evidence they need to link AIDS with JFK.

When I bought my copy of the *Guide*, in April 1997, it was copy 7,832—they are numbered by hand—and edition 4.01. It cost $15. That day, Campbell was in Vegas, where he spends most of his time. He has done quite well on it all, granted that his revenue would be a little over $100,000 in the course of four or five years (from a mass of work). His guide includes the cover note "Banned at the Little A'Le'Inn," as well as a full account of the inn and what it offers.

Down the street, however, a different approach to history prevails. The Travises hired Chuck Clark to write *their* guide, *The Area 51 & S-4 Handbook*, first published in 1997, and also available for $15. Clark is an amateur astrophotographer, and his guide is not without interest or value. But it cannot match Campbell's for scholarship or style, and censorship has ordained no mention of the *Viewers' Guide* or of Campbell's extensive research. That much stern obscurantism goes with this much open-mindedness (under "Reflections and Speculations"):

UFOs may originate from one or more of the following sources:

1. Another dimensional reality which co-exists with the reality that we are a part of. This reality may occupy the same space that we occupy, but at a different vibrational frequency.

2. They may carry time-travelers from our future . . . perhaps historians or anthropologists that have come to study their past.

3. They may be extra-terrestrial probes or space ships who have traveled here to study us. . . .

It certainly is not beyond the realm of possibility that UFOs are a currently unknown natural phenomenon. They might be living organisms of extremely low density and mass that move through the air in a manner like jellyfish or squid move through water.

Anyway, Rachel requires more than one brief stopover if you are to appreciate its span of human thought or reflection. And what other tiny patch of our wilderness can claim two guidebooks? Will Joe Travis and Glenn Campbell face off some high noon on the straight stretch of Highway 375? Or are they even, in their Odd Couple way, in cahoots, bringing modest lucre into a town that hardly deserves to exist, or which might need to consider the fact that it stands most directly in line with the prevailing winds that carry the air, the legacy, and the stories from the Nevada Test Site?

OF COURSE, IT ALL DEPENDS ON THE VISIONS YOU SEE: Triangular black forms maneuvering in the sky are as cute and negotiable as movie starlets. Yet try telling the story of a real star. Try saying that one day, up a dirt road south of 376 where you had gone to find a quiet picnic place, you saw this eighty-year-old woman, still glorious, dressed in a cerise silk pajama suit and high heels that never slipped in the sand, and she said, "Hallo, I'm Hedy Lamarr, still. Remember me?" I've told that story, and you just get laughed at. No matter that Miss Lamarr is alive still and said to be a startling version of her temptress self.

19. Area 51

You don't have to think about the life and times of
Rachel too much to realize how fortunate Glenn Campbell and Joe
Travis are to have each other. Isolated at opposite ends of the small town
and its straight, arid drag, they are like a comic version of *High Noon*. Not
that foolish feuds in the American West can't sometimes end in some
surge of adrenaline, armaments, a seizing on insult, and the awful perma-
nence of headlines. Wouldn't that be the making of Rachel? And it's a
short step from there to wonder if their antagonism isn't as set up as the
house rules in Las Vegas. Instead of that ugly, boozy confrontation late
one night, did two halfway decent and naïve American sharpies sit down
and stumble on the scenario of their hostility, seeing how it might put
Rachel on the map, and keep them as players? Did those two even reckon
that, one day, they might get it turned into a movie? It could be a version
of *The Odd Couple*, with Jack Lemmon and Walter Matthau as two men
with contrary views of the rational and the heavens who find that, inadver-
tently, they have invented a new game for Nevada. Or you could even
play it as the cunning plan of old friends who become tragically driven
apart by the con they've worked out — that could be a Preston Sturges or
Frank Capra film, and it might require some friendly alien, an angel
named Clarence, even, to bring about their reconciliation.

One of the ways we seek to explain life now is to suppose that this or
that situation became a movie — somehow, the clichés and genres of the
screen, its rhythm of seeing and being seen, have become answers to (or
containers for) our many mysteries. But there's another model available,
another "they" that might have put the story together so as to explain away
weird phenomena — the "they" of government. I remind myself that
Campbell and Travis need not be simple, or authentic, folks. They might
be spooks from Central Casting, figures cast to divert anxious attention

from what is, after all, a large, real, and troubling place — call it Area 51, or the northern end of Nellis Air Force Base, or the Nevada Test Site. We have taken it for granted over the years that the object of that site is to test weapons or vehicles of war. But suppose there is another quest at work — to test what we will believe, or can stomach, to find out just how fervent a land of imagination this might be. For sometimes it is far easier, and prettier, to imagine than to face the facts.

The basic facts are startling. Within the squeezed rectangle made up by highways 95, 15, 93, and 375, from southeast of Tonopah through Rachel and coming close to Alamo, and then from Beatty by way of Mercury to a spot about fifty miles northwest of Las Vegas, there is a land where no American may go without official permission. The only license granted covers bus tours of the Test Site, where no cameras or recording devices are allowed, and where the tourists must do exactly as they are told.

We will take that tour — and describe its marvels — while noting that it can cover only some of the things to be beheld at the Test Site itself. That area is 1,350 square miles, 860,000 acres. Yet the old Nellis Air Force Range, which surrounds the Test Site to the west, north, and east, is about three times as large. Area 51 — the bases at Groom and Papoose Lakes — is largely contained within Nellis (though it breaks into fresh, open territory to the northeast) and is itself close to 800 square miles. The total area fenced off against ordinary American intrusion, therefore, is a little larger than Connecticut.

Now, there are many acres in that state barred to us because they are private property. But every one of the forbidden square miles in Nevada is owned by the U.S. government, or by us. So, in giving up the chance to go there, or to be there, we make a bargain — we and the United States — that most of us abide by. Granted the exigencies of World War II (for which we hardly volunteered) and the Cold War that followed (our will is far tougher to measure here), we can see the sense in picking that uneventful desert as a place where the military could test artillery and bombs, carry out exercises, and even, eventually, prove the potency and the toxicity of bombs that were beyond ordinary ones.

Why not do it there? people ask, pointing to the evident "hole" in the state in 1930s road maps, the southern half of Nye County, too hot and parched for farming, and never a productive area for mining. In 1940, there was only one significant military facility in Nevada, the Naval Ammunition Depot at Hawthorne (just by the southern end of Walker Lake). Its origins are very telling. In 1926, a serious fire and multiple explosions overtook the Naval Ammunition Depot at Lake Denmark, New Jersey. The damage to life and property was so great that American wisdom thought of relocating the arsenal somewhere "out there." Hawthorne had had its own fire the same year, enough to erase almost completely the small place that was a railroad junction built originally to link up with the rough road that went over the mountains to Bodie and Aurora. Senator Tasker Oddie displayed classic Nevadan opportunism and begged the navy to come to Hawthorne. They took over 300 square miles and built row upon row of bunkers for shells, bombs, bullets. . . . The depot was commissioned in 1930, and Hawthorne's population tripled within a few years, climbing to nearly seven hundred. By 1945, the military was employing more than 5,500, in and out of uniform, at Hawthorne.

The Nellis Gunnery Range was founded in 1941—initially for gunnery tests. Stead Field was set up outside Reno in 1942, and other bases were established in the wartime years at Fallon and Tonopah. All of these operations, and even the Proving Ground (now the Test Site), were on the nation's books. They were owned-up-to budgetary items for the nation's exchequer, and it was possible that they were in the national interest. The Test Site was certainly organized with that sort of pragmatic approach: If atom bombs were to be exploded in the atmosphere of Nevada, then they were located at such a place that (and arranged to coincide with) prevailing winds carried the fallout in the "safest" direction, away from Las Vegas, Phoenix, and Los Angeles and into that "empty" quarter that was Nevada and southwest Utah. In those bizarrely positive moods of the late forties and fifties, the government offered statements and maps buoyant enough to let one think that any fallout was as close to beneficial as stardust. The bombs bursting in air were a great spectacle, a proof of American supremacy—the odd word *cool* was even applied, as in hip, modern, knowing, and sophisticated.

In 1997, on the Test Site, the rugged, handsome ex-military man who was our guide observed an enormous hole in the ground and reckoned that it was "cool"—by which, I think, he meant not just a fabulous bit of magic (as matter went to emptiness) but also a phenomenon of American technology and know-how, and an inspired exploitation of what was otherwise a wilderness. In the military and scientific personalities (and they are often close, even if historically they have been kept apart), there is a sense of being enthralled with colossal achievement; even the Los Alamos physicists were said to see a "sweetness" in what they had done, a kind of mathematical completeness, an emphatic order and calm.

Area 51 is a different kind of place just because it has never been directly or explicitly or revealingly acknowledged or described by the government, and because its budget is hidden in the Black Book* area that our government has employed to keep us in the dark. There is no doubting the amount of terrain used by the Groom and Papoose lake operations. Many photographs testify to the buildings, the runways, and the residential accommodations. Flights can be seen to come in and out every day from Las Vegas. People are employed there, and required to sign oaths of secrecy. Over the years, massive evidence has accumulated of unusual airborne activity coming out of the area. It seems close to certain that the U-2 and various forms of the stealth fighter and bomber were developed there. Another secret aircraft project, the Aurora—the name of that dream gold mine less than a hundred years ago—may well be based at Groom Lake. Some even claim that there is a warren of underground tunnels in the area where other tests go on. There are even those who say that UFOs are kept there and tested, along with the imprisoned aliens who piloted them to Earth. Let me add this wild tale: that in the tunneling that went on at Groom, discoveries were made of a mineral not yet added to the periodic chart, but of such exceptional properties that our government has resolved to keep quiet about it.

Or, if you prefer this one, that the Test Site has turned up the richest gold mine in the history of the world.

The government is very single-minded about its need for secrecy. Thus, above and beyond the regular fencing and security guards that protect Area 51, in 1993–1994 the government declared its intention to annex a further 4,000 acres (the Freedom Ridge and Whitesides Peaks, from which the best photographs of Groom Lake had been taken). This measure needed no more than the approval of the local Bureau of Land Management officer. Congressional support was required for actions involving more than 5,000 acres.

The first hearing on this matter took place in Caliente in January 1994. Col. Bud Bennett, a Nellis squadron commander, spoke vaguely of the need "to ensure the public safety and the safe and secure operation of activities in the Nellis Air Force Range Complex." A member of the Shoshone Nation claimed that the true owner of all the land involved were the Shoshone people. There were also several speakers, including

---

* Yes, a match. *Budgetary discretion* was the same term as Nevada has employed to list undesirables at the casinos. But do some names figure in both Black Books?

the rancher Dick Carver, who complained of the BLM meekness in the face of government authority.

In March, a second hearing took place at the Cashman Field Center in Las Vegas, with four television crews present. Colonel Bennett was there again, and he said that while no one in the services was confirming the base (which everyone knew existed), "visits" from the general public made it much harder to run. No "visit" was identified, or has ever been claimed. Then a variety of individuals, including Glenn Campbell, opposed the land seizure, some on solid legal ground, others because "this ain't America. . . . I was here when America was here, and it's gone. . . . We don't need this; it's top secret because if you found out what was going on, you'd stop it; we ought to decide who the enemy is, blow 'em to hell, and forget all this shit."

More than a year later, in April 1995, it was decided that 3,972 acres of public land in Lincoln County were being withdrawn (until November 2001) "for the United States Air Force to provide a safety and security buffer between public land administration administered by the Bureau of Land Management and withdrawn land under the jurisdiction of the Nellis Air Force Range."

The period of those hearings made Rachel and Area 51 national talking points. On June 26, 1994, the *New York Times Magazine* had run an article on it all, subtitled "The Cold War Still Rages in the Nevada Desert, Site of an Air Force Base So Secret It Doesn't Exist." In April 1994, ABC's *World News Tonight* carried an item on Groom Lake; in November, CBS's *Evening News* followed suit. And in October, Larry King came "live" to Rachel for a two-hour special on UFOs.

Meanwhile, the government spokespersons continued to be noncommittal on whether there was anything at Groom or Papoose. The same response greeted a suit filed on behalf of Helen Frost, the widow of an Area 51 worker, who alleged that her husband had died as a result of being exposed to fumes from waste burned in open pits on the Test Site. (Observers often reported seeing such fires from far away.) The suit, against Lockheed, had been taken up by Jonathan Turley, head of the Environmental Crimes Project at George Washington University. He broadened the case to include the EPA and the Department of Defense.

The government said it could not comment on the Test Site without causing "exceptionally grave damage" to the national interest. The EPA announced in April 1995 that it had just examined the base, concluding that compliance was full and proper but that the report was classified. A district judge ordered the report to be made public, but on September 29, 1995, President Clinton himself exempted "the Air Force's operating location near Groom Lake" from all environmental provisions with respect to solid or hazardous waste.

That was the most complete admission ever made by the authorities that there was a base at Groom Lake.

Why are our representatives so secret? Is it because the Aurora is being developed there as an aircraft that can take off and land like a regular plane while gaining the speed of a rocket once in the air? If so, is that anything to be ashamed of, or to be withheld? And remember that international treaties now permit the regular overflight of Groom and Papoose by foreign surveillance satellites. The Russians, say, know what is there. It is the American people who remain in the dark. In which case, of course, it is easier to believe that our government is using the base to explore activities that might be against our law, or against the general interest of the American people. What could that mean? Chemical or biological agents, such as we scold Iraq and others for attempting to possess? A prison for enemies of the state we are reluctant to name or charge? A secret seat of government in the event of insurrection, civil disorder, or breakdown (this is what *Independence Day* is based on)? UFOs and aliens? Lee Harvey Oswald, Lord Lucan, and . . . Howard Hughes?

By now we are in the shifting territory of *The X-Files*, the TV series that derived from the idea that government secrecy over something as farfetched as UFOs was really a means to conceal intrigue of a much more practical and immediate kind. Like, well, like the possibility that the base holds victims of fallout accidents or disasters, disclosure of which might cause panic over ordinary dangers we have all been exposed to.

I am not taking sides, except to say I do not believe in long shots. I don't think you will hit the jackpot at Vegas. I do not believe there is a single, profound secret to the universe at Area 51. I believe in the essential inefficiency of organizations and plots, which means that if Area 51 held anything so startling, it would have been leaked by now or it would have ended in mishap. Equally, I believe that if there was a conspiracy to kill John Kennedy, the news of it would have spilled out by now—some rascals would have book and movie deals; they'd be on *Larry King Live*.

However, here's the rub: If Oswald did it—that inept, that deranged, that clumsy man—on his own, then isn't one forced back on long shots and the extraordinary force of luck or chance?

It comes to this, I think: Just as we live in a society that puts irrational stress on the remote likelihood of hitting the jackpot, so we have a government that seems more inclined to cultivate the paranoia that says yes, it is doing something. The secrecy is a form of mystery in the intensely science- and computer-driven practice of government. It is a crazy urge toward mystery. And it is perilous.

20. Manhattan

"MANHATTAN PUBLIC LIBRARY," SAYS THE WOMAN'S VOICE. IT is rather dry, clipped, busy. You could easily imagine a phone that never stops ringing. But it turns out that Linda Hansen has time to talk. Manhattan is not what you'd think. About halfway down the Big Smoky Valley (between Austin and Tonopah), where very little in the way of man-made things competes with the curve of the road and the sweeping upthrust of the Toiyabe Range (with peaks over 11,000 feet), there is a turning to the east off Highway 376 that leads you to Manhattan, which is itself in the foothills of the Toquima Range, at 6,900 feet. Bald Mountain is to the north, at 9,275 feet. The town is in a canyon, or gulch. There are trees, and a weary kind of prettiness, even if the land seems disheveled—there was dredging there in the 1930s, done carelessly, the loose earth just tossed aside. No one since has had much thought of landscaping.

Manhattan, Linda Hansen reckons, now has about sixty inhabitants, though the number fluctuates, winter and summer. Open to the west wind, and at that height, Manhattan has fierce, frigid winters, a lot of snow. Some of the retirees go away then; they drop off south to Tonopah or Vegas, or Florida even, shutting their houses and letting them engage the wind. But in the summer, the view of Big Smoky is no small thing, especially in the mornings when the sunlight falls upon the land and the dappled ranges you're looking at. There's natural sculpting all over the Big Smoky Valley, and hardly a view that doesn't seem gracious. But summers pass, of course, and there are only so many videos in Linda Hansen's library.

They called it Manhattan because they were full of hope and bombast, long before that mixture was called "crossing your fingers." There had been silver finds in the gulch in 1866, but they stopped in a few years.

Nothing there to justify the name Manhattan. That came later, in 1905, when a cowboy named John Humphrey found gold at the foot of what was called April Fool Hill. Sure, there was always a lot of irony or gallows humor in the naming of things. They knew about the likelihood of losing.

By January 1906—the grimmest time of the year—there were several hundred prospectors keeping their backs to the wind as they hacked at the ground. As spring came, the population swelled to four thousand. There were over a dozen different mines, a mill, a telephone line, and what was called a "business district." The prospectors found gold, silver, and copper, and around $10 million of ore was taken out of the ground. Manhattan had had its own newspaper and company, Manhattan Consolidated. The population fell off, but there were fresh finds to stir up the old interest; those mining towns were so afraid of failing and so ready to jump at diversions and long shots. As late as 1939, the dredge was set up, so that there was a revival in the early forties.

There was hope again in the seventies and eighties, thanks to the Houston International Minerals Company, and there were still folks in Manhattan who would not have it counted as a ghost town. No sir! If you want a ghost town, you go to Belmont—that's the real thing, a classic! Belmont was fifteen miles to the northeast on a dirt road, a glory from another era. Back in the 1860s, Belmont had a thriving mine and became the capital of Nye County. A brick courthouse was built there, which is now a historic monument. Belmont once had a richer mine than Manhattan, with $15 million in lead and silver, but it's all gone now, and Belmont has nothing like a library, let alone people to use it.

I saw the Manhattan library building on a driving tour once, and I was tickled to think that Manhattan had such an asset, for there were only a few occupied houses that I could see and paved roads that turned into desolation, with hardly space to turn the car in. There is a little mining still, and there are people who have elected to live there, in retirement—for the air, the space, the light, the views, the silence, and the sheer lack of interference.

Linda Hansen comes in Mondays, Tuesdays, and Thursdays, from 10:30 a.m. until 4:30 p.m. The other days, she's at the smaller library in Round Mountain, another gold camp dating from 1900, ten miles to the north, a place where once upon a time you could see the gold in the ground and dig out pieces with hand tools. The two libraries are now part of the Smoky Valley Library District, which is centered on the new town of Hadley, a pretty little place a couple of miles west of Highway 376, a

town of paved streets and lawns, with a good nine-hole golf course (which
is advertised as far away as Highway 50). There is a grocery, and a swimming pool that is heated in the winter. Hadley is where the few kids in
Manhattan go to school, and that's the gathering place for the miners left
there and at Round Mountain, as well as the ranchers who work the valley
grasslands. That's where Linda Hansen lives. She is very pleased with
Hadley and what its modern facilities add to the grandeur of the Big
Smoky Valley. "Only fifty miles from Tonopah," people say if you mention
the isolation, as if Tonopah were something to hold on to. But why would
you go there, after all, when you're so close to Arc Dome, a superb peak,
11,361 feet, snowcapped, with hot springs in the valley floor, and with that
golf course of your own—which is more than Tonopah can boast, that
town that always feels as if it needs a decent tidying-up job.

At the Manhattan Public Library, Linda Hansen has eight thousand
materials—she prefers that term, since she deals extensively in videotapes
and audiotapes (as well as books)—and she fields an average of ten to
twelve calls a day from people who live in the town. There are days she
has no one, as well as times when "everyone" in Manhattan seems to be in
there. There are six or eight children in Manhattan—the number shifts
from season to season—and she runs reading circles for them in the
library. A kid could do much worse, she implies, and that's surely so. Manhattan is far, far from everything except the rapturous beauty of the land
and the sky, and the smaller miracle that society somehow survives there.
More gold in the ground would make the life so much less clear-cut, and
might drag in so many unfortunate consequences of the twentieth century. After all, if you've got nine holes that are grand and lovely and tricky
enough, who needs more?

In the late afternoon, you can see pairs on that golf course coaxing the
white balls along the lines of their own shadows on the polished greens. At
magic hour, the figures and the faces are washed in amber light. You hear
the chatter, the laughter, and even the merry dottling roll of the ball in its
hole. You see the lawns of Hadley and the sprinklers that keep them
bright. And you see nothing else but the distance, the desert, and the
rugged heave of the mountains. If one of those players chuckled and said,
"Isn't this grand? Isn't this paradise?" you'd be hard-pressed to argue. The
people live simply, perhaps, yet who really knows how plain the lives of
strangers are? Let us just say that they do not seem afflicted by anxiety, by
rush, crowding, or hard times. Their life balances out, just: They eat beef,
they sleep well, and they hold to simple certainties of existence that

nothing in the Big Smoky questions. Some people say the valley is an outpost of a tranquil nineteenth-century life. It may be it is a harbinger of
some future—after the fall—after the great pyramids of peoples and numbers are brought down, after the millennium, when the four of us left alive
golf away the daylight and sit alone together in the glow of those lamps
that confound the night. It would take something like gold again to dis-
rupt this calm. Nothing the world could offer in the way of outrage is wild
enough to disturb Hadley.

Not even the case of Sherrice Iverson. Sherrice was seven years old,
and she had been driven from her Los Angeles home on the Saturday
night and Sunday morning before Memorial Day, 1997. Her father,
LeRoy Iverson, fifty-seven years old, was driving, and her brother, Harold,
fourteen years old, was also in the car. They were driving on Interstate 15,
the road from Los Angeles to Las Vegas, and around 12:30 a.m. on Sunday,
they crossed the state line. That area is known as Primm Valley, and, as is
common in Nevada, there are casinos and hotels available as soon as a
road crosses the line, even if it is only another fifty miles to Vegas itself.
The Primadonna and Whiskey Pete's are on one side of the highway, and
Buffalo Bill's is on the other. Such places offer bargains and deals that
may persuade the traveler to stop.

The Iversons stopped, and LeRoy began to play in the Primadonna
casino. That casino has a fairground with an outdoor Ferris wheel—one
hundred feet high—set to catch the passing eye. The rides on that wheel
are free, and the lights on the wheel are famously pretty or hideous at
night, depending on your point of view.

That wheel isn't just an eye-stopper or a suggestion of Fortune's wheel.
It's meant to address what Barney Vinson calls a major family decision in
his book *Casino Secrets*—"whether or not to bring the kids. In the old
days, it wasn't advisable. After all, there wasn't much for youngsters to do
in Vegas. But in recent years, Las Vegas has been transformed into a
family-resort destination in an attempt to increase tourism. The reasoning
behind it is if parents can't bring their kids, they won't come either."

Gambling is illegal in Nevada for anyone under twenty-one. In all the
reputable casinos, that restriction is carefully enforced. And although the
casino floor is hardly avoidable in the big hotels—you have to walk
through it to reach a restaurant, the elevator to the rooms, and even the
check-in counter—parents with children are urged to keep moving. Stop
to have a conversation, and one of the floor attendants is likely to remind
you, politely but firmly, that kids are not tolerated as spectators or

bystanders at the tables. A small child lured to a slot machine by the lights, the big handle, and the gurgling noise is quickly removed and restored to the care of parents.

But in the early hours of that Sunday at the Primadonna, as their father gambled, Harold and Sherrice Iverson were left to their own devices. They crossed the highway to Buffalo Bill's, and not long thereafter, security found the little girl alone and called for the father to collect her.

It is not exactly clear what happened next. But at 3:48 a.m., videotape coverage picked up Sherrice playing hide-and-seek with a young man in the Primadonna casino arcade. The man is then seen to follow the child into a rest room. About twenty-five minutes later, the man emerges. And at 5:30 a.m., a security officer found the body of Sherrice Iverson, sitting on the toilet in a closed stall. She had been beaten, raped, and strangled.

There was widespread alarm in the Las Vegas area for several days. Radio talk shows were aghast at what had happened, and at the alleged statement by the father that he was prepared to waive any legal claim against the casino in exchange for a free room, $100, a case of beer, and an air ticket so that his girlfriend could come to Las Vegas. In a few days, a suspect, Jeremy Strohmeyer, was arrested—identified from the surveillance videotape—and people on the Nevada radio shows were saying that he, and even the father, should be neutered. Official vows of renewed vigilance were made by many casinos. The essential security of Las Vegas was reiterated, not to mention its excellent record as a place for family holidays. But no one could deny that, once that state line was passed, Nevada made available the means whereby a father or a mother could lose every penny their family possessed—or pass into the big time. In the larger hotel-casinos, they could do that in relative peace and assurance, while child-care specialists and counselors presided over facilities (open from 8:00 a.m. to midnight) where kids can do arts and crafts, play Ping-Pong, minipool, and Nintendo games.

All of which, I dare say, would cause a sigh on the golf course at Hadley and in all those similarly nineteenth-century parts of Nevada where kids are supposed to be content with the light, the space, the silence, and the opportunity for introspection.

Of course, Jeremy Strohmeyer was also too young to be in the casino. He was not allowed to play, and so he looked elsewhere. As the case developed, a further detail horrified the public. Strohmeyer had been at the Primadonna with a friend, David Cash, also eighteen and looking forward to starting his college career at the University of California at Berkeley.

*The casino complex in the Primm Valley,
contained within the roller coaster*

*Bare land to the southeast of the Primm Resort, the site for
M-G-M's new pleasure ground. Of course, all Las Vegas
looked like this once.*

Cash, it was claimed, had seen Jeremy in the stall with Sherrice, had seen the teenage boy struggling with the little girl, and had done nothing.

At the trial, with Strohmeyer defended by Leslie Abramson — famous from the Menendez case — Cash told every reporter that he had done nothing wrong, that the law did not insist that he should have intervened. Strohmeyer pleaded guilty, and Cash is working toward his degree.

As for the Primm Valley as a whole, rescue came in a strange, but Nevadan, way. There would be a new beginning. Maybe it was to redeem the name of Sherrice Iverson, or maybe it was just the spirit of fresh enterprise, but M-G-M, led by Kirk Kerkorian, moved in and bought up all the hotel-casinos in the valley, as well as stretches of land that reached out to the California border. They would build a great new park of rides, roller coasters, there on the happily flat land. Their guess was that the new playground would be close enough to Vegas for a day trip. By March 1999, the land was ready for work, one more polished dusty prairie waiting for "Fun!" And maybe somewhere a modest statue, tastefully done, to Sherrice Iverson and the spirit of childhood.

MILES OF VIDEOTAPE COME IN EVERY DAY FROM ALL OVER Las Vegas, not just the cameras that record transactions and missed meetings in the public places, but the cameras that watch over all the gaming tables and can call back the fall of cards, the shy distress of some players, and the deft cheating of others. The cans of surveillance, supposedly, are catalogued and stored in the warehouses on the edge of the city. So many minutes; so much short-lived action and excitement; and always the steady, listless beat of time peeling away. And so in the crushed spirit of a watched society, every mirror, every glass surface becomes the front for a clerical scrutiny — a little man, eating a sandwich, absorbing and being bored by your nakedness.

21. Tahoe

AT ZEPHYR COVE ON THE NEVADA SHORE OF LAKE TAHOE, some men were messing about with boats. The report in the papers was brief—it was one of those local curiosity stories that get into the national press—and I suspect, in fact, that the men were putting boats out on the water for the coming season. Zephyr Cove can be as gentle as its name, with a sandy, stony beach spread out for the afternoon sun to fall on in July and August. Well, this was May, and though the sun was shining, there is nothing calm or reliable about May at Tahoe. Some waves came up—not just swells, but real waves driven across the lake—and the small boat the men were in was simply tossed over on its side. Two of them grabbed ahold of something quickly enough, but a third was lost. You could say he was drowned, but to understand Tahoe, you have to realize that it was probably the cold that got him, paralyzed him, so he had nothing left but to drown. All of this in the clearest water you could ever hope to gaze through, and in one of the most beautiful places I know. Yet terrible, too, if you don't keep your eye on it.

Tahoe was discovered—or, shall we say, established for our history— by Frémont himself in the course of that journey begun on November 25, 1843, on the Columbia River. With twenty-five white men and some Indian guides, with some cattle to eat on the way and that howitzer gun with which to celebrate Christmas and warn off hostiles, Frémont had struck south and come down over the Black Rock Desert by way of Pyramid Lake. He had gone farther south, over the future site of Reno, and to what would be Virginia City, though the explorer had no idea of the gold his men tramped over there. How hard it is in life to journey and be open to everything. And so, in late January, with four or five feet of snow in the foothills, and despite immense warnings from his Indian guides and from other Washoe Indians found on the way, Frémont planned to turn west to

strike into the Sierra and pass over them in search of the Sacramento Valley, which he regarded as a place of biblical ease and plenty. They had
more than sixty horses, but the animals had the greatest difficulty making
their way in the snow and ice.

Frémont was brave, determined, and lucky. For in that country, in the
depth of winter, you may be forced to hole up in a place that offers no
food. As it was, Frémont's horses were gnawing at their saddle leather by,
let's say, February 14. Then on one clear, bright day, Frémont, along with
Charles Preuss, his mapmaker, left the trail they were trying to follow,
moved to their right (to the north) a little, reached what was probably
Steven Peak (10,100 feet), and saw, stretched out before them, this mountain lake. The day was so crystalline that, with his telescope, Frémont estimated that the lake was only fifteen miles long, north to south; it felt like
spring, he said, with the snow melting fast. But as soon as the sun dipped
below the peaks to the west, the rushing water on the peaks turned to ice.

The lake is actually twenty-two miles from Kings Beach in the north to
South Lake Tahoe, and at its broadest, it is thirteen miles across, east to
west. That day in 1844, Frémont called it Lake Bon Bland, after Aimé
Bonpland (1773–1858), the botanist who accompanied Humboldt on his
trip to Central and South America. But, as if alert to history and the sound
of names, Preuss wrote the name Mountain Lake on the map he made.
For a while, the lake was called Bigler, after John Bigler, an early governor
of California. But by the early 1860s, the name Tahoe had come into
use—a Washoe word meaning "big water" or "high water"—and by the
grace that sometimes figures in our dialogue with the world, it has stuck.
The name Tahoe does not just honor the Indian past—and those Indians
who had seen the lake long before Frémont, without knowing whom to
tell—it is a name that surely suggests height and clarity in the mouth.
There is something funny yet mystical in the word, something ineffable:
It makes the place mean that much more that, I think, people like to say
it—"Tahoe, Nevada." Say it to yourself a few times.

With the surface of the water at 6,225 feet above sea level, Tahoe is the
second-highest lake in the world, surpassed only by Lake Titicaca in Peru,
which lies at 12,500 feet and is over fifteen times the size of Tahoe. No
matter. Nevadans' sense of their own glory has always been either local or
infinite; the international, somehow, is a scale seldom employed. So
nothing really detracts from the splendor of Tahoe, thrust there in a savage split in the Sierra, and itself the consequence of glaciation. And
nothing quite settles the drama, or the tension between the size of
Tahoe—large enough, yet something that can be viewed and felt as a

whole from so many vantages—and the foreboding depth it has, the result of those scouring glaciers. For the exquisite range of colors in Tahoe, the enclosure of snowcapped peaks, and the evident invitation of the lake to all kinds of sport are offset by the knowledge that this lake has an average depth of 1,000 feet, and that at its deepest point, it goes down to 1,590 feet.

Tahoe today is a dangerously popular place. There is a short, intense summer season, and then there is the skiing in the winter. In the spring of 1998, Tahoe was optimistic about having those two seasons at the same time, for the snowfall that year was so great (we ascribe this to El Niño) that there was still pack on the ski slopes. For July 4, it was said, there would be skiing and swimming available. But in much drier years, the lake is fringed with boats, and the vexing water skis, the noise of which has been a matter of contention for years. You can see yachts and motorboats with water-skiers. There is even a preposterously "quaint" steamboat that goes between Zephyr Cove and Emerald Bay in the south, and which offers ignorant tourists a grotesquely bad dinner. In other words, the lake is busy, peppered with vacationers—not to mention the beaches where families sit out, barbecue, camp, and swim. So that it is startling to learn that this pretty, seemingly tame scoop of water, so gorgeous and changing in its colors, such a well-behaved, appealing place, is so deep and uncannily cold in its most secret places.

Not that measurement was always so simple. Up until 1940 or so, soundings reported varying depths—not by so much, yet enough to encourage the Nevadan hope (the local going over so quickly into the infinite) that the lake actually had no bottom, no limit, that there was at its deepest point an abyss, some plummeting chute, that went unendingly down into . . . well, some tunnel that comes up for air in Area 51?

Today, the depth is accurately recorded, at last; it is known—no matter if, from the level of the lake's summer fun, that depth strikes as oddly as the notion that there are spy satellites in the harmless deep blue sky, or that there are calculated arcs on radar maps far away that show the necessary passage of bombs to take out all those more recent outbreaks of civilization, or were, just a few years ago, when we lived beneath those arcs and had our spirits weighed on by them.

It is the harder to imagine that depth a mile or two offshore when one marvels at the clarity of Lake Tahoe. You can paddle around in the water in front of so many beaches, look down, and see the fine hairs on the knuckles of your toes. Swim, and it is as if a ghost goes with you, the white form of your own limbs with just the subtlest blue or green undertones. Kids in motorboats gaze down into the water, sure they can see the floor of the lake. And, if close to shore, they are right. We hardly know water any-where as clear as this.

Mark Twain visited Tahoe in the early 1860s. He loved the "vast oval"; "as it lay there with the shadows of the mountains brilliantly pho-tographed upon its still surface I thought it must surely be the fairest pic-ture the whole Earth affords!"

He ventured out on the lake in a craft, and then

> often, as we lay on our faces on the bow of the boat, a granite boul-der, as large as a village church, would start out of the bottom apparently, and seem climbing up rapidly to the surface, till presently it threatened to touch our faces, and we could not resist the impulse to seize an oar and avert the danger. But the boat would float on, and the boulder descend again, and then we could see that when we had been exactly above it, it must have been 20 or 30 feet below the surface.

He believed that under the right circumstances of light and stillness, one could see eighty feet down. Later experiments have established that white dinner plates could be spied at two hundred feet. Which is to say nothing of fish—trout especially—that seem as large, fresh, and available as your best dreams, or as bright as silver fish.

In late summer, on the shores of Tahoe, it can get as warm as ninety degrees. There are plenty of people in the water then, and the sand has been warmed by the best of July and August. But in April or May, on beau-tiful diamondlike days, when it is heaven to drive around the lake, seeing the tropic blues and greens, not to mention the strands of black and purple, in the water again, you can get out of the car and feel something like the airless draft from an open refrigerator coming off the lake. You go down to the water's edge and you cannot believe that anything can be both liquid and so cold. And so there are summer days when holidaymak-ers do no more than varnish their tans on the beach. A rippling in the water is too much to withstand.

It comes as a great surprise, therefore, to hear that Tahoe never freezes in the depths of winter—no matter its altitude, no matter that winter tem-peratures may drop to zero. There are some exceptions to this: In such sheltered inlets as Emerald Bay (nearly enclosed, and sheltered from wind by the sheer mountain faces that surround it), there may be several inches of ice. But out on the lake, on the turbulent sea itself, and despite that dread summer cold in the water, there is no freezing. Why? Because of the wind-driven motion, of course, but because of the depth, too. The winter never lasts long enough for that amount of stirring water to freeze.

One more peculiarity in nature springs from these circumstances. Bodies committed to the deeps of Lake Tahoe—by accident, by suicidal inclination, or whatever—do not rise to the surface. The reason for this is that they sink to such depths that the normal production of inflating gases in the body does not occur. And so the corpses stay down, and remain unusually resistant to deterioration. As in the cold, dry caves that the state offers, so Lake Tahoe does not give back its dead, but keeps them as nearly intact as nature can manage.

As I've said, the lake is not all Nevadan. The boundary between California and Nevada runs north to south and then turns east at an angle, hitting the south shore at—where else?—Stateline. Still, this rare facility of its water has a uniquely Nevadan appeal, where sometimes the need to convert people into their corpses goes hand in hand with the wish not to have the body recovered. I think of Fredo Corleone in *The Godfather* and *The Godfather, Part II*, the weakling older brother, a disgrace and traitor to his own family. Fredo betrays Michael, and then he is seemingly forgiven and allowed to live at the family house on Tahoe's Nevada shore. He likes to take his nephew, Anthony, fishing, and he has taught the boy to say a Hail Mary if he wants to get a fish.

Then one day, in the gray part of the year, Anthony is called away. His father says he has to go to Reno. Fredo will fish with just Al Neri as his companion. We see the two of them out on the lake in a rowboat. We see Michael watching from the house on the shore. There is the bump of a faraway shot, a shot in the back of the head, and Fredo keels over—to be tipped into Tahoe's cold, to sink slowly in the glass-clear liquid, to have the water soothe away the ragged bullet hole, and to stay down there, forever, as fragile and eternal as Fredo.

22. Tahoe Moods

LAKE TAHOE IS THE GREATEST NATURAL OPEN-AIR ATTRAC-
tion in the state of Nevada. And so it is the place above all where human
beings have to make some effort to balance their reveling in nature and
their cautionary urges to protect it. Elsewhere in the state, nature is so
enormous, so barren, so much dauntingly greater than, or oblivious to,
society that such issues seldom arise. But at Tahoe, there are recurring
ecological crises, and there has already been, for decades, that wistful
overture to great stories, "You should have seen it then. . . ." Most of
which are true, or valid; and all of which subscribe to the notion of Tahoe
as a magnet for glorious summer seasons, a place where people grew up,
had their fine days of idleness, romance, and awakening—with the added
luster of being rich enough to own the place. In the still-important social
circles of San Francisco, there are marriages that were made—and others
broken, or abandoned—during Tahoe summers. One way or another,
people are fond of the place, if in a bittersweet way sometimes. They look
at the intense cerulean colors in the water and see their youth, their great
days (so it helps that the water is so transparent). And when they look up
and notice the bustle and the business at today's lake, then they know how
much more has been lost. Yet every new generation discovers Tahoe for
itself. Yes, it is spoiled already—not the same—but you can see kids at
Tahoe being formed in their deepest imagination, just like Wordsworth at
Windermere.

Now, granted, I am stretching a point in claiming Tahoe for Nevada,
when two-thirds of the lake and its shores are Californian. And Tahoe,
especially at its northern end, is still very much the playground of San
Francisco and the Bay Area, just as Long Island serves Manhattan. There
are two ways to Tahoe for that traffic. One way is on I-80, which brings
you to Truckee—a boomtown for skiing—from whence you drop down to

the North Shore, which includes Tahoe City, Lake Forest, Carnelian Bay, Tahoe Vista, Kings Beach, and the state line at Crystal Bay, with the line going through to Cal-Neva Lodge itself, separating hotel from gaming room, and onto Incline Village, Sand Harbor, and down to Glenbrook (which is the oldest and classiest place on the lake). The other way in is on Route 50, a fork taken at Sacramento, a road that goes through more ski country and comes in by Twin Bridges and Echo Lake to the mess of South Lake Tahoe. Go on, to the east, and you reach Stateline itself (with Caesars and Harrah's, twin towers), and the twisty shoreline Route 50 will take you on to Zephyr Cove and so to Glenbrook (in fact, it skirts Glenbrook, which is too elite actually to be on the road).

The road has different numbers now—89, 28, and 50—but it goes all the way around the lake (which is exactly what you would expect, and dread). Not that the road is ever less than a great drive, with moments of hallucinatory beauty (and a testing onset of vertigo) as the narrow blacktop passes high above and between Emerald Bay on one side and Cascade Lake on the other. But too many amazed drivers have been killed—or gone over the edge—to make the driving comfortable. And summer fun around Lake Tahoe does put a lot of kids on the road who are bursting with beer and hopes of sex. There is a frontier spirit in driving there, and many battered vehicles in the parking lots.

Of course, the road system is a fairly recent concession. In the early days of Tahoe, travel was on foot or horseback, and then by boat across the lake. Within a few years of Frémont's glimpse of the lake, a trail had been made over the Sierra that touched the southeastern corner of the lake. That became a stagecoach run, and when the Comstock Lode was located in 1859, that was one of the principal routes to Virginia City. Glenbrook was founded four years later as a relaxing getaway spot for the most successful miners in the Comstock.

Then, within the space of a few years, the lake became not just a tramping ground for prospectors but also a forest that was ruthlessly cut down to build Virginia City—a place that still boasts timbered sidewalks. The unknown "vast oval," the desolate place, had fifty thousand travelers a year. All around the lake, pine trees were cut down and then barged and floated across the lake to Glenbrook. From there, the Bliss family—early tycoons of Tahoe—put in a narrow-gauge railway that climbed the four thousand feet to the east to Spooner Summit. The flats up there, Summit Camp—at ten thousand feet—were the scene of immense industry. Not only were the trees unloaded there for the railway but the ridge itself was scraped of growth. And all the lumber was then put in a flume system that took it down the steep slopes to the east, down toward Carson City, and then across the few miles of plain to Virginia City by rail. Look at the lake now, look at the slopes on either side of Spooner Summit, and the modern tranquillity is so striking compared to the photographs that survive of the desperate, mindless energies that were put into the effort to sustain the drive to get gold and silver out of the ground. In the 1860s, of course, our race was much less sensitive to the appearance of environmental brutality and unalloyed greed, which may only mean that we are just as blind to our excesses now.

By now, Virginia City is a garish tourist trap, the flumes and the sawmills are gone, and there is no one left to remind us that the very beautiful Tahoe we behold today was once so much more thickly forested. We forget that sometimes the apparition of monsters might glide over the lake—"rafts" of felled tree trunks, hauled or pushed by tugboat and locked up by strong cables or booms. Some of the rafts contained as much as 300,000 feet of timber. Today, such a sight, in the moonlight, would undoubtedly sustain the legend of Tahoe's beast—that creature that comes up from the great sink at the bottom of the lake. Whereas the real monstrousness lay in the cheerful scarring of the land and the remorseless commitment to the Comstock Lode.

But in the rush and the frenzy, sophisticated people noticed Tahoe and wondered what it might be. Fine hotels were built at Glenbrook and Tahoe City. A rail line was brought in to the latter from Truckee. And so the tradition of great houses on the lake began: Glenbrook House, the Grand Central Hotel at Tahoe City, the Grove near Tallac, Ben Holladay's house at Emerald Bay, the Tahoe Tavern, south of Tahoe City.

From the 1870s to the coming of the automobile, those households and hotels made up a polite society on the lake. It was a gathering place for the rich, who allowed special membership only to the eccentric or to those richer than themselves. And people kept in touch by way of boat trips across the lake. To this end, the Duane L. Bliss family (it was said that at one time the Blisses owned three-quarters of the lakeside property) ordered the building of a steamer. It was called the *Tahoe*, and it was constructed in San Francisco, shipped in parts by rail to Reno and Carson City, and brought over Spooner Summit by wagon and mule. Then, at Glenbrook, the parts were reconstructed as a 170-foot vessel launched on June 24, 1896.

The *Tahoe* carried two hundred passengers and had a top speed of eighteen and a half knots. There was a dining room for thirty people, and lavatories that had marble fixtures and hot running water. The ladies' cabin had plush crimson seats and was lined in teak and mahogany. The gentlemen's smoking lounge had Moroccan leather and cedar paneling. The "public" were allowed on the *Tahoe* by all means—to the extent that strangers were likely to require it. Essentially, the steamer was a club facility, running people across the water for dinners, parties, picnics, and social gatherings.

But then, in the years 1910–1912, the first road was built, just a stretch near Tahoe City—a one-way road with turnouts. The touring car appeared at the lake, its noise and intrusion every bit as offensive and far more vital than the Jet Ski that has been such a source of contention in the last fifteen years. By 1930, there was something like a road all around the lake, and thus the several businesses of wayside filling stations, restaurants, and local real estate had begun. The *Tahoe* became uneconomical, and not private enough.

It was withdrawn from service in the mid-thirties. Then in August 1940, at the end of that summer season, William Seth Bliss had the boat towed out into the middle of the lake and sunk. It is down there still, and likely in icily good condition, a little bit of *Titanic* in the Tahoe story.

There were hikers and adventurers, too, fishermen, painters, and hunters, and there were few restrictions then on any of them. You could camp out, as Mark Twain did, if you had enough blankets. He felt sure that

> three months of camp life on Lake Tahoe would restore an Egyptian mummy to his pristine vigor, and give him an appetite like an alligator. I do not mean the oldest and driest mummies, of course, but the fresher ones. The air up there in the clouds is very pure and fine, bracing and delicious. And why shouldn't it be?—it is the same the angels breathe. I think that hardly any amount of fatigue can be gathered together that a man cannot sleep off in one night on the sand by its side. Not under a roof, but under the sky; it seldom or never rains there in the summertime.

There was talk of making Lake Tahoe a national park. There were schemes developed in San Francisco for scooping away just a little of the lake's uncommon water, in which the citizens might bathe and sluice their cars. There were development schemes, with thousands of lots of lakeshore frontage sold, and then reclaimed, as the Depression hit. But the plan for a park was abandoned because speculation was already so rife that, by 1935, "ruthless commercial enterprises" had already altered the natural character of the place. Yet, at that time, there were probably no more than a thousand people who lived year-round at the lake.

The water was saved. By the mid-thirties, limits were established for how low the level of the lake could sink (a minimum of 6,223 feet above sea level). Any surplus was carried the much shorter distance for the farmers of nearby Nevada, for the Smith Valley and Yerington, as far as Fallon. Still, in the great periods of drought that California is susceptible to, there are newcomers who look at all that water—so cold, so clear—and marvel at the "waste." Also, in the summer season of 1935, Metro-Goldwyn-Mayer came to Lake Tahoe for its own eleven-week season to film *Rose Marie*. The large unit—producer Hunt Stromberg, director W. S. Van Dyke II— set up its base at Camp Richardson on the South Shore. It made its Canada thereabouts and hired, or rounded up, as many as one thousand "Indians," a search that went far afield. These extras were made to live at the camp. They were discouraged from leaving and were fed on fifty cents a person a day. Watermelons were shipped in, wrapped in straw; and the Indians used the straw for bedding. Extraordinary, paranoid precautions were taken against their getting drunk.

And many of those Indians—Washoe and Paiute—patiently stood in for the nations of Canada, and filled in the background of so many scenes. For the momentous occasion on which Nelson Eddy sang "Rose Marie," the setting was the enclosed Emerald Bay. It was said that the echoes of Eddy's noble voice could be detected a full five minutes after he had finished singing.

The stranger thing is that the Indians who lived near the lake then retained a legend of the time when the lake had been surrounded by more level country. By then, there had been upheaval—we are talking of all the centuries of volcanic and glacial activity—and the lake was lifted up by the squeezing of mountains. But the Indian legend also told of a cave on the northern shore, Spirit Lodge—its location has long been uncertain—where a warning noise could be heard sometimes.

In the language of the 1940 *WPA Guide to 1930s Nevada*:

Tahoe is a lake of many moods. When untroubled, it lies under a full sun like an enormous pavement of colors, with long slender paths of silver across the broad belts of green and blue. In early morning it is so soft and shimmering that it looks unreal; and under a low Western sun burning in cloud bands, it is a mighty plateau streaked with gold.

23. Wingfield

VERY SOON AFTER HE GOT HIMSELF INTO NEVADA, GEORGE Wingfield had his picture taken—and what a fellow he is, sitting nonchalantly sideways in a fancy wicker chair, his legs crossed, looking out past the photographer, keeping his thin black cane propped against the arm of the chair. He is in his very early twenties, his hair slicked back from a center parting, utterly sure of his handsome self. In truth, he was a cowboy and a saloon gambler, but he was fit to be an actor playing those roles, and his fearless gaze was ready to take on anything Nevada could offer. Yet nothing is quite right about the picture: His jacket doesn't match the pants; his shoes are leather and suede brogues; his bow tie is something less than reliable, and the cane can hardly escape being an affectation. But George is simply terrific, holding the show together, and, in his dark, rather cruel-lipped way, being a frontier knockout. His being so smooth an actor, or go-between, just adds to the thrill that this recent cowboy was on his way to becoming "the owner and operator of Nevada." Why not? The state needed every bit of help, and every canny knockout it could get. Consider these bare facts. Nevada, less than forty years a state, was in decline. The great riot of the Comstock was over. The mines at Austin, Pioche, and Eureka were all used up. The population of Virginia City was in rapid decline—it would be about 2,700 by 1900. In that year, the inhabitants of the entire state would number just 42,335—the number had fallen by 20,000 in twenty years. The state was depressed, largely vacant, and generally too dry for agricultural development. More or less, it was a desert across which the Central Pacific Railroad passed.

Wingfield, the son of a rancher, was born in Lakeview, Oregon, in 1876. Lakeview was about eighty miles east of Klamath Falls, on the edge of the desert that is eastern Oregon, and just a few miles from the northwest corner of Nevada. The boy had a limited education and spent too

George Wingfield as a young man
(courtesy of Nevada Historical Society)

much time with his father and the other cowboys working the cattle ranch. Even as a teenager, he had won a reputation as a cool gambler, and a generous winner. When he won a hand, he would buy cigars for the buckaroos he had defeated.

In the spring of 1896, he set out to help drive nearly three thousand head of cattle to the nearest railhead, at Winnemucca. That trip would take close to three months, and it would mean negotiating the great gradient out of Oregon to the plateau of Nevada, and then making a way across the Black Rock Desert in early summer. This is still close to empty ground, where golden mountains break up the graveled plain and let the wind skid and scream off their slopes. This is something like the true

Old West, with no spectators there to behold it. And Wingfield had handled it.

Winnemucca charmed him, no matter if the wind howled down its street. It was a town of one thousand people, and it was on the railroad. In a couple of hours, he could be in Reno, which had about four thousand inhabitants, as well as photographers' parlors with wicker chairs that were a mass of spirals and curlicues. The cowboy liked the town, and the saloons, and the way his gambling skills could make him a living there. Yet he was appreciated, popular, and trusted; no one who lost to him—and most did—ever accused him of sharp practice.

By 1899, it was said, Wingfield was worth $40,000, a remarkable piece of self-manufacture, and a history that he could never quite shrug off. For if persistent victory at poker doesn't mean cheating, then doesn't it require a certain cold scrutiny of weakness in others? That's what you see in the face of the young man, along with a complete lack of shame or shyness about letting his natural intelligence work for him.

In a spirit of entrepreneurship, Wingfield took his money a few miles east, to Golconda—also on the rail line—where copper had been discovered. He began to buy saloons, and he fell in with a woman named May Baric. Much later, she would say that if it hadn't been for her, he would never have gone to Alaska—there was a gold rush there, too, and $40,000 is more plausibly the result of Yukon luck than of steady application at poker in Winnemucca. Whatever the answer, May Baric had claims on George Wingfield.

In saloons, where there was gambling, there were also prostitutes and women who expected no more than an attachment to a strong man. So many men had come to Nevada on their own, to be on their own, to put their courage, their gambling instinct, up against the house and respectable society. And equally isolated women might make a living off that—off the loneliness of the men, their urge for celebration or consolation, or even the whimsy that a woman's knowing look at a hand of cards could make it a winner, and her a beauty. There were women in Nevada who were whores, thieves, parasites, and whiskey madams. And there were some who were far ahead of their times and their gender, ready to make apple pies free of the infernal dust, ready to listen to the incoherent dreams of losers who were falling asleep, ready to be lovers.

And if Wingfield was exceptional—industrious, adventurous, handsome, watchful, very skilled, and lucky—let us suppose that May Baric was his equal, or his match. They were together several years. She said she was his common-law wife, and he never really disputed that, no matter that she had become an inconvenience, or not what he wanted in the new moment. Suppose they were a real couple for those several years early in the century, companions, lovers, people caught up in some passionate exchange. Look at his face, and ask if he would have settled for less.

Golconda had its brief glory and its consequent pretensions. In the copper rush, the population went up from twenty to five hundred. The town got saloons and its own Jockey Club. George was a member; he loved horse racing. He met useful people—John G. Taylor, who would become the biggest rancher in Nevada by 1930; George S. Nixon, a banker who would go to the U.S. Senate; and a young mining engineer named Herbert Hoover. And almost certainly May was there, in the background, or even on show as the prize in George's life. In Nevada, then, everyone would have understood and accepted the arrangement, even the wives. For it was a man's world, a place where his dreams were carving open the land.

Golconda would fail soon enough. Wingfield lost money on his saloons, and he was in debt to Nixon, who was, by 1901, the president of the First National Bank of Winnemucca. Then word came north that silver had been found at Tonopah, 250 miles southeast of Reno. In fact, in May 1900, a rather halfhearted miner named Jim Butler had gone over to Tonopah from Belmont and found "bold, black croppings of fine-grained quartz" that were assayed as 395 ounces of silver to the ton. Another find proved to be 640 ounces of silver to the ton. Yet Butler was busy with other matters, he said, and it was not until August that he properly filed his extraordinary claims. He went back with his wife, Belle, and she named one of the claims the Mizpah.

Tonopah took off, with Butler entering into easy verbal contracts with prospectors that leased them the land in return for 25 percent of the profits. Within a few years, as Tonopah swelled in size, it ousted Belmont as the seat for Nye County. George Wingfield was there by May 1901, and he set up the Tonopah Club, which would be one of the town's most prestigious saloons. It was from that base, with George Nixon's capital support, that Wingfield turned himself into a great businessman. He gambled in his own saloon and more often than not he won—with cigars and champagne to the losers. Those losers were miners with plenty in hand and dreams of more. Over cards, they talked of bigger and better seams they had seen, and Wingfield got into the trade of financing them, as did Nixon. He never mined, but he would drive out into the desert to look at the ground. And he was as good or lucky with his hunches there as he was at cards. By 1904, it was said, Wingfield was worth $2 million personally.

Nixon, who was elected to the U.S. Senate in 1904, was Wingfield's mentor. He urged the ex-cowboy to think less of card playing and more of stocks and banking. The lesson was taken in whole, and it reached fruition in 1905, when Wingfield moved a few miles south of Tonopah, to Goldfield, which was on its way to becoming the bigger and more lucrative of the two.

It was in Goldfield that Wingfield made himself the most powerful figure in Nevada. Although still acting with and for Nixon, Wingfield was in charge on the ground. He bought up mining claims, he formed banks, and he would own the great Goldfield Hotel, built in 1908 for $500,000. He formed and led the Goldfield Consolidated Mine Company, and he built the vast one-hundred-stamp mill that dominated the town from 1908 onward. One of his mines, the Mohawk, delivered $6 million in nine months. Goldfield Consolidated was capitalized for $50 million. At the same time, Wingfield was engaged in running battles with the Industrial Workers of the World over charges that miners were stealing ore (it was a common practice), and over rates of pay and conditions of work. He even had troops brought into the town, and on several occasions, there were outbreaks of violence.

The dirty work of mining was always rapidly subordinated to the will of those who ran the industry. And Wingfield's wealth and eminence made him many enemies. But he was in most respects a fair dealer, and he was unusual for the time in urging that the wealth of Nevada be kept in the state and reinvested. Although Wingfield declined several offers of political office, he had enormous, idealistic visions for the state. He believed that mining's wealth should fund agriculture and irrigation. He wanted a sound basis of banking. He wanted business to grow. He guessed, ahead of most others, that Boulder Dam would be the turning point in state history, and as early as the 1920s, he had bought land in that place called Las Vegas because he reckoned it would boom one day enough to support a grand hotel.

His efforts to develop Tonopah and Goldfield meant new life for the state, so in fact few envied his personal profit. By 1910, the population of the state had increased (since 1900) by 93.4 percent—it was up to 81,875. The figures for mineral production tell the story even more dramatically. In the great days of the Comstock, Nevadan mineral yield had gone from $1 million in 1860 to $16 million in 1864 and $30 million in 1874. But after 1880, the figures fell off fast, and at the turn of the century, there was only a little over $2 million a year. Then see what happened as Tonopah and Goldfield came to life (in millions):

1903	$ 2.8
1904	4.4
1905	6.4
1906	13.2
1907	16.3
1908	14.4
1909	25.8
1910	31.4
1911	33.3
1912	35.5
1918	48.6

Wingfield put on weight. He drank too much. Within a few years of success, he was less striking as a man. And with his power, he had to face up to the facts of May Baric. Wingfield was a friend of the most important people in the state, and yet in Tonopah and Goldfield, May was with him all the while. She said that they had entered into common-law marriage in 1902. But then in March 1906, as Mrs. May Wingfield, she filed for divorce, asking for alimony of $3,000 a month, as well as attorney fees of $50,000. One of her attorneys was Patrick McCarran, a sometime crony to Wingfield and later to become a U.S. senator. She said that George had beaten her and infected her with syphilis.

May failed in her claim, but Wingfield made a private settlement: In March 1906, he effectively paid her off. The details are not clear, but she got money and some property in return for a signed affidavit that they were not married.

But May did not give up that easily. She would sometimes burst in on him, drunk and threatening violence and, worse, exposure. Two years later, in 1908, George married Maude Murdoch, the seventeen-year-old daughter of a San Francisco banker. It was a demonstration of his moving up in the world, just as it was the city's way of gaining an interest in Nevada's wealth. But Baric was still around, demanding and getting pay-offs. She gave press interviews to the effect that George still saw her, still paid her bills, and had even said that if she had behaved better, she could have been the "official Mrs. Wingfield." She filed a breach of promise suit in California, seeking $500,000, and announced, "I can prove all that I will claim in this suit, for the whole State of Nevada knows it. He broke me down physically and left me without a cent after living with me as his wife for seven and a half years. He introduced me to hundreds of people as his wife, including Senator George Nixon of Nevada."

May never won an action, but she never gave up. Somehow, you know there was love there once. And poor George was disappointed in Maude. They had children. They lived in a fine house in Reno. But she preferred San Francisco and she liked to spend her money in the stores there. There were separations, and times when George put out notices in the San Francisco papers that he would not honor his wife's bills. They were divorced in 1929; she got $2,500 a month in alimony and child support, a lump sum of $58,000, and their house on Pacific Avenue. George was a Nevadan still, and ahead of him lay the great crash—the Depression—and his bankruptcy.

All well and good. He found another mine later on, and his fortunes revived. But he had been a cowboy once, and then the champion of his state, and together he and May had had wild times in the heyday of Goldfield, which—you will likely have guessed this—is now a wreck of its old glory, fallen stones on the bare sand.

24. Tahoe Summer

IN THE MONTH OF AUGUST, AT TAHOE, THERE ARE EVENING barbecues on the beaches of Incline Village, Sand Harbor, Glenbrook, and Zephyr Cove that are likely to be reunion parties for some of the tonier private schools in San Francisco—Town, Hamlin, Burke's, the Sacred Heart, Country Day, Waldorf. The mothers and the children live up at the lake for that month; it is a system, and the families have the same condo or house every year, the way they have 49er football tickets. The dads make the drive up for long weekends, staying in cell-phone contact with the brokerage house, the venture-capital operation, or the law firm. The dads do business as usual on Saturdays, when they play golf. During the week, the wives take tennis lessons from pros who can recognize both the women who are just constitutionally disappointed but controlled and those who plan a full divorce as well as they can see the neurotic flinching, the self-pity, in a backhand. The wives have salad lunches together and dish the teak and maple pros just as they get into the niceties and nasties of prenuptials.

The kids can play on the sandy beaches where, by August, the shallows have a chance of being warm enough for paddling around in. They can dive off the dock that comes with their rental. They may go riding in the mountains. They can have Jet Skis hired out for them—at $55 or $60 an hour. They could go gliding, hot-air ballooning, sailing, or waterskiing; just about anything you can think of is available. And the kids feel it's okay, because most of their friends are there, and, anyway, at Tahoe you can pick up the San Francisco television stations. The mothers have their summer reading lists, and the kids may be getting into the first relationships of their lives—or just studying the opposite sex in bathing suits. After ten or so, who knows if in the closed rooms of the condos, the mothers and the kids aren't masturbating, to different rhythms, the kids full of hope and astonishment, their elders wistful. Tahoe cannot help but be a romantic place—the most lovely and love-filled in Nevada, I dare say. At the same time, Tahoe is getting to be so crowded that the summer regulars sigh and groan and consider doing something in local politics. You can even feel that you can see paradise slipping away. One of the summer distractions is the noise of buzz saws on the construction sites—new places, new estates, are being carved out of next to nothing every year. There's always a smell of fresh-cut timber; it's the cause of one of the several allergies that Tahoe mothers have to keep count of. Where will it end? they say at their parties, and they feel the steady intrusion of newcomers—tourists, visitors, the day trade—people from Reno, Sacramento, even San Francisco itself, who think nothing of a day at the lake, and who have to squeeze in somewhere to get their glimpse of it.

There are Tahoe people now whose grandparents told them about the house parties and boat trips from one house to another, and there are Tahoe residents still who remember a time when the entire population of the lake (or of the villages on its shore) was no more than one thousand. Not even the road system of the 1930s, or the attempt to sell off lakeside land, had caused that number to rise.

See what has happened in the sixty years since. By 1950, it is estimated, the lake had about 2,500 permanent residents, with as many as 35,000 total summer visitors. By 1978, those two figures had climbed to 45,000 residents and 186,000 visitors. The most recent figures—dating from 1995—suggest a resident population of over 52,000 on an average Friday in August, with 55,000 visitors (on that same day).

No one in an egalitarian society has any right to dispute a hundredfold increase in the number of people anxious to get a look at and the feel of glorious Tahoe. And why should we doubt increases still to come? In the summer of 1998, with people able to ski in the morning, play golf in the afternoon, and swim before dinner, Tahoe had everything to offer. The buzz saws went into fiercer discourse than ever. The south shore casinos booked the biggest acts they could find, and in Reno the "Hot Summer Nights" campaign of August mounted. Alan Greenspan had felt compelled to say he had never seen anything quite as good, and memories were fresh of the visit made by Bill Clinton and Al Gore, with their assurances that somehow the health of the economy and the purity of Tahoe would be preserved at the same time. "There cannot be an artificial dividing line," the president had said, "between preserving our natural heritage and growing our economy."

Of course, there is always a very artificial, very flexible line between our hopes and realities; that's so much of what being American, and Clinton, means. (In the summer of 1998, the same president had very high approval ratings, and the legend of Miss Lewinsky sustaining his cocky, yet sly grin.) Tahoe has already been altered beyond repair. Its future is largely a matter of the rhetoric we employ to describe, and disguise, the alteration.

The road system made the change, for one thing, and the postwar sense of driving as an American right, and the way in which after the war the United States became converted to winter sports. The true cause of the growth in residential population around Tahoe is that it has become a place for year-round play. To the north, on I-80, Truckee and the land that goes up into the once-desolate Donner Pass area has become a suburb of ski lodges that also serve as summerhouses. For it is a quick and easy drive from Truckee down to the lake, and it passes Squaw Valley—site of the 1960 Winter Olympics—maybe the single greatest example and spur in the development of the area.

At Stateline, on the south shore, since the late 1930s there had been a few cafés with slot machines. Sahati's State Line Country Club followed by the late forties, with rooms open all year round. And in the early 1950s, Harvey Gross and Bill Harrah built the first of the hotel-casinos. Today, at Stateline, there is Harrah's, Harvey's, Caesars, and the Horizon. At Incline Village, there is the Hyatt Regency. And at Crystal Bay, there is the Tahoe Biltmore, and the Cal-Neva, actually the oldest lakeside establishment, dating back to the 1930s, when it was an escape for the fast crowd and the gangsters in Reno.

But it is not really the large establishments that characterize Tahoe. Rather, the lakefront in its most crowded stretches, north and south, is an untidy assemblage of filling stations, of small shopping malls, restaurants, cafés, and burger joints, of realty offices where keys may be claimed and deposits paid for a week in this or that condominium. There are campsites and the stores that cater to camping. There are places to buy everything required for fishing, hiking, and rock climbing. There are ski-outfitting stores, and there are the big supermarkets where the wives or even the au pairs may load a dozen brown bags into the trunk of the big car—with ground round, buns, catsup, relish, potato chips, dips, franks, ribs, mustards, all the fun of the cookout. There are video stores where you can get an immediate summer membership. And five-and-dimes where you can pick up all the thongs, sunblock, insect repellent, goggles, golf balls, and condoms you may have forgotten. In one quick predinner errand, you can pick up caviar, pornography, and new software for your computer and be back in twenty minutes, by the time the ribs are done. All you have to do is drive and park, reverse and park, and know which little slip roads are one-way and at which junctions you have the right-of-way. Knowing isn't everything, though, and Tahoe cars are likely to be a little battered at the corners.

Over the decades of its development, so many residues have been produced by Tahoe. Whenever a new building goes up, the land is cleared—the weeds, the flowers, the ferns, the trees, and the exposed soil bleed a little into the water. The crystal air has had to deal with auto-mobile exhaust, the charred air from barbecues, the fumes from Jet Skis, and the viscous filigree of suntan oils. The condominium throws out the cellophane that wrapped the ground beef; the slithering innards of honeydew melons; the old newspapers; the bottles; the tennis balls that have lost their bounce; the paperback novels that fell in the dip; the million cardboard tubes that held so many rolls of toilet paper.

No one will ever again see the place Frémont saw, because the air and the open intervals of visibility will never be so empty. We have been here, discarding as we came and went. There are sewage systems and there are cemeteries by Lake Tahoe now. And there are lawyers' offices were you may consider suing over some encroachment on your space and purity. It has been counted up so we know there are sixty-three creeks and streams by which water runs down into Lake Tahoe—as well as the Truckee River, which joins it to Pyramid Lake. And with the counting goes a measuring. The water is not what it was.

In 1978, the Tahoe Research Group reported that in the previous ten years, sediments and nutrients entering the lake had increased to such an extent that there was 50 percent more algae than there had been. "You can see some of the signs yourself," said *Sunset* magazine, "mossy-looking algae called *periphyton* attached to piers and rocks; slime on boat hulls, ropes, piles; muddiness near shore; and a greenish algae 'bloom' that sometimes shows on the edges of the lake, especially at the south and southwest corners during spring runoff."

That was twenty years ago. Today, the Lake Tahoe area receives over a million visitors every year. To take just one example of what those num-bers entail: In the early 1990s, the Tahoe Regional Planning Agency—set up in 1969, and the single most active protective force in the area—reported that recreational Jet Skis and small motorboats dumped 775 gal-lons of unburned fuel into the lake and the air every day.

The Jet Ski, a kind of waterborne motorbike, capable of reaching 60 mph, is one of the modern rages in places like Tahoe. Sales in all of the United States had gone from zero to nearly 1 million in the ten years after 1986. In 1996, Jet Skis were involved in over four thousand accidents, with fifty-seven deaths. On Lake Tahoe, the minimum age for driving Jet Skis was raised from twelve to sixteen early in 1998. But still, the vehicles were very controversial because of their fuel wastage, their noise, and their interference with animal life.

The Tahoe Regional Planning Agency therefore announced that it would ban all two-stroke engines on the lake.* There is no question but that such a measure would hurt some local businesses, and reduce the "pleasure" of citizens. Already, there have been attempts at compromise, and active in those has been Steve Wynn, not just the head of Mirage Enterprises in Las Vegas and the most prominent of the modern casino owners but also the at-large member of the Tahoe Regional Planning Agency—if only because he then owned a magnificent lakeside property at the eastern end of Incline Village (in fact, there are several such properties there, and Wynn had Michael Milken and John Travolta as neighbors). In August 1997, Wynn announced that Bombardier Motor Corporation, manufacturer of the Sea-Doo, planned a new kind of ski, powered by fuel injection, that would be cleaner and quieter.

That came only a month after the Presidential Forum at Lake Tahoe, convened and led by Clinton and Gore, at which $50 million was pledged from government agencies over the next two years, as well as twenty-five initiatives "to help improve Tahoe's declining water clarity, dead and dying forests and clogged roadways."

The two leaders went out on a boat and gathered samples of plankton and algae. Vice President Gore took a dip in Fallen Leaf Lake, and the two guys appeared in pale blue shirtsleeves to talk to some three thousand Tahoe residents. Some experts said that $900 million was actually required over the next ten years. Practical politics said that $50 million is "exactly what we need right now."

The photo opportunity left good feelings—as such things do—and it was a glorious day, on which the lake looked "perfect." But Lake Tahoe is a kind of desert that has been tamed, enjoyed, and altered in a hundred years. There is no going back to old forests, the absence of roads, or flawless water. The water may be helped. Trees can be replanted. But poor

---

* The ban went into effect June 1, 1999.

roads are only answered by bigger, better roads that cut more drastically into the land.

We live on a cusp—and it may last so long that *cusp* hardly seems the right word—in which it is natural for more and more people to want to see and experience the beauties of Lake Tahoe. But it is a Nevadan mystery, and only a matter of profound time, that in being seen, the spectacle must wither, and vanish. Deserts can be defied, and compromised with, for only so long. In June 1999, introducing a bill to save Tahoe, California Senator Dianne Feinstein said that there were no more than ten years left to repair the damages done to the lake.

25. Reno

SOMEHOW THE NAME RENO SOUNDS RIGHT FOR A SMALL western city in just the way the Brown Palace, in Denver, is a fitting name for a grand western hotel. And if you grant that Las Vegas is something more or other than just an American city, then Reno is really the only city in Nevada. Elko, Ely, and Winnemucca are not more than towns. And Carson City is a very pretty place for a seat of government, but a charming fabrication. Reno has life, gusto, and history of its own. It always seems to me not a bad place to live, and as a matter of fact, it had a time—in the 1930s, I'd say—when it might have been one of the great places to be. It's a marvel that there isn't a grand American novel set there at that time. You could call it *Reno-vation*, the sarcastic word Walter Winchell dumped on the place in that era, when so many well-to-do women went there to change their lives, when Reno was the new divorce capital of the American world.

Transformation is always the guiding light. In October 1846, the Donner Party—over eighty men, women, and children in wagons drawn by oxen—came to the sweet Truckee meadows, where Reno now stands. They had left Wyoming in July, skirted the Great Salt Lake, passed the 10,704-foot Pilot Peak (which is in the east of Nevada), and came on across the desert in September. They were exhausted, yet jubilant; they believed the worst was over. They could see the Sierra, and they knew those mountains meant California.

But the view west from Reno can be somber even now, the mountains ranging from purple through slate to black, unless snow is falling already. September and October in San Francisco are the real summer, but up in the Sierra, the snows can begin early. In 1846, from the meadows—so rich in grass and water, such fine farming land—the Donner Party could see snow. But they lingered, thinking to fatten their cattle and gather their own strength before the big final play. It was what killed some of them: Timing is at the heart of gambling, and you can either trust your knowledge, your instinct, your intelligence or settle for luck.

Despite the suitable conditions for a settlement in the meadows, nothing developed there until the discovery of the Comstock Lode. A railway was built from the meadows down to Virginia City, and a spot was chosen as ideal for a ferry or even a bridge across the Truckee River. A man named Fuller started the business there, but he was flooded out and sold the spot to Myron C. Lake in 1861. Lake built toll roads and a bridge, and he made himself rich and available as the Central Pacific Railroad came by. And so, in 1868, a stopping place on those tracks became a settlement, and it was named Reno after General Jessie Reno, a Union officer who had died at the Battle of South Mountain in 1862. By 1870, there were a little over 1,000 people in the place (when the population of the whole state was 42,000).

Lots were auctioned off, and there was a building boom, especially on the banks of the Truckee River. With its links to Virginia City and Carson City, and then later as the natural railhead and distribution point for Tonopah and Goldfield (boomtowns in the first decade of the twentieth century), Reno was the true center of the state, a city that offered the quickest transportation west and east, and was itself pleasantly located. Myron Lake was the first potentate to build himself a mansion there. Others followed—George Nixon, whose banking business began in Winnemucca and then shifted to Reno; his protégé, George Wingfield, who would live in Reno and set up his banking interests there; and, most significant of all, Patrick A. McCarran, who was born in Reno in August 1876, the son of Irish immigrants, whose family moved to a ranch a few miles to the east, but who went to high school and then the university in Reno, and who would be buried there in October 1954, having served in the U.S. Senate since 1933.

By 1871, Reno took over from Washoe City as the seat of Washoe County. In the same decade, Lake put up the splendid Riverside Hotel. In 1885, the state legislature approved removal of the state university from Elko to Reno—that opening occurred in 1886, when the campus had just one building, Morrill Hall. By 1890, the population of Reno was around 3,500 (in a state that still had only 47,355 residents).

So few people as yet, but still Reno was Nevada's attempt at society and distinction. In the last decade of the nineteenth century, Reno was a communication center for the agriculture and mining businesses, and a place where many of the state's power brokers chose to live (if only because it allowed them the quickest journey to San Francisco). Set at nearly five thousand feet, Reno was glorious in summer and hard going in winter. From its early days, it was vulnerable to conifer fires, rushed along by the fierce winds, and snowfalls that brought activity to a standstill.

But Reno was the emotional headquarters for those people who wanted to build Nevada. And with the rich strikes at Tonopah and Gold-field, Reno came into its greatest power. It was 250 miles from Tonopah (though the journey was not too hard), but there was no other alternative city. Thus, Nixon, Wingfield, and others saw the great need for banking support for the new prospecting fields, and thus the chance to direct prof-its to the state's precarious agriculture. By 1910, Reno had close to 11,000 people; by 1920, it had 12,000; and by 1930, 18,500—the latter in a total state population of 91,000.

By then, it had a developed university, which included the Mackay School of Mines; a business district and a residential area; parks, churches, and lakes for recreation; a new Nevada State Building, erected in 1927; and a flourishing State Historical Society, where Jeanne Eliza-beth Weir had begun a valuable archive of state papers that included the oral histories of pioneers. Which is not to say that Reno in the late 1920s was secure—against the mines going dead, against drought, or any other calamity in human affairs. Which is a way of saying that by around 1930, Nevada had scarcely emerged from nineteenth-century conditions. It was a frontier state, yet all the real frontiers had passed it by; it was on the edge, but the edge was a desert in which life was barely sustainable. Those classical parts of Nevada—the farming, the mining, and the general adop-tion of a cowboy's attitude to life—go on. But if they were all Nevada had, the state would surely have needed rescue long ago. Instead, an extraordi-nary new daring came to its aid, a recklessness so much larger than any-thing the Donners gave way to (trying to be careful).

Nevada felt it would weather the effects of the stock market crash of November 1929 better than other states. After all, the plans for federal aid to the state's road program saw at least a doubling of funds—in truth, from the twenties to the thirties, the money would triple, reaching an invest-ment of $29.9 million. Plans were in place for the ammunition depot at Hawthorne, which meant another $3 to $5 million. Most important of all, in December 1928, President Coolidge signed the Boulder Canyon Proj-ect Act. Some said that meant an investment of more than $100 million, and a scarcely imaginable transformation of the state.

When Governor Fred Balzar gave the State of the State speech in January 1931, he was buoyant:

> Most fortunately, the existing Nation-wide condition of financial stress is but lightly felt within our own borders, when comparisons are made with conditions prevailing in other States, and this is partly due to our solid financial standing and partly due to the large Federal expenditures which have heretofore been made within the State, and those authorized to be made.

That sounds like the bluff of a good cardplayer. For the state governor was in a position to know the way the wind was blowing. Mineral production in Nevada died (in millions):

1929	$31.4
1930	16.2
1931	9.4
1932	4.2

What those figures revealed was one of the more enduring things about Nevada's mineral wealth, and something that still obtains: There are metals to be had, but the cost of extraction is high. What struck Nevada in the early thirties was the drastic erosion of capital. And nothing figured as large in this as the sudden fall of Governor Balzar's political patron, the enduring George Wingfield.

Wingfield owned or controlled banks, and he had made extensive loans to sustain state agriculture. He had not done much to explain the pressure he was under. The first few banks failed. Wingfield got a loan of nearly $5 million from the Reconstruction Finance Corporation, but nearly all of that went to pay a debt to the Crocker Bank in San Francisco. The threat mounted. Governor Balzar was sent to Washington for more loans—without really knowing the depth of Wingfield's problem—and failed in the attempt. By the end of the year, the Wingfield banks had failed. By 1935, Wingfield was bankrupt.

Was Fred Balzar a cardplayer? Let's say he had it in his blood, for he was born in Virginia City in 1880. As a child, he moved to Hawthorne and went to school there (this helps account for his rooting on behalf of the ammunition dump). He was a very popular man, affable and good-looking, and he had learned practical public skills as a conductor on the

Carson & Colorado Railroad. He then represented Esmeralda County in the state senate, and from 1901 to 1926 he was sheriff of Mineral County, an entity he helped found. It was in 1926 that Wingfield promoted him as state governor, an office he held from 1927 until his death, on the job, in 1934.

Thus it was Balzar who, in March 1931—on the same day—signed into state law two crucial pieces of legislation. The one permitted casino gambling, and the other reduced the waiting period for divorce from three months to six weeks.

As to the first, gambling had been legal in Nevada from 1869 to 1910. Ever since the Comstock excitement, gambling had been taken for granted in mining towns; Wingfield had made an apparently respectable career out of it, and then daintily sidestepped into banking. But, of course, those making the most solemn effort of spreading law, order, and civility (to say nothing of prudence) looked askance at gambling. In the effort to make Nevada a respectable state, therefore (never stronger than at the turn of the century), there were many reformers intent on outlawing the practice.

Progressive reform won the day in 1910, whereupon gambling went behind closed doors. That status was much enhanced when the United States as a whole took on the experiment to abandon hard liquor. In the years 1910–1931, it was not difficult to gamble in Nevada, or drink, and generally the two could be managed at one place. Legalization in 1931 did not have disastrous effects on the state, but it was a shot in the arm for Reno.

Nevada had always elected to make divorce as straightforward as possible. The hectic change of status in the gold and silver mines, the fact that proper wives were left far behind in the rush, and the nagging of common-law wives helped justify the flexibility. But then Nevada—and Reno, its big city—began to attract a few famous divorce cases. A six-month waiting period was required. And so, in 1906, Mrs. William Ellis Corey, wife of the president of U.S. Steel, came to Reno, seeking a divorce on the grounds of her husband's adultery with the actress Maybelle Gilman. In 1919, Mary Pickford made the journey from California in order to split from the actor Owen Moore. He was a rough man, a drunk, and a lesser actor than Mary. She claimed "mental cruelty," one of the oils that has made the Nevada machinery work. And she had Douglas Fairbanks ready to marry her.

All through the 1920s, Reno was the transitional place for wealthy women. They had to stay there six months, to pay for the lawyers, and to

*In Carson City, on the main drag, the nineteenth-century splendor
of the old Mint Building (now the Nevada State Museum) confronts
the flimsier appeal of the Nugget, the oldest hotel-casino in town, and the
church for a kind of experience that has been preserved only in talk.*

gain the eventual clearance. In 1927, as the trade mounted, so Nevada sought to balance judicious time with the pangs of cruelty, hotel bills with the risk of having the ladies go elsewhere. Idaho and Arkansas, opportunists, went to three months, too, and so Reno made the last bold play— six weeks. By 1936, decrees were running at the rate of three thousand a year. In some quarters of America, Reno was called "Sin City," but in the downtown itself, they put up an iron arch that bore another label: THE BIGGEST LITTLE CITY IN THE WORLD.

26. The Biggest Little City

IF YOU WANT TO BELIEVE THAT, SAY, BENEATH THE DESERT sands of Area 51 there is a complex, an enterprise, a labyrinth as large as a city, where aliens and their lethal viruses are kept guarded, you are very welcome. In Nevada, people believe whatever they want, and in defiance of the sober pleas of reason and for the good of the family, they stick by number 7 if they choose. Or whatever. And, after all, you have seen something very like what I have described above—haven't you?—in the movie *The X-Files*. And you were likely having such a damn hard time following that, you hardly bothered to ask yourself whether or not you believed it. And we will leave for the moment the way that film blew up a building in Dallas—in ways that could only remind us of the federal building in Oklahoma City, the Murragh—because of the need to disguise the evidence that the building contained bodies of innocent and ordinary citizens, a kid and two firemen, who had stumbled on aliens. As if some people needed help, or nudging, in their believing.

But there is a more mundane fantasy that I wouldn't mind shifting, and offsetting a little. And it brings me to the defense of Reno. You are doubtless acquainted with the legend—you may take it for a fact—that Benny Siegel, reluctant to be called "Bugsy," invented Las Vegas and the heaven of gaming that has made Nevada what it is. No knocking Benny, who was a figure and a character, well worth his pages, and we will come to him. But you have seen the 1991 movie *Bugsy*, and that moment, driving back to Los Angeles from the generally forlorn area of Las Vegas, when Ben says, "Stop the car." He gets out and strides away into the desert. He gazes around him—at the space, at the scrub, infinity, the setting sun—and he has what deserves to be regarded as a religious experience. After all, even if you take the very worst view of what happened, there is no reason why Satan doesn't hear the heavenly charm and strings of inspiration. Scoundrels and frauds get gooseflesh, too, maybe more than the rest of us. We'll build it here, says Benny, and they will come.

Well, let us just say that, in 1944–1945, the time of this pioneering encounter with destiny, the real Las Vegas was shabby, dusty, heat-stricken, and far from glamorous, but still a place of over ten thousand inhabitants. There was gambling there, and a kind of showbiz, too, for adventurous L.A. souls. Indeed, Las Vegas was known as a discreet week-end getaway place for the gay community of Los Angeles. I'm not suggest-ing that that's why Benny and Mickey Cohen (Harvey Keitel) were driving there that day. Though I will claim that they could have stopped off in the real town and been entertained, and even flirted with, by a bril-liant and really very nice-looking Polish boy named Wladziou Valentino Liberace, who first performed in Las Vegas (the city where his museum may be found; it should not be missed) in 1943.

All of which is to say that proper gambling, with its profound threat to law, order, and stability, with its truly sinister attraction, was conceived and understood in Reno, in the years before and after 1931. That's where wickedness found its first liberty and overcame all shocked responses and pious rebukes. That's what made Nevada what it became, and that's where gangsters first operated, including people who would have talked to Ben and given him much more concrete ideas than sublime visions in the desert. But, there you are, we like the big scenes, and there is something about the desert that requires them. Give Liberace credit: Somehow at Vegas, amid the dry heat and the sage and whatever, he smelled the heady air of camp.

In fact, the criminal use of gaming premises in Reno went back to before the 1931 legalization. The Bank Club—at Center Street and Dou-glas—had been operating since before the 1920s. It was owned by Bill Graham and Jim McKay, and it was a "secret" place in that gaming and then drinking were both against the law. Everyone in town knew what it offered, and the law made very little effort to intervene. In the same way, it was understood that gangsters from Chicago and the northern Midwest were in the habit of driving to Reno to launder their money. The very real notion of ugly fat men laboring to carry bags heavy with paper cash in and out of these casinos began at the Bank Club. Graham and McKay owned shadier places still—the Willows and the Stockade, the latter a factorylike brothel staffed with $2 whores.

These were the pioneers, and they were recognized by those other founders of Nevada—men like George Wingfield and Pat McCarran. For the political establishment made natural use of the facilities, and surely admired the way in which, say, $100,000 of bootlegger or bank-hold-up cash was purchased in Nevada at fifty cents on the dollar. Keep it in the state was always Wingfield's credo.

McKay and Graham were nabbed in 1934, on mail-fraud charges in connection with stock frauds. By 1939, they were in jail, but in the mid-forties, Senator McCarran himself petitioned for, and got, their release.

The Bank Club welcomed legal gambling, of course, and expanded, yet its whole stance was sultry, behind closed doors, and keep the lighting low. The attitude of legal gaming, as we shall discover, is rather different, though a sentimental case can be made for preserving some vestiges of the dark days. What really marked Reno's future was the introduction of two new outfits: Raymond "Pappy" Smith's Harold's Club, on Virginia Street, in 1935, and then Bill Harrah's place on the same street in 1937. These were wide-open establishments, brightly lit and so constructed that you could walk in off the street, instead of through the small "front" operations, a tobacco shop at the Bank Club. Smith was also a gimmick promoter: He had a version of roulette that used live mice instead of balls, and he hired pretty women as croupiers. Pappy drew a new class of ordinary middle-class people and tourists into gaming; he made it seem fun, relaxing, convivial, and sporty. And here, without question, is Ben Siegel's desert vision. But gambling was only the half of it. The other industry was divorce—five thousand a year by the late 1930s—and the way in which that altered the reputation of the town. For Reno became famous for the steady arrival of wives, most of them with some money to start with and hopes of much more, coming to Reno for their six-week stay. There had to be adequate hotels for them—the Riverside, the Mapes, and the Golden. Moreover, the ladies needed company and smooth lawyers, and so the "Reno divorce lawyer" grew up as a type, handsome, usually single, a good dancer, a shoulder to cry on, and so forth. Divorces were granted, which is not to say that romance ever died.

There were drives into the country—to Tahoe or Pyramid Lake even—and the waiting women could go riding at the dude ranches that sprang up, with the good-looking "cowboys" who might split their time between Hollywood and Reno. Equally, the town developed an unusual share of dress shops, makeup parlors and hairdressers, refined cafés, and dancing establishments. For a Reno divorce was almost always the privilege of the well-to-do, the sophisticated, and those eager for more. Rather more than the gambling, the culture of divorce split Reno itself. All over America, Reno's profits from these trades were held up as a mark of moral iniquity and dangerous law bending. The respectable people of Reno were alarmed—and the visiting ladies were seldom invited into the town's social circles.

The WPA Guide to 1930s Nevada, a book that has many eloquent passages as well as all the current information of a good guidebook, suggests the woe that these ladies could arouse:

> Women with money—and most of the newcomers are female— live in the smarter hotels, expensive furnished apartments, or on nearby ranches, and the rest live as well as their pocketbooks permit; a few even do housework or clerk in stores to maintain themselves during the necessary period. How these divorce-seekers spend their time depends in part on their means, in part on their up-bringing, and in part on their state of mind. To the majority the breaking up of their homes is a heart-breaking business and they react according to their natures; some grow reckless, gamble and drink wildly, invite attentions from any men they happen to meet, while others live quietly and are rarely seen in the cocktail rooms and nightclubs. It is the former who provide a disturbing element greatly resented by Renoites, in spite of their determined tolerance for human frailty and their appreciation of the revenue brought in.

There you have it. There were Reno promoters who used to salt the Truckee River bed at the Virginia Street bridge with old wedding rings to support the custom of newly liberated women casting off the last symbol of their chains. The pillars of the courthouse bore the imprint of kisses of gratitude, and these are just early gestures toward neon celebration, and the general air of advertised abandon that many find vulgar—not least those stalwart cities of Reno and Las Vegas, where business had been based on the overthrow of order.

Reno has never looked back, even if divorce has passed into the American bloodstream, where it has had the effect of a couple of Tylenol. The city's population surged forward, by more than 40 percent a decade:

1950	32,497
1960	52,470
1970	72,863
1980	100,756
1998	164,600

It is now built upon winter sports, Lake Tahoe's attractions, several types of light industry, and the general notion that it is a good place to live. To the north, especially, housing estates are spreading into the hill country; and to the east, Reno has merged with the town of Sparks. There is an efficient modern airport—Reno-Tahoe—only a few miles to the south. And the downtown area is a cheerful packed jungle of hotel casinos—Harrah's, still; John Ascuagua's Nugget, rising like a turret over I-80; the Silver Legacy; the El Dorado; and the Peppermill, which is south, toward the airport.

And there is one vital way in which Reno is not just still the Biggest Little City in the World but also the most intense Nevadan experience. By contrast, the Las Vegas Strip is huge, and built to the spatial rhythm of immense establishments and their parking lots. Indeed, the Strip still has space in it, bare land nearly, and that makes it a rather prolonged, desolate promenade. Most people cab it from one casino to the other.

But Reno feels all there in a very cramped space. The arch itself and most of the downtown casinos are all within short walks of one another. The streets are thronged on summer nights, and it is fun to walk on them and feel the packed crawl of cars anxious to find parking. Valet parking has tamed and regulated Las Vegas, but in Reno, the driver suffers that itch he feels in any American city of having to search for a place. The casinos are all in a row—big splashy places to be sure, syruped with neon, yet more compact than the casinos in Vegas, because space is at a premium.

The proximity of people and places does something for their sense of power, I think. In Vegas, the very size of the city tells you you are bound to lose. You may be dead on your feet from walking before you slump on a stool. In Reno, you are part of the crowd and you take a sucker's hope and courage from it. You feel the bustle there must have been once in Tonopah or Goldfield, where everything was in the range of a few hundred yards or so.

Still, Reno has a bigger trump to play. For only yards south of the famous arch runs the railroad itself. There is no fence, no warning—just the tracks in the concrete and a crossing gate on Virginia Street. And then, every now and then, the gates come down and the crowds gather as a huge train—standing twelve feet or so above the ground—lumbers through the city on what is still a coast-to-coast railroad. You can feel the frontier still, and how men have grabbed hold of the desert. The engineer—if that is what they are called now—leans out and waves to the mob. He is like a ring on the Truckee River bed, the perfect detail you hoped to see. The train, usually a freight train, takes minutes to pass.

Then the gates come up and the crowd surges forward, ready to play. I stood and watched such a train once on a July night, with a two-year-old sitting on my shoulders whooping and shouting at the clanging train. He had never seen a train so huge, so close, let alone one with all those palaces of transformation at hand.

Don't miss Reno.

"SANDY" IS VERY LIKELY SEVENTY NOW, BUT SHE COULD PASS for a smart fifty-five, running the coffee shop in one of the big Reno hotels. She moves people in and out with a deftness the establishment doesn't want to lose—she keeps it all in her head, the big parties, the kids who want booster seats, the honeymoon couples who need a window: she's reckoning split in a year, but she knows how to give a guy a little touch in his lower ribs so he feels like Clint Eastwood. Sandy knows such things; she knew them as a child, let alone in her hooking years and then when she was promoted to management just because she can keep people waiting without getting surly or impatient. Flattering them. And she still has the sweetest, admiring smile—surprised at how great people are—and her way of dropping a few secret words on every customer, the inside stuff just for them, no matter that in the early fifties she knew exactly how and when two of the girls were going to be taken out (because of the threat of starting their own business) and knifed and dumped on the roadside outside Lovelock. And she wrote the letters to their parents, in longhand— that's what management means. And she hasn't forgotten a detail or let it sour her smile.

"Don't ask," she says, smiling, if you ever try to ask her. "You really don't want to know, not if you're here for a good time. And I know you are." And then she'll slip you her little touch so that not even your wife sees it.

27. Kicking the Ground

WE COULD VERY EASILY ESTABLISH A NEVADAN LEGEND OF the man who kicked at the ground and changed not just his life but also the history of the Earth. You can play it any number of ways. He is driving along in some rolling semidesert terrain, or he is carefully nursing his four-wheeler through the folds of hills. He stops. He gets out of the vehicle. He is drawn out into open space by the prickling silence of the day and the sustaining waft of the dry heat. He feels that he could float above the ground, the gravel, the rock, the shale. He knows where his car is, so he walks on into the light and the openness. He smells the fumes of sage and the faint metallic tang in the air beaten out of the rock by the sun. He is on the very edge of the aloneness that is Nevada, that same creeping solitude that can overtake a gambler at the table when he knows he is making the inspired play, the one that will alter everything.

And so, like an owner in Paradise, let's say, or even like John Wayne in *Red River* when he comes upon the sunbaked ground that he will make into a great ranch, he leans over and scoops up a handful of the dry earth or he kicks at it with the steel toe caps on his fancy Tony Lama boots. He *is* dressed for Nevada.

It goes like this: As the dust settles, he sees a jagged vein of green or gray, like bad teeth, in the disturbed ground, and he knows it is silver. Hours later, when he is burned in the sun but unaware of the pain, he realizes he is in a field of silver ore. He needs only to pick it up.

Or, the flash of his toe cap blinds him for an instant to the rattlesnake that was resting from the blaze of day beneath the rock. So he hears it before he sees it: the rattle, the hiss, the whirring in the air. And he feels the wicked slap on his hand and the nearly instant swelling. The snake hurries away, and he stares in amazement at his pierced hand and the sudden drunken rush of venom. The car is only a few hundred yards away, but he feels a kind of seizure in the hand already—a panic—and wonders if he can even get the key out of his tight jeans pocket.

Or he hears a snap, then notices that his stray kick has broken the ulna in an arm—a skeleton's bleak angle—arising from the ground. He crouches down and carefully smooths away the gravel until he realizes that he has come upon a corpse, swathed for the most part in some fabric so ancient, it begins to drift apart in the air and the light. He moves the earth back and makes a marker that will one day celebrate the discovery of some missing link in the prehistory of man.

Then again, he may just appreciate that he is at the site of some hurried, unofficial burial. There is a sleeve and there is some pulp within it that is not quite the softness of flesh, but the easeful substance of decay. There is a hand, rotted away in part, but with a ring on a finger still, as bright and hard as crystal. It is a buried body, the burial rather casual, as if two or three hundred yards removed from the road were enough to let time do the rest. But our man may be offended, moved, or curious; he may search out authorities deserving of the report. You may think I am becoming a little more fanciful—you must hope that is so—but the toe cap on the boot begins to sizzle and dissolve as it touches some fundamental, unshakable core of potent toxicity in the ground. That, or the guy kicks a stone at a can, and the can goes off in an explosion that makes the rest of the cloudless day seem depressed or obscure. No single piece of our man is ever found that is larger than seven and a half millimeters in length. But it is admitted that, by unhappy mischance, he had simply wandered off into an area where there happened to be some unexploded bomb or artillery shell. No one knows exactly how it could have occurred—but Nevada is a state, isn't it, in which sometimes very long odds come through? Supposedly, one attraction to Las Vegas's location for those who sought to run the place was the proximity of great expanses of uncongenial open ground where tourists were unlikely to explore. In the tough but wonderfully naïve running commentary to Martin Scorsese's film *Casino*, the desert is alluded to as ideal for burying the bodies that may arise naturally as a by-product in some businesses. It seems a reasonable suggestion: The ground is generally light, dry, and easily worked; the winds will cover up tire tracks or footprints; and in most desert spots, you can count on being undisturbed.

Eventually, in *Casino*, that is what happens to the Santoro brothers, Nicky and Dominic. Although in this case, the desert is a clearing in a verdant cornfield where the plants are taller than the guys. Then, because Nicky (Joe Pesci)—let's face it—has been a pain in the neck, a loose cannon, and a ham all through the film, he and his brother are brutally offed. Part of the charm of the scene, however, is that the leader of the gang of executioners is played by Frank Vincent, perennial sidekick, who had been abused, humiliated, maltreated, and horribly killed by Pesci (in *Raging Bull* and *GoodFellas*).

Now, the glossy silver-haired worm has his turn. Nicky and Dominic are turned to pulp—rather more tomatoesque than fruit—with the use of aluminum baseball bats. Then, stripped down to their underpants, they are dragged across the fleshy trampled cornstalks and tipped into a dusty ready-made grave. If you're in the corn business—and Hollywood and Vegas always have been—you have to nourish your crop.

Scorsese is so good at showing us things like this, it's hard to believe that scene is simply a fiction. But I am prepared to believe that in the last fifty years or so the surrounds of Las Vegas have been occasionally salted. There is even one case dear to my heart where "they" didn't even bother to bury the body, which may be enough to argue that "they" had nothing to do with this one.

Not that Wardell Gray could ever have counted as a gangster. That's another of the reasons why, in the 1940s and 1950s, a black man out of Oklahoma City would think to make it as a boxer or a musician. What other ways were there? And Gray was too skinny to impress himself, let alone an opponent, in the boxing ring. Being content with heroin can do that to you. But Wardell Gray was plainly one of those people who cannot help but face the terrible challenge to impress, or convince, oneself. You can hear that in his playing—a style that manages to be both lyrically desperate and stoned laid-back. And you can still hear the extraordinary meaning of Gray, even if not one in a hundred Americans has heard of him forty years after his death; and even if, at the time, they didn't even bother to bury him, but tossed him out of the car on the edge of town because, after all, he was nothing but a black jazz musician.

Born in 1921, he was found dead in May 1955 and his body was picked up on that rough land where the concrete of Las Vegas tapers off into the gray sands of the desert. The liner notes on the *Wardell Gray Memorial* (a two-volume set) admits that the death "has not been completely cleared up." Bill Moody, in his fond novel *Death of a Tenor Man*, argues that the failure to clear things up began and ended with the lack of a police report. As if to say, Such things happen; and in some of the great cities of America, there are purple periods in the cities' plunder of the world when the police managed to behave as if theirs was a very dull beat where nothing much happened.

What happened? As a junkie, he could easily have owed more money than drug dealers were prepared to wait for. Moody wonders whether Gray was having an affair with someone marked down as the property of important people. Tenor men have that kind of reputation. On his last job, Gray had been playing at the Moulin Rouge, short-lived, but the only hotel-casino of that age where blacks were welcome as more than performers, and from which, it was said, white gangsters were carrying away the money, skimming, in all and any containers they could find.

There's no saying now what happened, or why. After all, in *Casino*, Nicky Santoro is buried alive, as an example to others. And so one night, Wardell Gray was playing in Vegas—lagging along a waver behind the beat, with all the lonesome eloquence of don't leave me behind, don't forget me—and the next day his chair was empty on the stand and the talk was that he had been found in a heap outside town. Wardell Gray? Did you know him? Wardell? Yeah, sure, I believe I heard him at the Hula Hut Club in L.A. Didn't I hear him there? Or maybe I'm confusing him with Dexter Gordon, or was that Sonny Stitt?

It's a fair question now when, more or less, the legacy of great American jazz is hard to track down. And Wardell played with Gordon and Stitt, and admired them both. And even if it would take a connoisseur, a buff, now, to know whether Sonny Stitt is dead or alive, Dexter Gordon is among the elect. He made a movie, *Round Midnight*; he was nominated for an Oscar for his acting in it, no matter that he behaved in that sweet lost way for years. But Wardell Gray died so much younger, and was . . . well, I don't know about "so much," but was better. There ought to be a statue to Wardell Gray—a thin, stooped guy, leaning back against the marlinlike surge of his own horn—out in whatever weed-lined stretch of suburbia it was where they found him. But, of course, Las Vegas prefers the statues of mythic Caesars to those real heroes it has, like Ben Siegel, Frank Sinatra, Howard Hughes, Wardell Gray, or Steve Wynn. Not to mention "them."

Still, I wish you'd listen to Wardell Gray, instead of just taking my word—to "Twisted," "Sweet and Lovely," "Blue Gray," or "Lavonne," and never mind whether or not Lavonne was the wrong woman, the one he was crazy about. Wardell was really mad for the music and his horn, and you can listen to anything of his and hear the ghastly, lovely sense of time running out. When he hit a solo right, he never faltered, but kept on straight to the end, having seen the end and knowing that the beauty of the improvised melody was surely fatal, and had to stop. At which point, even a great genius, and one who made records—surely there are some

*Formations in the Red Rock Desert, close to Las Vegas,
and on the way to a burying ground*

who didn't—had to start to play the game of chance called "Will anyone remember in forty years? Or four thousand?" None of which is very long, not by the standards of the half-lives of those virulent compounds, so passionate still, left by bombs and so forth. And name me one musician who played four thousand years ago.

So tread lightly, in case that rise in the ground is really Wardell Gray, or some unexploded bomb. We are not supposed to see the beauty in such things as bombs. Show us the famous photographs of great tests conducted on Pacific atolls (thereafter unfindable) or even in the Nevada desert, and we are meant to fold up in horror and mortification at man's dire folly and mindless cruelty. Well, okay, but the fact is that in the fifties, people in Vegas used to go to the higher floors whenever a test was scheduled to the north, so they could see the flash and feel the building rock. It's playing with fire, in every sense, but face it, the entire known history of mankind doesn't really stretch much farther than four thousand years, and that's a small win in the larger emptiness of time. What the desert teaches you, for sure, is that the whole thing can go on without you. And maybe will. The desert is only waiting to make its move.

You feel that in Richard Misrach's photographs, which are another version of what can happen if you kick at the desert of Nevada without due consideration. Starting in 1986, and with the help of a few locals, Misrach began to explore the area known to the U.S. Naval Air Station Fallon as Bravo 20. This is part of the alkali flat, the Carson Sink, between the Humboldt and Stillwater ranges of mountains, about thirty miles northeast of Fallon itself. To the south, this area fades into the Stillwater Marsh area, which is subject to major flooding a few times in a century, and which consequently is a fascinating exploring ground for wildlife. Many species of fish and bird are found there. What is more, the Northern Paiute Indians have always frequented the area because of these riches. In 1984, there was serious flooding in the area, so that when the water receded, hundreds of Indian graves were found that testified to forms of society at least two thousand years old and maybe three thousand.

Such discoveries sharpened the attitude of those who deplored the way the naval air station and the U.S. government as a whole were exploiting the area. *Bravo 20* is a book of Richard Misrach's photographs, with an accompanying text by his wife, Myriam Weisang Misrach. Near the end of that text, this passage sums up its approach:

> A piece of wilderness that includes a sacred Paiute site was taken over (albeit in a national emergency), bombed to smithereens, and polluted with extremely noxious materials. This was done expediently, without consideration for Indian rights, archeological remains, the local flora and fauna, natural resources. It was simply cheaper and faster to use Lone Rock, a highly visible target located close to the naval base. Besides, in the words of one Navy official who obviously does not understand the meaning of climax ecology, "It's a desert out there. Nothing grows on it."

Bravo 20 makes the case that the area had been used, since the early 1950s, as a practice ground for U.S. Navy aircraft. That involved extensive low-level flights—sometimes at only two hundred feet—by aircraft that may exceed the speed of sound (something that is forbidden to civil aircraft flying over the United States). In addition, the aircraft have bombed targets, fired missiles, strafed areas, and over the years jettisoned enormous amounts of aircraft fuel. The navy scarcely bothers to deny or mitigate these charges. Instead, it says that such activities are part of its proper duty, and that Nevada is the best or most ideal part of the United States for such work. In general, both the Federal Aviation Administration and the Bureau of Land Management have looked favorably upon the government's claim that it needed certain airspace, and that in some situations it was obliged to buy out the few people who lived on the relevant land beneath.

Misrach's somber yet very beautiful photographs show a kind of desert or playa landscape pitted with small craters, with pieces of shrapnel, with the ruined targets—everything from tanks, to buses, to trucks, to military personnel carriers—as well as thousands of shells and bombs, some of which are reckoned to be defective or unexploded. He also photographed large craters that contained pools of brilliant yet unnaturally colored liquids—pinks, reds, greens, the hues of childish paintings.

The navy agreed that the area might be dangerous. When Misrach and some others insisted on driving into the area and even camping out there, the authorities issued warnings and sent Jeeps and helicopters; in certain cases, they seem to have sent personnel to watch over the intruders. Arrests were eventually made, though charges were never pressed in court. In turn, Misrach and the others claimed inalienable rights to be there, sometimes those of prospective miners. *Bravo 20* is a very partisan book, crying out for a return of the wilderness to its natural uses. It is a book that takes for granted a certain callousness or indifference in the military. It is also written in such a way that the death of one of the concerned citizens, in a plane crash, is delivered with pregnant paranoia, as if some "they" had to be involved. The book laments the very few obstacles that confront the U.S. government in having its way with Nevada. It resents the occurrence of maybe one hundred supersonic flights a day, of school buses being buzzed by dangerously low-flying aircraft, and of the general fear and alarm such things cause in cattle, the young, the elderly, and those who simply cherish the peace and silence of Nevada. In Misrach's photographs, we can see the peak of Lone Rock—sacred to the Paiute—a feature reduced maybe by as much as half by persistent navy bombing.

Misrach echoes his wife's text. Yet he is also a photographer, content to see, and surely aware that there is beauty in all things. His pictures, I think, are more profound than the book's text. He camped often in the Bravo 20 area; he nearly lived there for part of the 1980s. And he documented the look of the eerie landscape. He got used to being afraid or lonely there, though, as far as I can gather, no unexploded bomb has ever gone off there, or hurt anyone. He easily enough fell in with the cause behind his wife's text:

> The landscape boasted the classic beauty characteristic of the desert. It was also the most graphically ravaged environment I had ever seen. I found myself at the epicenter, the heart of the Apocalypse. Alone, no sounds, no movement. No buildings, no roads. No indication of life, no promise of civilization. Only the smell of

rusted metal. Bombs and lifeless holes. Side by side were great beauty and great horror. . . . The landscape of Lone Rock is a graphic reminder of our failing stewardship of this Earth. It should be returned to the public domain for all to see.

Well, "stewardship" is a convenient word. It seems to stand for decent, judicious respect toward all things. But stewardship failed whenever great amounts of gold and silver were taken out of Nevada's ground; witness the vast, spectacular gougings that mark the copper mines of Ruth, outside Ely. Stewardship may be assailed for insisting on the great Hoover Dam on the Colorado River. It surely abandoned purity, prior existence, silence, and desolation in letting Las Vegas grow up as it has. And stewardship itself now admits the torturous, nearly eternal problems in all things nuclear. There are still guardians to our welfare, or moral stewards, who would berate Nevada, and America, for its laxity in being so ready to experiment with divorce, prostitution, and gambling. Would it have been better that Wardell Gray live out a long, dull life in Oklahoma—he could be alive still—doing nothing very much to risk being remembered, or reviled, let alone offed? Or will we settle for the "tragedy," and maybe the greater misery than we can ever grasp, that he was dead at thirty-four, violently, a heroin addict, a "wreck," as they say, and one of the great tenor saxophonists of all time if only because of "Twisted," for which a few years later Annie Ross supplied the lyrics:

> *My analyst told me*
> *I was right out of my head*
> *The way he described it,*
> *I'd be better dead.*

One doesn't have to be a philosopher or a depressive to find Las Vegas awesomely terrible. The many abandoned mines of Nevada—with all those names like Hope, Wonder, Aurora, Climax—speak to our greed, our recklessness, our irresponsibility. We cannot shrug off the consequences of nuclear waste—just as we cannot fathom a place to put it. We may regret the atom bomb and the hydrogen bomb, and we may yet be swept aside in a hurricane of fire as those forces find expression.

On the other hand, it's not too remote an argument to say that the bullion made the residential splendor of San Francisco, or that the bombs, the testing, and the dogged strafing of Bravo 20 helped bring something like liberty (with all its scars, excesses, and errors) to Prague, to Budapest, to Warsaw, and even to Saint Petersburg.

There is a vanity and a righteousness in the "stewardship" of the Earth that defies all the natural forces of alteration—the drift of continents, the upheaval of earthquake, the rage of fire and rain—that would go on whether or not the Earth was inhabited. For myself, I feel that sense of history in Nevada as much as the sensible need to preserve things.

In other words, I believe that the instincts that lead toward gambling, the overthrow of marriage, the desperate tearing at the ground for wealth, the putting on of martial airs, and playing the saxophone are natural and human. They merit their own stewardship, or at least they had their chance at the larger gaming table and they may be the number we choose to play. For things do grow in the desert, and in the very end of it all, I am against nothing—except to be moribund, to be dead in advance. We have no right or reason in nature, and no evidence in history, to think that living is safe. Or was ever meant to be.

What I see in Richard Misrach's pictures, and what I hear in Wardell Gray, is something I find in life and human nature—and something as bright as the sun in Nevada: It is the inescapable adjacency of beauty and horror, even to the point that we might not understand, or see, one without the other.

PART TWO

Suspects

The end of night. Stars recede and go out, the sun's rim appears above the sea of hills, and the sky swiftly catches fire. . . . The eye tires of distance and seeks detail, and rapacity emerges; a rabbit hops from under a sage bush and a shadow passes over it. A hawk, serene, floats in narrowing circles above. . . . A butterfly lights on a stone and a chameleon's tongue flicks out and takes it.

—Arthur Miller, *The Misfits*, 1961

*"It's here!" The figure of Vegas Vic as first erected on the Pioneer Club,
Fremont Street, Las Vegas, B.S. (Before Siegel)
(courtesy of Manis Collection, University of Nevada, Las Vegas Library)*

28. Noir

BECAUSE I NORMALLY WRITE ABOUT FILM, THERE HAVE BEEN people who looked at me askance when I told them what I was trying. "You mean films about Nevada?" they'd say. "Las Vegas movies?" And I've tried to say no, not that, perish the thought. You see, getting into movies in the first place was really no more than an accident, and if I sometimes seem to concentrate on film, why, really, it's just a way into life, and words, and wondering what you can believe. And I've said, over and over again, that Nevada has been—this above all—a chance to get out and be out there in the light. "Give me the light!" I've cried, hardly knowing why I needed it. Which is a way of telling that dark and its illusions to get lost.

Why, I'm not even going to do more than just say, flat out—without any explanation—that *Hard Eight* is my favorite Nevada film.* And you've likely not seen or heard of it.

But if the light is so precious, is that because of too long spent in the dark? In other words, gaze at the daytime as long as you can, absorb its vistas, and still you may find that your thoughts about it are shaped by apprehension of the dark.

I have to admit that at the start of this part of the book—the recent history of southern Nevada—because I know I have been unable to escape a kind of intertwined crosscutting for it, a little thread of noir in the broad daylight. Maybe there have been so many movies in my past that my nervous system converts everything to their level. Read for yourself, and consider how calm or objective you can be about it; or whether we are all audience to a reckless show.

---

* *Hard Eight* (1996), was written and directed by Paul Thomas Anderson. It is a fable—mysterious in many ways—in which Sydney, a sort of angel (Philip Baker Hall), attempts to guide a young couple in the ways of fate and chance.

29. Someone Wins

THE BUSBOY COMES TO THE FRESH TABLE WITH FOUR TUM-
blers of ice water. They grow out of his hand like cold bulbs. Sometimes
you have to ask for this little detail with the big dinner, but as a rule it is
taken for granted. After all, even if the party is going to order wine, or
cocktails, it's nice to see those sweated glasses and hear the chimes made
by the ice. For they tell you that here in Las Vegas, even if the temperature
has been over 111 degrees eleven days in a row, it's a sign of assurance if the
house can still put down four pints of clean water as starters. And people
drink the water, because you want to keep a clear head at the tables, and
liquor won't make a sap of you as easily if you water up first.

A lot of these people have their quaint ways of not being suckered.

Moreover, if you're going out in the heat, even if it's just crossing over
from New York, New York to the M-G-M Grand, you'd be advised to drink
your water. "You know, I heard that for a long and healthy life, Cloris, an
adult needs six or eight glasses of water every day."

And Cloris says something like "God, Arthur, with a prostate like
yours, you'd never be out of the john!"

And the party of four howls with laughter, and the ice in the water
glasses shivers and whispers with the fun of it all. You won't go ten minutes in Las Vegas without meeting the need for a certain defiance in
human attitudes. A robust "fuck you" toward the elements and all the possible doubts goes hand in hand with the wistful promise over the filet
mignon, "You know, Lenny, I really feel I'm going to be lucky tonight."

At that point, an absolutely terrific guy passes by their table, spreading
a smile and a few words of good cheer, giving of his generous self, meeting
the public, pressing the flesh, and being simply terrific.

What do I mean by "terrific"? Well, it is that he looks so young, while
you know he must be older than you think—all of which makes one of the

most intriguing philosophical conundrums of southern Nevada. He is also as primed, complete, and coolly ready as those glasses of water, and at least as optimistic.

What is he doing, spreading bonhomie and that feeling of confidence as thin and convenient as Kleenex tissue? Is he the eternal master of ceremonies, your host, or just the front man for the girl in tights with the armored bra who will come around to take a picture of the table for four as a personal souvenir? He could be all of that; he could be just the ghost of "Is everything all right?"—the water that flows too fast for a reply—but, look, you were at least asked, weren't you, and look at those sensational glasses of water, won't you, ladies—they were in Lake Mead this morning, did you know that? "Everything at the Mirage is fresh," says the terrific guy, and he looks at the quieter lady in the party of four and says, "I bet you'd get fresh if I gave you half a chance."

The lady blushes, for, truth to tell, the sheer, terrific talk of the guy has left her smitten. And he surely picked her as the natural dreamer at the table. And he pauses there, hovering—just as if, were he alive, he would be flirting. "What is your name?" he asks. But then he tells her no, that he'll guess. "Give me three guesses." And he is really good—is he, maybe, a magician, a guy with a true calling who just can't help laying it on?—and he gets her name, third guess, Ruth, so that she knows he can see into her soul.

And he says, "You know, Ruth, I have spent my life in Vegas."

"Really?"

"Cross my heart. [She would. She would!] And one thing I can tell you—this is my oath."

"Yeah?"

"Every night."

"Yeah?"

"Someone wins."

As he says that, he straightens up, his arms extend, and his smile takes in not just the entire dining room, the Ristorante Riva, but all of the Mirage, and even all of Vegas itself. For this guy is not just promoting himself and his own hotel-casino. He is promoting the city, Nevada, the desert that can furnish four tumblers of iced water as *your* miracle; he is promoting promotion. Call him Stephen A. Win.

And remember that he is one of the guys who wins every night.

Don't worry, we will come back to Steve. But, for the moment, cut from his absolute and knockout spiritual smoothness to the immense roughness of Octavius Decatur Gass. It is a natural cut, for these two men are true sons and fathers of Las Vegas. They seem civilizations apart, and yet Gass—who died in 1924—could have been Win's grandfather.

Gass was born in Ohio in 1827. He was one of the many drawn to California by reports of the gold found there in 1848–1849. He took a ship around Cape Horn, came to San Francisco, and for fifteen years or so led the life of a disappointed prospector and acquired the reputation of being unlucky. He was six feet tall, and yet he had a proud, defiant gaze that tended always to look upward. His brown hair was receding, but it was balanced by a long, wavy beard that reached down to his second shirt button.

In 1864, he was mining on the western bank of the Colorado River, at El Dorado Canyon, in what was then Arizona Territory. A year later, for reasons no one really knows, he moved north and west and came to the abandoned Mormon fort at Las Vegas. With partners named Lewis and Cole, he took it over, rebuilt it, and began to work the fields. It was the Las Vegas Ranch (the site is where Las Vegas Boulevard North crosses Washington Avenue).

Ten years earlier, this was the place where William Bringhurst had established a Mormon colony, and where the thirty colonists built a fort, 150 feet square. The site seemed promising—as it had been to Spanish missionaries (January 1830) and John Charles Frémont (May 1844)—because there were natural springs there. Moreover, as the years passed, Las Vegas proved itself in the sinking of many artesian wells. There was water there, which meant as much as gold, and which sooner or later was far more important in the mapping of history. To this day, there's no other boast that means as much, or is as close to being put in doubt, for Las Vegans.

Bringhurst's settlement had failed and been officially disbanded by Brigham Young when too many of its members were lured away by the lead mine at Potosi. That is how Octavius Decatur Gass found the fort and began to turn it into a ranch.

At last, Gass found something he was good at. Employing local Paiute Indians, he devoted himself to cultivation and irrigation. There were fruit orchards that included peach, apple, apricot, orange, and fig, and fields given over to grains and vegetables, most notably pink Mexican beans.

Gass took a wife, Mary Virginia Simpson, a tall, dark-haired, attractive woman from Missouri. She and Octavius were married in Pioche (a more important and developed town then) in February 1872. They had seven children, two of whom died in infancy.

But the marriage came relatively late in Octavius's life, after all the labor of mining and ranching, and after his career in politics. In the mid-

1860s, he was elected to what was then the Arizona Territorial Legislature, for which he helped to found Pah-Ute County, and then later cast a deciding vote that moved the territorial capital from Prescott to Tucson. But then, in 1866, Congress passed the legislation that brought Pah-Ute County within Nevada.

The ranch had flourished; the most significant development Las Vegas had ever seen. Even so, as late as 1900, it is estimated, there were no more than thirty people (or white men) resident in the Las Vegas Valley. (Technically, Vegas was not even listed in the 1900 census.) By then, Gass and his family had moved on. He was a wanderer still, and he could not see how his growing children were to be educated properly in Las Vegas. He had taken a mortgage on his ranch, and a couple of bad years found him in money troubles. In 1881, he was compelled to sell out, to Archibald Stewart, for a little less than $6,500. The Gasses went to California. Octavius did some more prospecting, without luck, and he died in Bryn Mawr, near Redlands, in 1924, at the age of ninety-seven.

A few years later, Stewart was killed by a man named Henry in one of those intense feuds, left well alone by the forces of law, that characterized the history of what we call "the Wild West." Stewart's widow then ran the ranch, and by the close of the century, there were other ranches in the general area. But the nineteenth-century history of Las Vegas—hardly known, let alone considered in the city today, or at the tables for four in the hotel restaurants—concerns the great difficulty in maintaining life, business, or order. This was land that many Arizonans had felt themselves well rid of. It was still a place where gunfire might settle a dispute, and go unrebuked. If one man, and one family, had made a life and farm there for a few years, the long-term viability of Las Vegas was still unproven. After all, the Mormons, no easygoing pioneers, had elected to write the place off.

Las Vegas now is the thriving place of leaders like Steve A. Wynn. It is the heart of the fastest-growing state in the union. It is a city that seems ready and able to gulp down fresh bits of desert every day. Wynn's new creation, the Bellagio Hotel, opened in October 1998, at a cost that easily exceeded the $611 million he had paid to build the Mirage. The Bellagio was a national event, like a big new movie or a moon shot. There were commercials on TV, and a feature in *Vanity Fair*. The Bellagio was the next step, or progress, as well as a harking back to old Italian bliss; not just a casino and a compelling hotel but one man's art museum, too. It advertised not Elvis or Streisand, but Matisse and Picasso.

The progression in numbers and money from what Gass got for his ranch in 1881 is phenomenal, and American. But watch the growth of Las Vegas—the way in which fresh stretches of desert are cleared and plumbed for estates, for houses, for ranch-style dwellings, "all within easy reach of the Strip," for the fast-growing city remains small—and be wary. In Las Vegas nowadays, a vital part of construction is demolition, clearing the ground for new dreams. The flimsy structures come down faster than they go up. Look at "development" in terms of still photography and it may not be clear whether Vegas is growing still, or being folded up, broken down, and put back in its boxes, as if someone had just found out that the water was drying up, or was contaminated.

Of course, that's a gloomy, historical view in a city that dislikes clocks, let alone the long-term view. Steve Wynn can wipe away the worry. The Bellagio, he will say, everything we do in Vegas, it all comes under the rubric of what God would have done "if He'd had the money." It is one of his terrific jokes, without a trace of keeping his fingers crossed.

As if God, or His possibility, is going to be tamed, or appeased by being put in the league of entrepreneurs. After all, a God or even a god can read between the lines and know the much bleaker humor in today's paper— that telescopes have picked up the smear of light out there at the far edges that may be 12 billion years ago. As if Picasso or Matisse, let alone Steve Wynn, were playing in that game.

And, anyway, God has other shows in southern Nevada—and part 2 of this book is show time, the Vegas experience and the altogether fabulous light in the sky. Which brings us to Brenda.

30. Journey

IN THE FIRST PLACE, YOU HAVE TO CALL BRENDA, AT A Nevada number. She doesn't exactly advertise. There are no TV spots promoting what she has to offer; she doesn't figure in any of the standard guidebooks to the Las Vegas area. In the hotels and motels that have wall-sized containers of pamphlets, leaflets, and flyers for all the amazing attractions of Nevada—from ghost towns to horseback riding with cowboys—there's nothing that recommends this tour. I only came upon Brenda's number in the best guide to Area 51.

Not to beat a dead horse, but what Brenda offers is no small thing. And I have to wonder, Does she—do they—want you to go? I mean, do they think they've got a product, or not? And if they're going to the trouble of doing it—and of making the place and so many of its details available to be seen and explored—why aren't they more confident about it? On the other hand, if the enterprise really is too much fuss to be profitable, or if the risk of some loss of security is too great, then why get into it at all? In all of America's governmental affairs, I don't think I've ever seen such discretion, or shyness.

In any event, Brenda takes down some basic information about you—more than they ever require at Hoover Dam or Circus Circus—your name, your address, your citizenship, your Social Security number. You have to assume that she or her people will be running some kind of checking procedure, a screening. After all, with that much data in this day and age, they are going to be able to get their eyes on anything about you—whether you were turned down for health insurance, or convicted on charges of espionage, say. So you're put in a supplicant's position at the outset, not that Brenda is anything other than friendly.

But, thinking ahead, you do wonder what the day is going to cost. After all, what you're getting is close to nine hours of entertainment and enlightenment based on one of the biggest investment programs man or God has ever undertaken.

Oh, there's no charge, says Brenda, as if it was sweet of you to ask. They're giving it away. It's almost as if they take the attitude that it belongs to us anyway. Yet we're well accustomed now to having to pay a modest fee to see our national parks. We recognize that such places have to be maintained, and we're especially anxious to believe that this one is well looked after. If it isn't, I'm not going.

A little later, and a week or so before your due date, a letter arrives confirming that you have a place on the tour, or the visit, of such and such a date. As you plan your date with Brenda, it doesn't seem as if there's more than one tour a month. It all feels stranger than ever: Day trips in southern Nevada that are free should be booked way in advance. I mean, imagine this kind of attraction in the hands of Steve A. Wynn.

The letter, from a public affairs officer at the Department of Energy, supplies a map and an itinerary. It stresses that no one under fourteen is allowed on the tour, and that anyone from fourteen to seventeen will require a parent or a guardian. Everyone attending will need a driver's license or some other kind of photo identification, though connoisseurs of such language may note in passing that the driver's license does not have to be valid. Firearms, cameras, recorders, and binoculars are prohibited, though there is no word about the taking of notes.

"Casual clothing is recommended," we're told, but that is immediately brushed aside by other instructions: "Wear sturdy shoes, no shorts, no skirts, and no sandals." Just like that! Be casual, but get yourself some boots. The odd imbalance between attitudes that are loose and militaristic is followed up by this wistful admission: "Cafeteria services are no longer available." Is it that the place has seen better days? That there just isn't the will any longer to make another buck or two on your basic selection of fast foods? After all, it's going to be hot out there—one way or the other, with no shorts or sandals tolerated—and there isn't even a soda machine!

There's a final warning not to count on anything: "There is a possibility that the visit may have to be postponed for operational reasons. If that happens, you will be notified immediately."

You are called to assemble at the Public Reading Facility of the Department of Energy, which is at 2621 Lozlee Road in North Las Vegas. You are to be there by 7:30 a.m. And on that sunny morning in late May, you find about a couple dozen people carrying their packed lunches and several bottles of mineral water and looking ready for a rough hike. Your names are checked off a list by a friendly staff member. A driver and a guide appear. The mood is now very chipper, as if to say, We're all going to have a very good day. Indeed you are, so long as you're not averse to some fairly deep thought as part of a good time. You are on your way to the Nevada Test Site.

How much of this story, this testing, do we all know by now? How stable or closed a state has the story reached? Or are we, even now, the victims of our own credulity if we take any of it on trust? This is something a little more potent than six-week divorces, no income taxes, licensed prostitution, and letting gambling drive a state. And this is a matter that goes beyond the confines of Nevada itself. Indeed, we may not yet be sure just how far this experiment reaches.

Nevertheless, in the years that followed Nevada's decision to authorize gaming, as the population of the state closed in on 100,000 (the crowd at some big college football games), there was a war, begun in Europe, yet swiftly made available to the rest of the world. Enormous armies were mobilized, great fleets, flocks of aircraft. More or less, and granted the language of promotional materials, the forces of fascism opposed the nations of the free world. The central Communist force in the world, the Soviet Union, having been a little uncertain at first as to which side it should take, threw itself in with the lands of the free.

There were anomalies. The side of the free included India, as well as several other nations in Africa and Asia that felt dominated by British rule. The Soviet Union was as suspicious of its allies as it was of its enemies. And there were people helping to run the war effort of the free world who felt ties of sympathy (even of blood) with the fascist enemy stronger than any alleged bonds with Russkie allies. It was a messy business, yet as wars go, it was recognized both at the time and ever afterward as a just war. For anyone who had doubts on that account, there would be the unmistakable evidence that the fascists—or at least the German fascists—had made conscientious efforts to eliminate all the Jews on the Earth. By no means was every citizen of the free world wedded to the cause of the Jews. Still, the spectacle of that slaughter—so cruel, so thorough, so clerical— was one of the two most shocking events of the war period.

The other dawned more slowly, or gradually, and it was something that the ordinary person only recognized once it had happened. We always knew how cruel we might be; we had a collective sense of history that numbered horrors and outrages. The genocide of the Jews was startling when the camps were liberated (and presumably it shocked those few who knew of the camps years earlier). But it was in line with, in the family of, the terrible things our race had done in the past. The explosions in August 1945, demonstrated for the Japanese and all other onlookers, were so much more than anyone had anticipated.

For, more or less, people reckoned that the very big bangs of World War I—mines, bombs, howitzers, tank attacks, machine-gun fire—were par for the second course, granted some natural improvement and enhancement, such as the greater ease and accuracy with which aircraft could bomb enemy cities.

But some scientists knew there might be more—much more. From Stockholm, Lise Meitner, a physicist, advised colleagues in the United States and the potentially free world that Germany—or German scientists—was making moves that indicated some thought of atomic weapons, a way of bombarding and splitting a uranium atom that could unleash a hitherto-unimagined explosive power. There is even charm and intrigue in the story of how some of those colleagues in the United States, refugees and Jews, sought out "the old man," Albert Einstein, as someone who might alert President Roosevelt to the fact that this arcane science (hardly grasped by more than a score of people) could affect millions—or everyone.

The penny dropped. And so, as "regular" war went on, in North Africa, Europe, the Pacific, and above all in Russia, the United States and that free world began a most secret inquiry into a new kind of war, or power. It became known as the Manhattan Project, and it was a large collaboration, or conspiracy, among scientists from several countries and the American military to achieve a new kind of weapon—one that would work—before the Germans could get it.

The intensity of the American effort—the secrecy and the thrill, for the science of it was intellectually ravishing—did not rule out doubts and foreboding. Some of the best and most vital scientists wondered if they were interfering with nature, delivering into military hands an awesome power, and doing things to the atom that would result in uncertain yet probably very prolonged, and possibly very dangerous, aftereffects. Still, many of those scientists knew directly what Germany had done already in Europe, and they dreaded such a weapon in those hands.

As it happened, Germany was not nearly as intent on, or advancing, with the new weapon as we feared. Did "we" or "they" know that? Should it have deterred or slowed our effort? Or, under the pressure of world war, was it inevitable that so large a search for knowledge could hardly be controlled, just as the knowledge, once learned, could never be forgotten?

And so, in the early 1940s, at Los Alamos, New Mexico, amid high security, a band of brilliant scientists and wary military men developed what would become the atom bomb. Why not in Nevada? you may ask. In truth, because Nevada then was so little known or noted in the eastern United States, where such decisions are taken. And because enough of the scientists knew and loved the New Mexico countryside.

By the spring of 1945, the new bomb was tested in the New Mexico desert. It was pronounced a great success, yet some who had understood the power (and its "disaster") on paper were uncommonly and eloquently affected when they saw and felt the fireball itself. Some word of the bomb's existence was passed on a few days later to Stalin at the Yalta Conference. But he knew as much already, for espionage had been at work in Los Alamos. Klaus Fuchs—a betrayer, or a hero; it is hardly clear which yet; let us say both—had conveyed crucial theoretical information to Soviet agents. Though, as yet, at war, and more ravaged by it than any other participant, Russia could do very little with the knowledge.

In August 1945, atom bombs were dropped on two Japanese cities, Hiroshima and Nagasaki. President Harry Truman gave the final orders. Those bombs killed about 215,000 immediately; altogether, 340,000 were dead from the bomb and the aftereffects six months later. This was the second shock, though it was appreciated at the time that many Allied lives—maybe 200,000, maybe half a million, maybe more—had been saved in that there was no need now to launch a final land invasion of Japan. The numbers were . . . well, theoretical. A very novel kind of gambling was at work. It was not for the squeamish or the unsteady, and Truman himself often barked at the scientists' timidity. All they'd done, he said, was create the damn thing. He had to make the decision. And there were some, even then, who advocated dropping more atom bombs on the Soviet Union, straightaway, to get the whole thing over with.

31. Auction City

PULL BACK THE BLINDS; LET IN THE LIGHT. CAN YOU BE sure, at first, whether it is the break of day or the close?

Promotion, persuasion, and possibility are the trinity of Las Vegas, and in their odd way they are only variants on the darker yet transforming vision felt by Robert Oppenheimer at Alamogordo when the atom bomb was exploded on July 16, 1945. Just forty years earlier, on May 15–16, 1905, Las Vegas observed its first great promotional miracle as, in a temperature that approached 110 degrees (it was only May), about $265,000 was paid in return for utterly vacant, very dusty, but dazzling lots in the new township of Las Vegas. So solemn was the enterprise, and so dedicated the spirit of progress, that many of those engaged in the dealings wore ties, vests, and either derby or ten-gallon hats. By sheer purchase and possibility, Las Vegas began to come into being. In the ten years from 1900 to 1910, its population jumped from about 30 to 945.

Of course, that sort of rate of increase is not unknown in Nevadan history, but in nearly all circumstances, it would have been prompted by the discovery of gold or silver. The bullion of Las Vegas has always remained in the neon and the transformational rhetoric. The town itself was, from the outset, only a service center, or a factory that dealt in state of mind.

At the turn of the century, Las Vegas was still no more than a few viable ranches, notably the Las Vegas and the Kyle ranches. It was dwarfed in significance by the silver or gold towns of Pioche and Delamar to the north, and Searchlight to the south.

It was in 1901–1902 that the railroad was brought to southern Nevada. There were disputing schemes at first, but the contest was won by Senator William Clark (of Montana) who designed the San Pedro, Los Angeles & Salt Lake Railroad to make the link between Uvada (in Utah) and Manvel (in California). With a staging point in mind, Clark and his railroad com-

pany bought the Las Vegas Ranch and its water for $55,000. The work
went on through 1903–1904, and by October the last tie was laid. The
potential for Nevada was far greater than any immediate plans, but the relevance to Los Angeles was larger still. For in the period 1890–1910, that
city grew from 100,000 to 400,000 and began to cultivate the special form
of industrialized fantasy for which it would become famous.

The position of Las Vegas had another boost when, after the major discovery of silver at Tonopah ($125 million, eventually), and then the open-
ing up of Goldfield, Bullfrog, and Rhyolite, a spur line—the Las Vegas &
Tonopah Railroad—was constructed to carry in supplies and material, as
well as new fortune seekers. And so Vegas began to grow: saloons, restaurants, stores, and a hotel, even if most of these were glorified tents or very
simple wooden facades and a canvas interior.

The railroad track from Caliente, Pioche, and Utah came in at a diagonal, running northeast to southwest. This was of some importance in the
unruly but open-market frenzy to decide just where Las Vegas should be.
Furthermore, it helps explain the somewhat sprawling nature of the modern city.

A young urban genius, a surveyor and engineer named J. T.
McWilliams, had been hired originally by the widow Stewart to establish
the boundaries of the Las Vegas Ranch in dealing with the railroad. He
made claims on an 80-acre piece of land, mainly to the west of the rail-

*Less than ninety years ago, Las Vegas (the view from the southern edge of
the developed city) looked like this.*

*The industrialization of fun: corridors giving access to uniformly
superb rooms at the Mirage Hotel — three such arms spread out from
the elevators. Each corridor is more than 100 yards long.*

road tracks, and in the northern part of the modern city. That was where
the first tent city sprang up, and it was much enhanced by the location of
an ice plant on the tip of the 80-acre lot, just to the east of the rail line.
This piece of land was also very close to the Las Vegas Creek, which ran
west-east and was the most accessible form of water for newcomers.

McWilliams set up the Las Vegas Townsite Company and announced
an immediate sale of desirable lots. But the official depot on the railroad
line was south of the creek and a mile or so farther down the track. Its
sponsor was J. Ross Clark, president of the Salt Lake Railroad and brother
to the Senator Clark who had done so much to get the railroad there in
the first place. Clark's Las Vegas Townsite, another gathering of tents, with
a putative hotel, was adjacent to the depot. It boldly, and nearly surreally,
drew up a grid map of city blocks and proposed to sell the lots, by auction,
on May 15, through the agency of the Las Vegas Land & Water Company.

The advertising was as heavy as the capital letters, and it was largely
conducted in Los Angeles and Salt Lake City on the principle that this
sparse, burning desert was a boom and a boon in the making. None of this
materialized for many years. But the point about promotion is to build an
idea, and as we come closer to the legend of Ben Siegel, rather than give
him all the credit for perceiving a vision in the desert, we should see that
McWilliams and Clark had recognized—with how much collusion, no

one knows—that one absurd idea was all the more far-reaching if put in competition with another fanciful scheme.

Las Vegas had water: not just the creek but also the supply that became available when new settlers discovered that they had to dig only to twenty feet or so to get themselves a good well. There was a fine spring harvest of fruits—figs, apples, peaches, and cherries—and the auction would be in the spring. The depot was placed as a junction of sorts, and it was prospering from the mineral discoveries to the northwest. But those boomtowns would wither, as others had, in which case no one would be able to dispute the long summer or its torrid heat, let alone the essential condition of desert.

Clark's people laid on auction trains from Los Angeles and Salt Lake City (any purchasers would get a rebate on their ticket price). They announced a city with streets that would be eighty feet wide, and alleys twenty feet wide. The streets were all given names well in advance of their existence—First, Second, Third, and so on, and Stewart, Ogden, Fremont, Carson, Bridger, Lewis, Clark, Bonneville, and Garces. Fremont Street was a line drawn directly away from the depot. Ordinary lots were reckoned to be available in the range of $100 to $500, while choice corner lots might go as high as $750. All sales would require 25 percent down, with the balance in sixty days.

The McWilliams Townsite was not put off by the pie-in-the-sky map, and its backers were pained to think that any decent town had ever existed so close to a depot: "The promoters of the so-called Railroad Townsite of Las Vegas now propose to sell their lots at auction. They have been asking from $350 to $700 for unimproved, so-called business lots, 25 × 140 feet on streets without a store or other buildings on them and within so many feet of the depot, just as if it was necessary to have the depot close to the best business section of the town, which it is not. Very few good towns such as Las Vegas is going to be has its depot near the best part of the business section."

Of course, there was wisdom in that: One day, not too far away, the shining jewels of Las Vegas, the Strip, would be tossed down on the ground well to the south of Fremont Street and the depot.

The advertising was gloriously unrestrained, and as the ads ran, so the promoters tried to throw together some semblance of what they claimed. To the north, in a tent city, where McWilliams looked forward to "a city of more than 10,000 in a short time," he claimed a bank, six stores, fourteen lodging houses, and many good restaurants. To the south, workers struggled to get the Las Vegas Hotel ready in time for the auction, while others drove markers in the ground to indicate where the illustrious streets were meant to be.

By the day itself, May 15, the towns were jammed. A wooden platform had been built for the auctioneer, Ben Rhoade, a known Los Angeles performer. The auction took place on ground just to the north of what would become the Union Plaza Hotel, and it began at 10:00 a.m. on a hot morning. The results exceeded all expectations. Hard money changed hands for plots of ground in the future. But when the pioneers sought to retire to the Las Vegas Hotel, their hotel, for lunch and a cold beer, they found that its interior temperature had reached over 125 degrees. For the builders had had time so far for only one layer of canvas in the roof, and one layer served to increase the force of the sun. The beer was all the more welcome. A few nights later, as the revelry continued, there was a dance, at which shots were fired, enough to earn that section a reputation as the rowdy part of town. But there were enthusiasts who went to work and put up buildings on their new lots. It was crucial that mining activity continued in the Bullfrog area until at least 1910, for those few years of prosperity and commerce allowed the dream of Las Vegas to get a footing as the service base for mining towns.

At the same time, the new citizens discovered the heat, the wind, the dust storms, the almost natural condition of fire, and the awesome nature of hard labor in those circumstances. It was remarked that Las Vegas was "the creature of a day, so to speak," that the state was optimistic on its behalf in the very way it needed to believe that the workings at Rhyolite, say, would never dry up. In those first few years and decades, as Vegas was built, as the lone buildings slowly developed into real streets, and as the population grew—from 945 in 1910, to 2,304 in 1920, to 5,165 in 1930—and as Rhyolite became a ghost town, so the city waited to rediscover the true lesson of May 15, 1905—that it had been the product of make-believe and magic, that the old rugged frontier might be turned into a circus tent in a few hours, that the trick might be pulled off.

That's why Ben Siegel is so important, and such a truly Las Vegan mix of good and bad luck. He saw the desert and the great game of transforming it. And like the first citizens of the place, he knew the virtue of moving a little farther out into the desert and starting again. For the desert is a romantic place, and Vegas must never threaten to defeat or alter it with water and the dull routine of wall-to-wall plush carpeting.

32. Your Guide

BY NO MEANS THE LEAST THING ON SHOW DURING OUR DAY AT the Nevada Test Site (NTS) was the guide. I will call him Rick, a handsome western type, deeply tanned, maybe as old as forty-five. All day long, he was eloquent, wry, patient, quietly confident about what there was to behold. He could have walked in and out of one of those reliable buddy roles from a World War II film—and even if, on the road to Mercury, we had been waylaid by terrorists, I wouldn't have been astonished if his sensible pale khaki pants and blue shirt concealed a secret firearm and expert evasive drills. Enough of an aura, one hoped, that the assassins' bullets would have bent around us.

He was a very helpful guide, and so immediately, plausibly, and availably a good guy—so western—that one could not erase all thoughts that he might have been an actor, a bit of a con, or an ingratiating fraud. When that sort of westerner talks so much and so well—I am reminded of Steve Wynn or Ronald Reagan—your fingertips may reach back to hang on to your shirt cuffs.

Rick was ex-services, he said, though he wasn't precise. He had worked a spell at the NTS and was doing the guide job chiefly to keep up his clearance with the Department of Energy, in case they ever got back into rehiring. (The Ricks of the world live on the dream that it's all coming back.) Apart from that, we learned that he was a fitness nut: He liked to bike in the midday sun or mess around on Lake Mead. He had a wife and some kids, nearly grown, but he made them seem a little like casting. He had a Jet Ski rental business, as far as I could gather, and he was as brisk and vague about it as most men are with fronts, things that could be reappraised before 5:00 p.m. or in the next rewrite.

I liked him, or I responded to him. I admired the deft, wide-eyed, but grinning way he deflected a question about Area 51—"Oh, I never heard anything about that. Is that so?"—and then threw us a bone with a little giveaway on what all the fuss was about, when there were nuclear weapons being stored at Nellis, for heaven's sake, practically in the suburbs of Las Vegas. As if to let the wise, or would-be wise, know that there were bigger things to worry about than Area 51, which might have been floated, one fine day, as just a grand piece of camouflage. If you want something to be scared of, folks, look in your suburbs.

Rick answered nearly every question put to him. When he didn't know the answer, he said so, and then mentioned a place where one might research it. As it turned out, there was opposition on the bus, a warning voice, a couple of pale kids who wanted to distribute leaflets, to the effect that there were still immense nuclear dangers. Rick grinned, and said, "Sure, that's fine," and let the leaflets be passed around. He sort of let his tan and their pallor tell their own story, without a word of underlining. And, altogether, there was that air about him that, sure, his marriage and his business might go belly-up by cocktail time, but he might also be true-blue Secret Service, not a mean man, either, but ready to let democracy and free speech have their moment with some of these issues. After all, for God's sake, this is a frightening world we're in, and don't let's kid ourselves it isn't. Am I right, or am I right? Put it another way: Rick was just another professional gambler, but more so—he'd have done it for no money; he enjoyed risk for its own sake.

And he liked his work. He might have let it be known that the practical matter of clearance was his motive for being there, that and its chance of more government work, if America ever yields again to insecurity. But it was plain that he enjoyed the talk, the promotion, as well as the opportunity to draw attention to efforts that even the American authorities had once preferred to hide under a bushel. He relished the cause and the decisions it had made on how to protect itself. He was a believer in what, in its days of high secrecy, may have been a greater hazard than we ever knew. He took comfort now that the fierceness over the years had neatly freed faraway countries that he need have no thought of visiting. The United States, after all, had been challenged for decades, and called, and it had had the cards and the solemn resolve to keep them ready. The country had not folded—no, not even during the worst throes of organized weakness and forgiveness. The military had held firm and said, You see if I'm bluffing, Ivan, you just see. However one looked at it, there was no getting away from the confidence that came from winning.

Not that this was any ordinary victory, one from which the money might easily be lost again tomorrow night. No, this was a decisive win, where firepower held ready had broken the back and the economy and the spirit of an evil empire. This was a win where the house itself had been on our side, the house and its God.

So Rick could easily have been insufferable, or cocksure. He was not. No one on the bus could have taken personal offense, or seen him as someone not trying to do his best. He was a government employee, to be sure, only hired and cleared because he knew what to say, and what not to say. Not that the government was going to pay him much for his day. So most of us tipped him, and thanked him, and realized that his shining face and clear-cut, communiquélike information had been a vital part of our pleasure. He was vigilant, yet cool, fierce but good-humored, inflexible maybe, but a true gambler.

Rick was not a brilliant man, not an intellectual, let alone a genius. And he had earnest respect for those things. There were several occasions on our tour of the Test Site when he volunteered his complete admiration for what the scientists had done, rather in the way of a fan admiring while being incapable of the rare, penetrating insight, and the arm that threw the ball down the dotted line, of Joe Montana, say, guiding the San Francisco 49ers to victory. But Rick was not daunted by all the extra things artists or geniuses possessed. For he knew the military wisdom whereby, sooner or later, ordinary, solid guys—like Rick—will take the decisions toward which the great minds have been reaching and feeling, in the dark, whether they know it or not.

One aspect of the Manhattan Project—and of any such enterprise where the government enlists its very highest experts—was that men trained in decision and leadership, like Rick, had waited for genius to give it the bullet and the trigger. Yet the best minds had been so caught up in the extraordinary difficulties of making those things that they need not have thought too much about whether they would ever be used. More or less, the American triumph in World War II made manifest the notion that uncommonly fine minds (but maybe not the most worldly people) would furnish a weapon or weapons, the use of which could be trusted to steadfast common sense and absolute military pragmatism. No one in the American command would have considered leaving the executive decision to the scientists who had made the bomb, and conjured it up out of the clouds of mere possibility. And in hindsight, even the most tender of the scientists recognized the implausibility that such decision makers would be granted a new tool, a fresh ploy, and not use it. For their decisions, all along, had been based on such things as the superiority of firepower and the favorability of a thing called odds.

We sometimes remark on the contrast between Harry Truman and the extended family that includes Oppenheimer, Teller, Niels Bohr, I. I. Rabi, Enrico Fermi, and so many others, including even Einstein and Klaus Fuchs. The great minds could speak languages unknown to Truman; they could entertain concepts, doubts, and proofs that the Missouran might as well have left the room for. But Truman was protected in his own mind, as he has been in American history, by the notion that common sense, sound instincts, and the willingness to make decisions are what mark great leaders. And surely, in time of war, it is much easier for a nation as a whole to make that distinction. Even if the proposition had been put before the country as a referendum—whether to incur so many Japanese casualties to avoid that many more in the event of a land invasion—there's little doubt what the result would have been.

Luis Alvarez had been a physicist at Los Alamos. He made several important contributions to the work there, and he flew in a plane—a B-29 called the *Great Artiste*—behind the *Enola Gay*, to measure and observe the effect of the atom bomb. On the way back from that mission, he wrote to his four-year-old son: "What regrets I have about being a party to killing and maiming thousands of Japanese civilians this morning are tempered with the hope that this terrible weapon we have created may bring the countries of the world together and prevent further wars."

That is a very decent communiqué, fit for a world of four-year-olds. In the decades since 1945, presidents and ordinary citizens have sheltered beneath it and crossed their fingers in the hope that its language covered the terms of the gamble. For, in truth, folding or playing is never just an immediate, isolated moment at the table. Gambling cannot be considered properly except as a link in the chain of events. And gambling affects the future, just as surely as the life of a big winner is altered, or as vaguely as he hopes it will be.

One such consequence is that, with the efficacy of gambling so clear, it becomes harder to argue that our decisions pertain to higher or more far-reaching issues. Gambling is a pretext for taking action; it believes in activity more than reflection; and sooner or later, brutally or practically, with pride or humility, it takes the consequences. As witness Curtis LeMay, describing the policy of firebombing Japanese cities before the dropping of the atom bomb. These raids, carried on in the spring and early summer of 1945, were actually more destructive than the incidents at Hiroshima or Nagasaki:

> Killing Japanese didn't bother me very much at that time. It was getting the war over that bothered me. So I wasn't worried particularly about how many people were killed in getting the job done. I suppose if I had lost the war, I would have been tried as a war criminal. Fortunately, we were on the winning side. Incidentally, everybody bemoans the fact that we dropped the atomic bomb and killed a lot of people at Hiroshima and Nagasaki. That I guess is immoral: but nobody says anything about the incendiary attacks on every industrial city in Japan, and the first attack on Tokyo killed more people than the atomic bomb did.

Of course, a fallacy was gradually revealed for those prepared to see it—not just an aversion to elitism and intellectuality but also some feeling that to dispute commonsense decisions is undemocratic, or unegalitarian. That it is, somehow, contrary to the American way and its trust (in God—let's not forget that) and the decisive, if perilous, actions of men.

LeMay may have been correct in saying that the Tokyo raid of March 1945 killed more than the Hiroshima drop. But the Tokyo raid killed quickly: The death toll was settled within a few days. The legacy of Hiroshima was and is prolonged: Decades later, suffering and deaths occur because of that drop. What happened in 1945 begins to reveal the awful truth that perhaps only the very brilliant, the very knowledgeable, perhaps only the inventors, were in any position to make decisions about the bomb's use. For only they foresaw what use entailed and how long the consequences could last. That quandary seems great enough with the use of nuclear weapons and power, yet we are close to chaos because of the decision, and on the edge of greater dangers than we care to recognize. How much greater may be the confusion that comes from the alteration in nature made available by genetic research.

Yet, still, we honor the gambler's creed that common sense and steady nerves will make the play—for us, and for succeeding generations. What I am trying to suggest is the extent to which gambling entered our system around 1945.

33. The Dam

THE DESERT AND THE ELEMENTS WERE NOT MUCH IMPRESSED by the cheek with which Las Vegas had set itself up in 1905. There were buildings, to be sure, some as fine as the Spanish-style railway depot. There was the Armour Ice Plant and there were new railroad yards, an area where freight cars and carriages could gather and age in the sun, as well as a shop and a turntable for repairs. There were a few hotels and a couple of what were called department stores. There was a telephone system in the town, but there were many open sites, scrub and desert, still, where the wires drooped in the heat from one street to another. Las Vegas could boast ten miles of graded and curved streets. But in that first decade of the twentieth century, Nevada had several bigger and far more prosperous places. For the most part, Las Vegas seemed to be sustained by the railroad, and it was dusty and stupefyingly hot much of the year.

But in the spring and fall, Las Vegas could still seem an idyllic place, with the sunlight on the mountains, fine fruit from the nearby ranches, and the Arizona Club in town for entertainment. Year by year, that establishment improved, going from timber construction to concrete block and brick, adding a thirty-foot bar as well as fancy French mirrors. In 1907, under its new boss, Al James, a brothel was added upstairs, and the promise was made of "Service in Keeping with the Surroundings."

It was a Wild West town, still, ignorant of its actual future, yet all too well aware how rapidly Nevada could turn a place into a ghost town. Vulnerability was made much more real early in 1910. A severe winter storm caused heavy flooding in the Southwest, and much of the railroad north of Las Vegas was swept away. For nearly six months, no train got through from California to Utah. The population of Las Vegas fell to below one thousand, and many of the buildings were emptied.

Five years earlier, as Las Vegas jumped up, clamoring for attention, a far more devastating flood had overtaken the Southwest.

Ever since mankind had been in the area, respect had been owed to the whims of weather and the Colorado River. Coming south, out of Wyoming and Colorado, the river had been fed by the melting snows of the Rockies. As such, it had had the force to cut its way through the canyon country of southern Utah, and frequently flooded as it served as the border between Southern California and Arizona. An irrigation canal had been made for the river to the general area of Indio and Palm Springs, but in 1905 the flooding was so great that the canal was washed away. In addition, the inland Salton Sea was hugely enlarged, from 22 to 500 square miles. The area was devastated: Crops, houses, roads, and railways all had to be replaced. Yet, ironically, in summer, when the agricultural area risked reverting to desert, the Colorado was often no more than sticky mud.

The disaster of 1905, along with the emergence of Los Angeles and Southern California, prompted attention to some way of controlling the river. It was the most significant piece of government intervention that Nevada had yet known.

Secretary of Commerce Herbert Hoover arranged a conference to consider the matter. The parties met in 1922, representing not just Arizona, California, Colorado, Nevada, New Mexico, Utah, and Wyoming but the nation of Mexico, too. For the Colorado meets the sea — in fact, the Gulf of California, between Baja and the mainland — in Mexican territory. The central purpose of these meetings was to determine the water rights that the parties had upon the Colorado River. There was an agreement made by the end of November 1922, subject to ratification by the states, but then Arizona reneged on it. That was enough to delay the project until 1928. However, in outline at least, California was set to get two-thirds of the water, with Arizona and Nevada dividing the other third.

The Boulder Canyon Project Act was passed in 1928, with $250,000 allocated for research. Engineers and surveyors for the Bureau of Reclamation investigated the area and decided that Black Rock Canyon offered the most likely site for a dam. When Edmund Wilson went to look at the place, he found

a steep narrow gap between two immense burnt-out cinders. In summer, the heat of those cinders suggests that they may still be smoldering from the primeval volcanic disturbance which has left the whole landscape an infernal desert: hard blue and black hills, full of metal, that look as if you could ring them with a hammer, seem to lie with their heads down in the plain like monstrous pre-human animals; sunken mirage-like marshes in which it is impossible to tell from a distance whether the dried-blood red is water or earth.

"Infernal" is not an exaggeration. When we marvel now at the transforming effect of the dam, and if we wonder whether it may be the most beautiful and stirring thing men have made in Nevada, we can't underestimate the terrible conditions under which it was built. Boulder, or Hoover, Dam changed everything, and it is often referred to as one of those benevolent improvements of the New Deal, but in truth its construction was so primitive and cruel, it seems to have come from the Dark Ages or the Egypt that made the pyramids.

The rock in Black Rock Canyon in summer was too hot to be touched. In the first July of construction, 128 degrees in the shade was recorded, and daytime temperatures were consistently over 100 degrees. Moreover, while the neat and rather pretty little town of Boulder City, ten miles away, is regularly posited as the place where the workers were housed, that is far from the strict truth. Indeed, Boulder City was built as construction headquarters in 1932, but work had begun in 1931. Many of the workers lived at the site itself—and died there. For although Hoover Dam seems like a great civic undertaking, it was actually contracted out to private companies that were able to ignore many state laws in their hiring and treatment of workers.

To make the dam, the waters of the Colorado had to be carried around the site of the dam so that excavation and clearance work could go on there, prior to the erection of the concrete barrier itself. It was the decision of the then president, Herbert Hoover, that the government should not do the work itself. Instead, it accepted the joint bid of six companies—Six Companies, Inc.—to build the dam for $50 million ($5 million less than any other bid). Secretary of the Interior Ray Wilbur signed the contract that called for nonunion labor, with special consideration to be given to ex-servicemen, and with Orientals barred. There were to be no regulated wages, and the idea that 80 percent of the workforce should live in Boulder City was abandoned, simply because their housing was not yet ready. In due course, some workers did live there, along with the administration and technical staff and the many services that were called into being. But the labor force that did the brute work—dynamiting and clearing tunnels, hacking out the rock, and then mixing and laying concrete—

lived in shacks close to the site. The nighttime temperatures in those baking rooms often reached a hundred degrees. The food was cooked on the site, and without refrigeration, much of it perished. For all the cases of heatstroke, there were many who had stomach illnesses, to say nothing of the danger of accident, falling rocks, and mistakes due to fatigue. Six Companies was allowed to ignore Nevada state provisions, and so men were sent back into the new tunnels fifteen minutes—as opposed to sixty—after nitroglycerin blasting.

Edmund Wilson reported the hardships:

> . . . the men at the river camp had no means of refreshing themselves: spending all day in the tunnel with shovels and drills, so hot that they always worked naked, they could not even get a shower or a cold drink. The only water they had for drinking or washing was the water of the Colorado River, which, full of silt from the decomposing tufa, is always an opaque yellow like coffee with too much cream; and this, with no water-coolers, would get tepid or hot in the tanks. As the weather became hotter and hotter, the water began making people sick. Nor were there any facilities for cooling the barracks. The nights were so suffocating and uncomfortable that one welcomed the diversion of work. And for the shift that got its rest in the daytime, with the sun glaring through the windows and heating the shack like an oven, sleep, if they managed to get any, became a heavy, sweating curse.

Laborers on the dam project were paid $4 a day. The excellent tours of Hoover Dam do not announce how many people died on the project, and there is no official listing of names, but it is reckoned that as many as one hundred men were killed.

Such details pass and fade away. The laborers were almost all of them victims of or refugees from the Depression, people who came to Black Rock Canyon desperate for work and not likely to complain. But visitors and tourists who wince at the high summer heat when they come out of the air-conditioned movie theater may reflect upon the ordeal of the men who worked there, and the serene way in which their suffering has been eclipsed by the dam itself.

Hoover Dam stands 726 feet above the base level of rock. But what seems like a wall is a magnificent splayed pyramid, 45 feet thick at the top, and 660 feet—220 yards, a furlong—thick at its root. That great form thrust between Nevada and Arizona, and the burning walls of Black Rock

Canyon, is 3.25 million cubic yards of concrete. The curved crest of the dam is 1,244 feet across. Imagine that form standing free in some open desert—an object of such amazing pent-up load and force, requiring several minutes for it to be walked around. And then think of it being crammed into the mouth of Black Rock Canyon, with such tender finesse and forgotten suffering.

What I want to suggest, above all, is that it is a lustrous, beautiful shape, so massive, yet so curved. It speaks of bulk and voluptuousness, with as much strength in its flex as its mass. But it stands there, backing up the Colorado into what is one of the great man-made lakes of the world, Lake Mead, a reservoir and a place for sport and play, a water mass with 550 miles of shore and 35.2 billion cubic meters of water (if the level reaches to the dam's spillway, its top).

The work was completed by 1935, earlier than expected, and only a couple of million dollars or so over budget. Franklin Roosevelt dedicated the dam on September 30, 1935, and in a little over a year the power plant came into operation. It has never faltered or crumbled; no floods have overtopped it. Just as Lake Mead, suddenly, became a place of glorious recreation—to such an extent that some later generations now reckon it was a natural lake—so the Colorado makes its gentle regulated way to the sea, watering the cities and the farmlands of Arizona, Nevada, and Southern California. Something like 15 million people have lives made possible, and pleasant, by the dam's grip on the river. A million acres in the United States and another half a million in Mexico are irrigated because of it. The power plant has a capacity of 1.92 million kilowatts. About 25 percent of the energy provided goes to Nevada, 19 percent to Arizona, and the rest to Southern California.

The tour that is available—and which has had nearly 30 million visitors since 1937—lets you see and feel the flat expanse of Lake Mead urged up against the dam wall; it lets you enter the slipway tunnels, where you can feel the pressure of the river's passage beyond the containing walls; it lets you see the turbines, the drunken pylons leaning over the gorge; it lets you drive back and forth from Nevada to Arizona; and it offers up the unerring classicism of the 1930s architecture—the towers that adjoin the dam and stand in Lake Mead; the Egyptian-like fortress of the power station beneath the dam walls; and the bright, graded facade of the dam itself, a hand that has never wavered, but which lets its own sweet curve tell us that all such things can be done.

America was so recently wilderness, and Nevada's beauty rests so much on the unspoiled quality of the place. But Hoover Dam is one of

Hoover Dam, with the lake it holds back

the great, bold, simple, and lovely human assertions—it says, We can think of this, do it and make it, and some will die in the doing, but we will alter the dynamics of nature and make it serve us. And even if it all comes tumbling down eventually, because the raw, innate upheaval of land cannot be quelled, or because our games with explosives go too far, still, anyone who sees Hoover Dam will know and remember that men gave

Another view of the dam wall and the tamed
Colorado River that flows south

wildness and nature a terrific game, and won the game with grace and ingenuity.

In the end, it is not the statistics of transformation that mean so much about Hoover Dam, or which sustain the great upthrust wings on the two bronze figures by the road that crosses the dam. You can outline the advantages and the permission given to Los Angeles, San Diego, Phoenix, and Las Vegas. You can point out the other complexes farther down the Colorado, at Lake Mojave and Lake Havasu. That is not really it. For, truth to tell, the constructions of the area often seem flimsy or temporary. Phoenix is no more convincing than Las Vegas as a city that has taken root in the ground. Their style has to do with transience and illusion. But Hoover Dam has a strength that is directly emotional. You can imagine the Southwest empty of people because of one hazard or another. You can imagine yourself as the last spectator coming up the river in an open boat and seeing that mighty wall. And somehow the dam works, even if the people have gone: The turbines roll, the spillways control the water level, and the Colorado does the dam's bidding.

Hoover Dam is glorious because it lets you know that sometimes mankind can play the great game of creation and look good doing it. Elsewhere in the West, I know, at Lake Powell, farther up the Colorado, a lake was made, for fun and hydroelectricity, and great beauties and old Indian cities were consigned to the deep, like dead bodies. It is a close call, in the West, how much of ourselves we should allow. But Hoover Dam is the place in Nevada where anyone must be ready to be moved. And even if the amount of water is very great, still a few more human tears are appreciated.

34. Over There

OFTEN ENOUGH IN NEVADA, SOMEONE WILL SETTLE A CON-
versation by nodding at the distance and saying something like "Just the
other side of those mountains there." The mountains are golden and
mauve, gray and red, depending on the position of the sun. They are
those mixtures of rock and shale that count for mountains in so much of
Nevada, a state that has thousands of such peaks, more than anyone could
know or care to count. And you know intellectually, and you have seen, if
you have ever flown over the state, that yes, indeed, there is another side
to all the mountains. They have their beyond, which is usually one more
empty valley with more rows of mountains, all different, of course, yet so
alike, lounging, slung back, so clear and silent in the still air, so lovely, yet
so numerous that the traveler takes them for granted much as he accepts
that there are mountains on the moon.

But still there is the legend, the suggestion, or the rumor that there is
something over there. That is the great question mark, full of wide-eyed
wonder or paranoia, with which Rachel regards Area 51. And it is the sort
of thing that mining people—eccentric prospectors, especially—still say
about the possibility of extraordinary finds beyond those ragged cones. So
you walk on, or drive past. There are, eventually, too many mountains in
Nevada for us to stop and explore them. So paranoia and hope knit
together and the "interior"—that part of the world beyond, deeper than,
or farther in than where you are—becomes a mythic place. You might die
there, from the sun, or from some blast you set off; or you might find gold
there glowing like danger, and choose to stay with it, to live with it, to be
with and in it, rather than come out and tell the story that turns your private place into a gaudy suburb. More or less, in Nevada, you have to
decide whether you are going to live in America (the organization that
claims it) or the desert (the condition that will never yield).

You cannot get such thoughts out of your head as the bus makes its steady speed-limited way along Route 95 to Mercury, the real township that marks the Test Site—well, I could not, for I felt in advance that I was going to a kind of holy but perilous place. Those feelings, I dare say, speak for the dread and the sense of wonder of growing up in Nevada's light—not just the real glare of the day but also the illumination of *Dark Sun*, the title of Richard Rhodes's excellent book on the making of the hydrogen bomb.

That confused state of anxiety and eagerness seems almost the soil of my life. I can easily see that in every age of man there has been so much to be afraid of, yet so much to hope for. But, still, as someone born early in 1941, and just about four and a half when the bombs were dropped at Hiroshima and Nagasaki, I know what the alternative means to me. It's my mother telling me, "Everything's all right now," with such relief that only the reassurance let me know how afraid she had been. We lived in south London, near the railway line to Portsmouth and Southampton. The area was bombed regularly, and I am told that our house was hit—one way or another—three times. No one was killed, but several feet of the house had to be chopped away in 1946 because the structural damage was beyond recovery.

I never felt the terror of the bombing raids, never understood the nearness of German invasion. I was too young to grasp such things, and I was sheltered by my mother, I'm sure. Still, fear can be conveyed in silent, atmospheric ways. This is a book that will have to consider the effect of fallout in milk, so I see no difficulty in wondering about the nervous stirs in the milk I sucked from my mother's breast. She was afraid of the war, and I caught that fear, at four and a half, in the way she began to relax. At the same time, there were pictures in the papers of gaunt figures, all in oversize pajamas, found in the places called concentration camps. It seemed to me, at that age, that concentration had done terrible things to them, and their general look and bearing hardly seemed to fit the everything that was all right now.

This is put in terms of a children's story. But, of course, the contradiction affected everyone, and I wonder whether the world had ever had to live before 1945 in such self-evident confusion. That question is more than just background to this book. The bus comes to the Mercury turnoff, to the right or the north, where the road is pinned between the Spring Mountains to the south and Paiute Mesa to the north. But there is something to see before the bus turns. On the south side of the highway stand the remains, or the resting condition, of what is called Peace Camp. It is

Bureau of Land Management land, which is to say that it is ours, yet it belongs to the United States in such a way that its agents could bar entry. (So much of Nevada is like that.) Which makes it worth stressing that for several decades the authorities let the land be a camping site and gathering place for all those people who had come to protest the testing of weapons. "All" sometimes was a few thousand; sometimes only a handful. They were mostly young, barely provided for, itinerant, hitchhikers trying to get to the wicked place where they could register their objections. As late as the 1980s, there would be people there crossing the road in the day to parade and demonstrate as close as they could get to Mercury. The campground is derelict now, though there are the frames of a few Shoshone sweat lodges that were shelter against the sun. There are the outlines of paths, and several small shrines and monuments to peace.

As if anyone, since 1945, except for Curtis LeMay perhaps, ever argued for anything else. But just as the campers believed in peace as a state of mind (or a serene anarchy), a kind of passive well-being that could be communicated to others, so the people on the other side of the road, the Ricks, believed in being damn sure about it. And in the end—if there can ever be an end to such a worry—that amounted to the expenditure of at least $4 trillion. For, if the Cold War was a gamble, the winner got no payoff.

Across the highway, on the road that leads up to the gates of the Test Site, there are two chain-link pens—one for males, one for females—where overzealous demonstrators could be confined, under the unopposed sun, if they had got out of hand. Occasionally, the Test Site was "assaulted"; once someone managed to chain themselves to the axle of a stopped truck; and often the demonstrators got in the way of the natural flow in and out of Mercury. So the pens held offenders for a while, until they were bused into Beatty, where they could be charged and fined, and even kept overnight.

I saw groups of protesters there in the eighties, never very many, though the numbers increased if the date of a test was known in advance. These were not belligerent kids, and if they had been, there was the heat of the day to sap them. The protests seldom made news, even in Las Vegas, but they were a steady fact of life, and something for young radicals to join in. As far as I can tell, they were gatherings of the seventies and eighties—which means to say that, in the 1950s, when their case was most urgent, such protests had hardly been thought of yet. In so many matters nuclear, reflection and wisdom came along well after decisive action.

As early as August 1945, Brigadier General Leslie Groves, head of the atom bomb project, received from the U.S. Army Air Forces a breakdown of the major cities and targets of the Soviet Union and an estimate of how many atom bombs would be required to destroy them—if the United States could make enough bombs and somehow get its B-29s within range. For several years in the American military, there was sentiment, most forcefully expressed by Curtis LeMay, that in the inevitable and inescapable antagonism between the United States (and the free world) and the forces of communism, the practical time to strike with nuclear weapons was before the Soviets gained their own strike force. It's unlikely in 1945 that Stalin knew of that breakdown of his cities. Soviet espionage was so much more concentrated on a full description of the atom bomb itself. Hostility was taken for granted; that's what propaganda and espionage do for you.

Of course, LeMay was technically correct, which surely proves the inadequacy of military thinking in the modern world. Further, it shows that even jittery industrial-military complexes aspired to some higher thought—some primitive fear of extinction, or responsibility: the United States and the Soviet Union did not actually enter into a spasm of mutual destruction in fifty-odd years of Cold War. But only because we could have done, argue Rick, Ronald Reagan, and so many others.

I wonder if there was ever another way, granted the emotional brink of 1945 and the limited state of its education. Or even greater danger than in the years of warming up that have followed the dispelled Cold War. Some terrors come to fruition only with relaxation.

The Soviet Union had suffered more drastic losses and intrusions in the war than any other country—not least to whatever vestiges of Communist idealism it had kept through the 1930s. The union had survived, and it had taken great parts of Eastern Europe into its empire, yet they would prove to be an added burden to its shattered economy. More than that, because of a few dedicated spies, even by mid-1945 the Soviet Union had learned enough about America's atom bomb to be able to attempt a reproduction. Did it have any choice in whether to follow that path? It is hard enough to abdicate from wicked secrets you have learned. It was unthinkable for the vulnerable Soviet Union not to equip itself with nuclear weapons. In the same pinch, the United States would have done exactly the same thing. Victory in World War II at such cost settled once and for all the question of whether the Soviet Union was to be Communist or totalitarian—it had no option but to be the thing the United States most feared and loathed. At every step, it behaved like the perfect monster in America's dream.

The United States had some reason to feel cheated. It had won, and it was at the apex of its own short-lived imperial glory. Beyond that, war had wrapped up its recession and would ensure a prolonged booming economy. It had the bomb; it had invaded Europe, crossed the Rhine, and pushed the Japanese back across the Pacific. It was the only possible salvation for those wrecked Allies that had helped win the war. But at the same time, it was hated and envied for its success (everywhere except in Japan); it was made to feel guilty for the extraordinary scientific work of making the bomb—and then dropping it. And it faced a Soviet Union that it could destroy, or suffer with, in the way the nouveau riche suffer with an odious, self-pitying, smelly, drunken, unstable parent. Years ahead in the nuclear race, the United States had little option but to turn neurotic over its citizens' loyalties, while trying to increase its lead. It was also bitter that it (and the Allies; Fuchs was an English representative at Los Alamos) had let so many secrets slip out through espionage. Only a very few were wise enough to see that spying, and its result, a kind of equity, might protect the world. But, having attacked others, and having served as the official fact finders at Hiroshima and Nagasaki, the United States was now terrified of being attacked, and of losing the ease and boom of victory.

Of course, there was also a moment of gesture toward a form of internationalism in which rivalries might be subsumed. In June 1945, three weeks before Trinity, the first atom bomb test at Los Alamos, the United Nations charter was signed in San Francisco. Later that year, a prestigious group of American leaders was brought together to ensure that "atomic energy" would not be used for destructive purposes, but would be put to "peaceful and humanitarian ends." That group included Dean Acheson, General Groves, Vannevar Bush, James Bryant Conant, David Lilienthal (head of the Tennessee Valley Authority), several industrialists, and Robert Oppenheimer. The group proposed an Atomic Development Authority, the only body on Earth that would be permitted to develop its own uranium ore and would seek to share new nuclear knowledge internationally. The plan was based upon a very penetrating idea: that only truly shared information would persuade any nation that it was practically protected against others.

The plan went nowhere, except to bring such people as Acheson and Oppenheimer under more anti-Communist suspicions as the years passed.

The military did all it could to ignore such scheming, and to pursue testing, for testing used up material, thus requiring replacement and something like a steady manufacturing of uranium products; testing brought some knowledge, and it meant more publicity.

Immediately after the war, the U.S. government asserted its right to use Eniwetok and Bikini atolls as testing grounds. The right was that of conquest, for the United States had captured Eniwetok from the Japanese in February 1944, and at the same time occupied Bikini. The two atolls are in the Marshall Islands group, about three thousand miles west of Hawaii and two thousand northeast of New Guinea. Eniwetok is a ring of coral islands surrounding the mouth of an old submerged volcano. Bikini, two hundred miles to the east, is a similar configuration. It was there, in June 1946, that U.S. Navy and the U.S. Army Air Forces anchored a small fleet of ancient and captured vessels so as to observe the effects of a nuclear explosion. It was called Operation Crossroads, and Curtis LeMay was once more in charge. There were Japanese and German ships that offered no further use, as well as a few American ships that were damaged or outdated. As it happened, the central vessel of that fleet, painted bright orange and named *Scarlet Fever* for the exercise, was the old-time dreadnought USS *Nevada*. As in so many such things, where a state has so little to boast of on the national scene, Nevada was very proud of its battleship. The *Nevada* had been launched at Quincy Yards in July 1914. Among those present were Assistant Secretary of the Navy Franklin Roosevelt, the governor of Nevada, Tasker Oddie,* Nevada senator Key Pittman, and Oddie's ten-year-old niece, Eleanor Ann Siebert, who actually christened the vessel. A little less than two years later, the *Nevada* was commissioned, the most powerful warship in the U.S. Navy.

Though it was never fired upon in World War I, it was the escort ship when Woodrow Wilson sailed to the Versailles Peace Conference. Thereafter, it was hit and damaged at Pearl Harbor, and it escaped only by sailing past the wrecked *Arizona*. Repaired, it served in the Aleutians and then gave supporting fire at the D day landing. It was sent to the Pacific, where it took part in the Okinawa campaign and was struck by a kamikaze aircraft.

---

* Tasker L. Oddie (1870–1950), a Brooklyn lawyer who came to Nevada in 1898, played a large part in the development of the Tonopah silver fields. He was governor from 1911 to 1914, and a Republican senator from 1921 to 1933, eventually defeated by Pat McCarran.

By 1946, it had no future except to be the target for another atom bomb. The blast did severe damage to the structure of the ship but did not sink it. The ship was towed back to Pearl Harbor, no matter that it was badly contaminated by radiation. As such, it remained at Pearl Harbor in a kind of quarantine until July 1948, when it was towed off the shore of southwest Hawaii and filled with explosives. Even after that explosion, the *Nevada* took artillery fire from ships, and fighter attack, before torpedo bombers at last sank it.

For a state that had no coast, this was a proud and defiant fate for a battleship, and it was enough to remind America's nuclear thinkers that Nevada might be useful one day.

35. Helldorado Days

IT WOULD BE HARD TO EXAGGERATE THE DIFFERENCE MADE by Hoover Dam, not just to life in Nevada but also to that more potent matter, prospects. The thought of the dam could turn dry, rational, and very intelligent men into boosters, as witness Richard G. Lillard in his excellent and important book, *Desert Challenge*, published in 1942, which is about as good a turning point as you'll find. Lillard wrote, "Boulder Dam is to Americans what Chartres Cathedral was to Europeans, what the Temple at Karnak was to ancient Egyptians. The clean, functional lines, the colossal beauty, and impersonal mass and strength of the dam itself are as symbolic as real."

In fact, the news of the dam was more far-reaching than Chartres or Karnak, for Roosevelt's formal opening was broadcast over every radio network, and photographs of the awesome structure appeared in all daily papers. What the news meant was that the desert was no longer, or not simply, dangerous—a place where civilized people died, like the two men at the end of Erich von Stroheim's film *Greed*. Nor was the dead land neglected any longer. It had been lifted up by national enterprise and attention. Yet maybe more important still, Nevada had been dignified.

Until at least 1931, and in many ways thereafter, there were those in the United States who reckoned Nevada did not matter, that it was beyond relevance or significance, that its very presence marred or diminished the idea of the union. Those with such feelings said that Nevada had gained statehood by a trick; that it was no more than a brief-lived silver mine that had bribed and bullied its way into the nation, only to end up corrupting the "noble" worth of silver. It was a place of outlaws and outcasts, "worse than California." There were many in Washington, and the East as a whole, who doubted that Nevada deserved any voice in the nation's governance.

Lillard quotes a Yale professor, William H. Brewer, who was opposed to statehood for Nevada:

> I see no elements here to make a state. It has mines of some marvelous richness, but it has nothing else, nothing to call people here to live and find homes. Every man of culture hopes to make his fortune here, but to enjoy it in more favored lands. The climate is bad, water is bad, land a desert, and the population floating.

The facts of the matter would lend credence to the professor's gloom. The silver did run out. There were gold finds to come, but in nearly every case there occurred a frantic routine of discovery—boom—ghost town in not much more than a decade. Reno had its roots, but Las Vegas was a place that might have been erased by flood or drought, or even wind. Never forget that in the 1880s the population of the state fell from 62,000 to 47,000; and then again, between 1910 and 1920, the number dropped from 81,875 to 77,407. Mineral production had fallen precipitately in the years after 1880, and it was not back on par again until 1906. There was another terrible fall in the figures in the early 1930s.

There were even times when some argued that Nevada's representation in Congress be abandoned. The *Chicago Tribune* ran an editorial that said, "The silver-mines which made her all she was have been exhausted. She has no other mineral wealth. She has no agriculture resources. She has nothing to attract people; and, as a consequence, she is flickering out."

Nevada behaved like the desperado its enemies pointed to. To get hold of people and their money—even their residence—somehow, it made divorce easy and gambling normal. All over the rest of America, there were sermons, editorials, and earnest opinions that this was damnation and outrage writ large in the sand. There are still many people who say or feel the same things, just as there are thoughtful people—some as close as California—who have never visited Las Vegas because they know they would loathe it. Nor am I inclined to give up the proposition that among the many practices and ideas that have been taken and pioneered in Nevada, we should never forget the one called "the end of the world." You do not have to play it tragically. Indeed, in our time, Las Vegas has helped find the right camp tone of voice. But black humor is often America's soundest social criticism. There was a song to convey the fraud and convenience of the upstart state:

Nevada, 'tis of thee,
Sweet state of liberty,
Of thee I sing.
State where our fathers flee:
State that sets mothers free—
Marriage, because of thee,
Hath lost its sting.

Against all that, Hoover Dam was an example of engineering vision and progressive genius being allied to the barely rewarded toil of common men to control nature for the benefit of society. The great enterprise had brought several thousand workers and a lot of money into the southern Nevada area. Boulder City had cost $2 million of government money to build, and it had housed as many as eight thousand at the height of the dam work. Run jointly by Six Companies, Inc., and the Bureau of Reclamation, it was a strange model town—"it is as spick and span as though it were in charge of Dutch housewives" declared a guidebook in 1940, when the bureau was in sole charge. They kept out gambling and ensured that property could be leased only on short-term agreements. And so by 1940, the population of Boulder City had fallen to about 2,500.

Nevertheless, between 1930 and 1940, the population of Las Vegas rose from 5,165 to 8,422. Its railroad importance increased when the line was taken over by the Union Pacific. In 1937, the railroad company struck an artesian well that produced 3.5 million gallons a day—the desert township had more water than it knew what to do with, as well as power from the dam. And people came to see the new wonder, and to look at the waters of Lake Mead. Most of them made the drive from Los Angeles, and gradually the idea of Vegas as a weekend getaway place developed. With gambling, of course.

In Vegas itself, there were several small casinos, all of them less sophisticated than the big establishments in Reno, and all suggestive of a frontier saloon. They were the Northern, the Hotel Apache, the Boulder Club, and the Las Vegas Club, owned by J. Kell Houssels, a businessman who believed in confining the action to the general area of Fremont Street.

These places were crowded with citizens of Las Vegas, cowboys, mine workers, and tourists. But the gambling business was nowhere near established as surefire. For too many of the gamblers were cautious and ill-paid. None of the casinos was spectacular or an attraction in and of itself. For no one yet had the funds to invest, or the vision that a hotel-casino might offer an entirely different way of life—a modern way. Indeed, the decor and the style of the Las Vegas casinos in the 1930s was a throwback—it conjured up frontier days, the prospectors' experience, and the general look of a shabby Western.

That mood was captured in the invention of Helldorado Days, a town celebration meant to attract tourists and keep the spirit of the past alive. Begun in 1935, the April festivity involved the putting on of cowboy costumes, riding horses—indoors and out—growing beards, rodeos, folksinging, "cowboy poetry," even, parades of western tableaux, the reenactment of scenes from frontier history, and an overall air of nostalgia and the archaic, enough to make Ben Siegel or Steve Wynn sick to their stomachs. Helldorado went on until the early 1960s, and it was a huge attraction, but historically it served to show us how little Las Vegas had yet foreseen its streamlined destiny.

However, there were signs. In 1931, the Meadows Club opened to the east of Vegas and on the road to Boulder City. It was a supper club, with dancing, but it had a gaming license and it was owned and directed by Tony Cornero, a man who has as much claim on legend as Ben Siegel.

Antonio Stralla Cornero had been a bootlegger in the age of Prohibition, bringing the stuff into the greater Los Angeles area from Mexico or Canada. He liked boats: Whenever he was arrested, he declared himself a mariner. While Tony was in jail, his brother Frank ran the business, but all agreed that Tony was the brains, the best-looking, and a class dresser. George Raft would have been lucky to have been offered the part, for Tony Cornero was a pioneer for the modern gangster.

The Meadows showed his acumen. It was a suave joint, with waiters in white jackets and bow ties, and a smart western style of decor that might have been borrowed from San Simeon (Tony claimed that he often ran liquor at the pier there for William Randolph Hearst). I'm looking at a picture of the place, and it's full of smart young people; you even wonder if there's a movie star there. And there's a guy in corespondent shoes, pale slacks, and a white shirt and tie who could be Siegel himself. But there's something else about the picture that's arresting. It looks as if the place is air-conditioned. Everyone seems at ease, whereas in just about every other 1930s interior photograph of Las Vegas, you can feel the stupor, smell the sweat, and sense that absolute atmospheric problem that confronted the city. I've never been able to find out whether the Meadows pioneered air conditioning, but Tony Cornero was the sort of guy who refused to sweat in public. So draw your own conclusions. Cornero was in and out of Vegas in the 1930s, but his real preoccupation then was gambling boats off the coast of Santa Monica or Long Beach. Tony claimed that if his ships—notably the *Rex* or the *Monte Carlo*—kept beyond the three-mile limit, he was safe. And so he ferried celebrities and gamblers out there by motorboat, and made somewhere in the region of $1 million a year until Attorney General Earl Warren put him out of business.

Thereafter, the details of Cornero's career are uncertain. The Meadows closed when Boulder City went quiet, but Cornero seems to have worked as a casino manager in Vegas during the 1940s. When he died in 1955, it was in Vegas, playing craps, as he planned and dreamed of a place of his own, the Stardust.

Earl Warren is a significant player in this story, for he represented a general move against the gambling that had been easy to find for the well-to-do in Los Angeles throughout the 1930s, not just on the Cornero boats but also at places like the Clover Club, off Sunset. Warren's attitude helped push the business and the market for gambling farther east, along what was then Highway 91, the road from Los Angeles to Las Vegas.

In 1938, Guy McAfee, a onetime Los Angeles policeman, had learned enough to open a roadhouse, which was located a few miles short of Las Vegas. It was called the Pair-O-Dice, and it did not last long. But McAfee stumbled into history. Recalling Sunset Strip in Los Angeles, he called the empty highway in front of his roadhouse "the Strip." Not long thereafter, however, a bruised McAfee moved downtown, where he opened the Golden Nugget.

Clifford Jones had come to Nevada, from Missouri, with his family in 1931. At the age of eighteen, he actually worked at the Hoover Dam site, then went away to the University of Missouri to study law. By 1938, qualified, he was back in Vegas. In 1941, for a 2.5 percent interest in the casino, he gave away space beneath his law office for the new Pioneer Club. In time, he got this interest up to 5 percent and established himself as the principal lawyer for the casino business. Later on, he would rise to the rank of major under Patton and became lieutenant governor for the state—as well as someone implicated in the interests of organized crime and the casino business.

The Pioneer, on Fremont Street, would become famous for the 60-foot high, neon-lit figure of Vegas Vic, a cowboy smoking a cigarette and pointing down with his thumb at the establishment below. Jones's law office came just about at the level of Vic's rolled-over boot top.

In the same year, 1941, Jones took a 5 percent interest in the El Cortez, an establishment on Sixth Street. That was owned by Marion Hicks, who had also been in the gambling-boat business off the coast of California.

But that was not all. Nineteen forty-one also saw the opening of El Rancho Vegas, owned by Tom Hull, a California hotelier. He elected to build outside the city limits because it was cheaper, and he had the luck to find good water on the land. The El Rancho was, for its time, sophisticated and exclusive. It featured a pool and private bungalows, as well as the peace and quiet of a south-of-town location. It was on the ridiculous "Strip" that Guy McAfee had named.

In short, the casino business was very active in the late thirties and early forties. But it was vulnerable. A lot of places came and went quickly, put out of business by the competition or by their owners' recklessness. No one with real money had yet taken the decision that it was a business to be in, and all of them might have taken fright if they'd known for sure that the United States soon would be at war. After all, a war would take away most of the young men, the most natural gamblers, and it would surely frighten off tourism and the taste for weekend excursions. So it might have been, but war would make Las Vegas, just as surely as Hoover Dam had given it its chance.

36. Mercury

The gateway to Mercury is like a tollbooth where vehicles coming and going must stop for security checks. The exit lanes include automatic radiation-detection equipment so that no vehicle may leave the Test Site with too high a count. The sign on the roof of the checkpoint has drawings of mountain ranges and three lines of type:

U.S. DEPARTMENT OF ENERGY
NEVADA TEST SITE
AN ENVIRONMENTAL RESEARCH PARK

Whereas the first two lines are unquestionably matters of information and labeling, the third is something else—a hope, a myth, or even the kind of insouciance with which a prospector might have called his piece of scrubland El Dorado or Eureka before he'd found anything.

The same description, apparently, is used at the Savannah River Site in South Carolina and the Hanford Site in Washington, those early adjuncts to Los Alamos, the places where uranium and plutonium were isolated and prepared.

All these sites, of course, were once so secret that they were of the kind officially denied by governments, like the Groom Lake base, or Area 51. Anyone confident that they existed, however, and able to drive up to their gates in the forties and fifties, and well after that, would have been barred. No use of the word *park* would have cut any ice, despite its air of something nationally owned where the citizen has a right to roam at will.

Even now, visitors at the Test Site are carefully controlled; they are taken here to specific areas and told what they are seeing, but they are not allowed to go to other areas or to make up their own minds. For good reason. There are "theres" on the Test Site where no one should go—for their health's sake. Though, doubtless, if some unlikely, long-odds accident got you there, there would be people with equipment and clothes for getting you out, whether you were alive or dead, and provisions for proper scientific research into the effects (on you), research so stringent that your body might not be returned to your dear ones for conventional burial. This is not paranoia or mischief making. Rather, it's a way of saying that there are perilous places on the Test Site, dire damage in the atmosphere, and every reason for the authorities to watch carefully as the subjects die. "Research" would require as much.

That is not what the word means on the sign, or wants to convey. No, I think that the attempt is to say, Well, once upon a time, things happened here that, more or less, were carried out as tests (as well as warnings to others). That's reasonably accurate. Bombs were exploded to test how well they fared in storage; to measure the effects upon large solid structures — everything from buildings to pieces of military equipment; to see how livestock fared; and to see how well troops performed in the rockets' red glare.

None of those things are what most of us understand the word *environmental* to mean. We take that to cover the land, the water, the air, the plants that grow, and the animals that live in a place. But since those were secondary, or neglected, "targets," in much of the early testing, the rather recent adoption of the designation Environmental Research Park must stand as an example of the nerve, the affectless ingenuity, and recasting abilities of government. Is there even some poker-faced black humor in applying that label to this peculiarly abused bit of land? After all, Nevada is the state where atmospherics and wishful thinking have also influenced official road signs — THE LONELIEST ROAD or THE EXTRA-TERRESTRIAL HIGHWAY, for instance.

The spirited naming of things and places is a tradition in Nevada, and I think it arises to counter that immense seeping pressure by which all places might be Nowhere, Unknown, Unnamed. That's why mining towns were given such ecstatic bull-market titles, names that now float ironically above ground that has been nearly fully reclaimed by the desert. That's why, in many thriving places, there's a nearby hill, outcrop, or mountain with a large white initial letter made of sun-blanched rocks, the first letter of the name of the place. To remind you where you are every fresh morning? Of course, this naïve practice is all over the West — there's a sign saying HOLLYWOOD over what is supposed to be a sophisticated metropolis — but the scheme is as heartfelt in Nevada as the neon that says MIRAGE, or whatever. It's a nervy, cocky gesture to the self, like Vegas Vic saying, This is the place as his thumb juts downward. It's like the sign that says WINNEMUCCA—AND PROUD OF IT, the great testament to the worry of all Winnemuccans that one day their tugging wind could just sweep the place away.

The busload of day-trippers has to get out at the Security Patrol Building—which, inside, is as pleasant, anonymous, and shabby as the waiting room at a busy HMO—for badge checking. No visitor to the Test Site can be admitted without a photo ID check-in and the issuing of a badge for the day. Our bags are checked, too, as at airports, for anything like cameras, telescopes, or weapons. There's time in this procedure to stand outside the office in the sun and get a sense of the township named Mercury.

The place was built by the government, on a good budget, with every thought of permanency. Military bases know no other way, and so the buildings have their foundation slabs; they are plumbed and wired in; there are roads with names; the various buildings are numbered; and everything is kept in an orderly, tidy way.

Nevertheless, Mercury begins to resemble the Nevadan phenomenon, the failed boom. Whereas, in its heydays—the 1950s, and then again in the 1980s—it might have had as many as ten thousand people (some of them resident, but many more bused in and out on a daily basis), now the staff has dropped below two thousand.

In one sense, there's satisfaction in that, for Mercury did its job. It was a testing place for weapons, and a signal of such military and political determination that its only evident enemy, the Soviet Union, cracked and broke up. And so the prolonged readiness for war, and in many cases the feeling out of aspects of it that were unknown and/or unthinkable, not only deterred the enemy from making such a war but eventually helped strain its economy and then undermine its political will.

Still, Mercury has the desolate air of an unoccupied place in many parts. It was a small city, ready to be self-sufficient. It had a power station and a water-purification plant, as well as a ten-bed hospital. There were dormitory huts capable of housing a thousand people. There were spacious parking lots for workers who chose to drive in from Vegas, for the buses that were available, and for the fleet of security vehicles that patrolled the entire Test Site. A running track was put in so that the security guards could keep fit. There is a gymnasium, a pool, a bowling alley with a snack bar (there are five lanes for bowling), tennis courts, and a softball field—there used to be a league, with teams from the different sections, so Security could play Analytical Chemistry, and so on. There is a cafeteria, large enough to feed several thousand people. There is a movie

theater. And then there are all the buildings for administration, mainte-
nance, storage, and warehousing—well over two hundred sheds, huts, or
Quonsets, all in as neutral a style as possible.

The great majority of these are now unoccupied, yet maintained. The
cafeteria functions still, but it is notable that it does not cater to the tour
buses—that's why visitors have to bring their own lunches. The buildings
do not lapse into disrepair. In an emergency, most of Mercury could be
made functional again very quickly. But it would take longer to bring in
the personnel, the scientists and the technicians whose job it was to
mount and monitor tests, all of which, since 1963 and the Limited Test
Ban Treaty, had been conducted underground. In the years following
1950—the Test Site opened in December of that year—one hundred
atmospheric tests of such weapons were conducted there, and over seven
hundred underground.

On September 24, 1996, even underground tests ended, when President Clinton signed the Comprehensive Test Ban. But that presents problems to the military and the Department of Energy, who give these official
reasons why some testing should continue:

(1) To periodically proof-test weapons taken from stockpiles to
assure reliability. (2) To test new safety features to assure the best
available safeguards to prevent accidental destruction or unautho-
rized use. (3) To test new weapons designs that are lighter, smaller,
more efficient, and/or that produce less fallout, and (4) To determine the effects of explosion-produced radiation on military hardware, such as communications, electronics, nose cones and other
components.

Such arguments are plausible, and sensible. Still, in terms of its old,
regular activities, Mercury is dormant now. There has been talk within
the government of closing the establishment, though that does not necessarily mean turning it back to the people or making it accessible as a park.
For there are those things or places that could not be responsibly given
up; there may even be some that the government would rather not yet
own up to.

So Mercury is poised between purpose and ghost town. As such, it
makes a striking contrast with Henderson, the modern city that stands
between Lake Mead and the road from Vegas to Hoover Dam. In 1940,
Henderson was unknown, and the place was desert as bare as the place
that would become Mercury. But in 1941, even before Pearl Harbor, the

government took steps to locate the Basic Magnesium plant there. Magnesium, it was clear, would be a vital component of the aircraft required in the event of war. And though this was not appreciated as quickly, the metal was what burned most brightly and savagely in the incendiary raids that were carried out over cities like Tokyo and Dresden.

There were large magnesite and brucite ore deposits around Gabbs, about fifty miles northwest of Tonopah. Basic Magnesium was a part of the Ohio Company, Basic Refactories, which owned the Gabbs deposits. The government contracted it to set up in what would be Henderson, using hydroelectric power from Hoover Dam. The plant was built and went into operation in the summer of 1942. The work there had cost $150 million, about three times the cost of Hoover Dam. The plant occupied a full square mile, and it had no equal anywhere in the world. Twelve thousand people were brought in to build it, and the beginnings of the town, as such; it was the largest single project that Nevada had known since the Comstock days.

The work was managed with astonishing speed, but there were political problems. There were union disputes and fears that the dramatic influx of working people would shift the electoral balance of Clark County from Republican to Democrat. Senator Patrick McCarran, a Democrat, acquitted himself very adroitly in making the changes without undue hostility or difficulty. Remember that in 1942, say, twelve thousand newcomers more than doubled the population of Las Vegas. Henderson was ideally placed in terms of Hoover Dam, for turning the magnesite oxide into metal required enormous amounts of energy. But it was a ferociously hot place, where many people became ill from the chloroform fumes. Indeed, Henderson was palpably a more dangerous place than anywhere on the Nevada Test Site.

The plant was an incredible success. By 1943, it was producing far more magnesium than the country or the war needed. A year later, production was stopped because the stockpile was so great. Henderson faltered. Basic Magnesium moved away, but then the state of Nevada, and Senator McCarran again, took decisive action. They decided to do all they could to maintain the city. In 1947, the state legislature approved purchasing the plant from the U.S. government and the facilities were then sold out to private industry. There was much talk of corruption in this process. Norman Blitz, a developer who had been bringing millionaires into the tax-free haven of Nevada, offered to buy the plant himself (and for his interests). But in the end, McCarran and the state kept the process in their own hands.

And so war's crisis played a vital part in urban development. The population of Henderson dropped; it was hardly a place for people to live without pressing reason. But the wiseacre talk of the grandest ghost town of all was averted. By 1950, Henderson was on the move again. Today, it has close to 100,000 inhabitants, and as such it is third to Las Vegas and Reno in the population centers of the state. It is also, whether it likes it or not, something like a suburb of Las Vegas; one day, for sure, the two will be joined by the steady sprawl of shopping malls, motels, fast-food places, and low-rent casinos.

Henderson, plus the other local wartime developments—like the opening of the Nellis Gunnery Base (on what would become the Test Site)—were crucial in turning Las Vegas from a frontier town into the start of a modern city. For as we come to describe, and decide, what made Las Vegas, there is no denying the way in which in the wartime years the population of the area had doubled with servicemen and industrial workers who had money burning holes in their pockets. These were people with little or no interest in the "old days." They were the new men, who reckoned they had won the war. They were ready. From 1940 to 1950, the population of Las Vegas would go from 8,422 to 24,624. And by 1950, the whole state was at 160,000—about the number of hotel beds estimated for Las Vegas by the year 2000.

37. Bugsy

THERE ARE THOSE WHO LAMENT THAT THERE IS NO STATUE of Benjamin Siegel anywhere in Las Vegas. After all, it is argued, didn't he invent the place? Hasn't enough time passed for a little wry honor to fall upon his dapper, shy shoulders? We don't have to buy all the explanations to be touched by the plea. In the invention of Las Vegas, Siegel played a vital part certainly worth remembering, yet it is hardly what the legend says.

Indeed, in any contest for such a statue, I would pass over such contenders as an eternally poised Bugsy on a stool at the end of some polished bar, his blue eyes estimating the trade; or even a sofa in the great lobby of a casino, with the Bug's corpse sprawled and shattered—so kids could have their picture taken sitting beside him—and one of the blue eyes (traced by a helpful dotted line) mashed into the tiled floor behind him. No, I would have the statue on the Strip somewhere, with the figure in the act of stepping off the curb, but twisted around, as if, while he made his businesslike way, some great noise or disturbance had startled him. He should be saying, "What the hell was that?" and he should be caught out, stranded, pickled.

Ben Siegel was born in the Williamsburg district of Brooklyn on February 28, 1906, and never finished school. But there are ways of life in America in which school is a rather defeatist path ahead. Siegel was out on the streets. He had a gang by the time he was fourteen, and they were experts at fast, minor robberies, rolling drunks and taking their wallets, and getting into the special booze business that was introduced by the Volstead Act. Siegel was violent, reckless, and quick-tempered: He got the name "Bug" or "Bugsy" because he was unpredictable and kind of crazy when he was roused. People were afraid of him, despite his sweet good looks. Yet Ben himself didn't want to be upset, out of breath, or out of control. He wanted to look good and cool. It was a mixture of talents and urges that drew him to the ladies, and—just because the "Bug" would jump out—every now and then he got in the way of rape charges. At the same time, he had married a childhood sweetheart, Esta Krakower, with whom he had a bunch of children. He moved the family out to Braden Road in Scarsdale, even though he kept a suite for himself at the Waldorf-Astoria. He was a success, and he ran an effective criminal enterprise with a friend from his childhood, Meyer Lansky. In their time, they had been rivals of and enemies to the Italian mob in New York—the gangs of Albert Anastasia, Johnny Torrio, Lucky Luciano, Frank Costello, and Joe Adonis—but as business prospered, so there was a politic merging of Jewish and Italian interests. The result was that thing called "organized" crime, as if anything is ever really or finally organized when it comes from the wellsprings of human nature and social congress. Still, the word *organized* says so much about our hopes and fears, and it addresses the rather romantic look often to be seen in the eyes of Ben Siegel.

For the *organized* in the term *organized crime* was a dream in which order, system, thoroughness—the net, let's call it—might one day purge or drive out those rowdy elements of crime—the violence, the bad publicity, the lack of class and refinement—and make it indistinguishable from all those lawful and respectable ways of running things.

Siegel branched out. He was often in Los Angeles during the 1930s, as if he sensed opportunities there that were novel compared with those on the East Coast. Did he ever wonder if he could have made it in movies himself? Or was he just eager to renew the friendship he had begun earlier, in New York, with the actor George Raft? It's an intriguing notion—as much a scenario, maybe, as actual history—that Raft (an uninspired actor and a rather frozen face) was hot in movies because he was reckoned to be either an ex-gangster or the friend of gangsters. On the other hand, Siegel was the authentic rogue who sometimes dreamed of being a player in show business. Let it just be said that show business and organized crime are worlds that have often leaned together, like climbing plants that thrive best when near each other.

There was work to do in Los Angeles: Siegel was introducing the Racing Wire network (an electronic system that let operators know race results before bettors), which had already facilitated gambling in the East. He became an investor in Tony Cornero's gambling ships, and once he prevailed upon Raft to borrow money from his agent, Myron Selznick, to help finance the boats. Siegel also had a small share of the Clover Club, the movie world's favorite gambling haunt in town. In addition to that, he became a minor celebrity on the social circuit, a handsome charmer who had that little extra clout of being rumored to be dangerous. He also ran a protection business for extras, being paid off by the extras and the studios to ensure crowd scenes.

Then, as war came, Siegel formed the California Metals Company, a gatherer of scrap metal for resale in the war effort. As far as anyone could tell, it was a solid, legitimate business. Why not? Siegel was patriotic, and you could make a fortune in scrap in those days. The wire service and the scrap business made odd companions. Yet organized crime was moving up in the world, and in many indirect ways the government was now dealing with it. Mickey Cohen, a Los Angeles outlaw attached to the Siegel enterprises, was impressed by the Phoenix office, headed by Gus Greenbaum, where mobsters engaged in earnest telephone calls with senators, all in splendid air-conditioned rooms. No sweat.

Siegel had noticed Las Vegas early on. He went there a good deal, and in the early forties he had modest investments in the El Cortez, the El Dorado, the Las Vegas Club, and the Golden Nugget. He knew the people who owned and ran the casinos; he was on good terms with Tony Cornero; he knew the criminal fraternity in Reno. All of which is to say that he can't quite be labeled an inventor.

But he was smart enough to recognize that Vegas was lagging behind Reno. He saw the dramatic increase in local population in the late thirties and early forties. He discovered that the legal controls on operation in Nevada were minimal. And he had that sort of general optimism that reckoned the war would be won one day, at which point Americans were going to expect good times. Plus, he had seen how much the rough mix of Hollywood style and air conditioning could improve on the old-fashioned western roadhouses that presently passed for casinos in Las Vegas. The words may never have formulated in his head. Siegel was not especially eloquent. But he had a vision, or he felt the need for a kind of fantastic luxury, like that of the screen, as if you were living in your dreams.

So the point about his originality is not quite that one day, driving in the desert with Mickey Cohen and his mistress, Virginia Hill, he suddenly thought of or saw his great casino. As a matter of fact, he was driving with Moe Sedway (a veteran out of the Lansky gang) in the area where the El Rancho and the Last Frontier already stood. So it's not that he parked his De Soto wagon, stomped off into the infinite sands, and imagined a place there. In fact, the land he chose was closer to downtown Vegas than either the El Rancho or the Last Frontier. But what he saw was a completely different kind of place. And since it was a summer day, maybe 120 degrees in the shade, he thought of air conditioning, too. What he said—you don't have to take this as gospel—was, "We're going to make Reno seem like a whistle-stop!" There wasn't even nothing there. The ground he wanted already sported a wrecked motel that had come to grief. And Virginia Hill wasn't there, either.

Even at that, it's doubtful that Siegel got the idea on his own. A lot of the talk had started with Billy Wilkerson, who owned the trade paper *The Hollywood Reporter*, as well as the Café Trocadero and Ciro's, successful nightclubs on the Sunset Strip. It was Wilkerson who preached the allure of a Las Vegas palace that would have a floor show with top Hollywood stars performing.

In September 1945, the land and the motel owned by Margaret Folsom were transferred first to Moe Sedway and then to the Nevada Projects Corporation. The work was done by a leading Hollywood lawyer, Greg Bautzer, who represented Wilkerson. Siegel approached the Los Angeles architects Stodelman & Russell, got a budgetary proposal ($1 million), and went about finding investors. The group he secured included himself, Meyer Lansky, Billy Wilkerson, Charles Straus (a banker from Phoenix), Louis Pokros (another member of Lansky's enterprises), and the Rothberg brothers, who were distillers. That does not mean that there were not other silent partners allied to the mob.

Siegel's vision to this point was touched by brilliance. He was the first person to see that the scale, atmosphere, and indoor climate of Las Vegas had been all wrong. He saw that the casino-hotel must be larger than life. And not least, he saw that it was a providence beyond anything they deserved for their business interests that needed money laundering. For Las Vegas as he saw it—and as it has come to be—was an undocumented cash business beyond anyone's dreams, with girls and booze and the loosest state laws anyone could hope for.

Siegel had been absolved of murder charges in Los Angeles in 1940—the victim was Harry Greenberg, and a key witness happened to fall out of a window—but still the Nevadan authorities readily agreed to his getting a gaming license, if he could build his place. He was going to call it the Flamingo, after one of Virginia Hill's nicknames. She had other love names, but they would hardly be suitable, fifty feet, in neon.

Once the building began, however, Siegel was always looking the wrong way. Organized crime may have neglected the principles of sound management, and the guy from Brooklyn and Los Angeles often found himself the victim of Nevadan cunning and chutzpah. The planning of the Flamingo was also vulnerable to his own chronic second-guessing; he changed his mind whenever a new idea occurred to him. Even at his new level of the grandiose, the place was intended to have no more than ninety-two bedrooms. But no one yet had really built a modern hotel-casino, and in the immediate postwar period, there was great difficulty getting the expensive materials Siegel envisaged.

Ground was broken in December 1945, with Del Webb of Phoenix in charge of the construction. Senator McCarran again used his influence in procuring some elusive materials, no matter that he had to deprive ordinary citizens to get them. Marble was imported from Mexico and Italy, and some said that Lucky Luciano himself—no great friend to Siegel—had personally supervised the shipment. But in Nevada, in the desert, there were stories of supplies being delivered one day, stolen back the next, and then redelivered and recharged. Naturally enough, no records were kept. Siegel was in the process of being divorced by his wife, Esta (she went to Reno), and he was keeping close company with Virginia Hill, a bold, aggressive woman who had ties to several other mobsters, and who had a tremendous innate capacity for collecting quantities of raw cash. To this day, it is unclear how loyal she was to Siegel, whether she was stealing from him along with everyone else, or just putting money aside for a rainy day. She and Ben were married in Mexico in the fall of 1946, and the legend has them as a beloved couple. But, in truth, when the crisis came for Siegel, Hill was far away in Europe. Which tends to suggest that by then Siegel believed in the Flamingo rather more than in the woman who had inspired the name. He may have seen that events were out of control, and that there was only one available fall guy. In which case, he would be known for the Flamingo.

It was set to open on December 26, 1946. But very few of the hotel rooms were ready in time. When Siegel was told that a great fountain in the forecourt—meant to be floodlit—had been chosen as a place by a cat to have its kittens, he ordered the animals to be left alone. A gambler never risks his fate with cats. The weather was bad. Only a few of his promised Hollywood stars showed up. There was a story that William Randolph Hearst was opposed to the venture and had tried to impede it. Still, the Flamingo opened, with Jimmy Durante as its opening act. George Raft made the trip, and other noted names included George Sanders, Charles Coburn, and Sonny Tufts. But those were not big names. Siegel was still learning: He gave the order, not friendly to locals, that no man should wear a hat, but he had to be told by Virginia Hill that he should put on a black tie and a tuxedo himself.

More or less, at this point, the Flamingo had cost or consumed $4 million. There was no way for Lansky and Luciano to see that as anything but a racket, or a measure of Siegel's incompetence. Worse was to follow. In the first few days of operation, the house lost badly, to the extent of $300,000. The only big loser among customers was George Raft, who (not content with loaning money to Siegel) dropped some $60,000 at the tables.

This must be the old Las Vegas speaking between the lines. It was natural for the old-time westerners to resent the newcomer, his arrogance and his slipshod, big-shot ways. They saw a sucker coming, and they provided most of the croupiers and table people. In Las Vegas, there has never been a proper way for the house to lose, even if a new casino is happy to have a few publicity-ready winners when it begins.

Early in the New Year, Siegel closed the Flamingo. He had exhausted the mob as a money source. He was scrambling, and heavily in debt, but he got the hotel to the point where the rooms could be occupied. The reopening was on March 1, 1947, and now there were customers. But the curse at the tables persisted—in the first few months of its existence, the Flamingo is said to have lost nearly three-quarters of a million dollars. Not all of that was at the tables, but it's likely that $500,000 of the red ink was due to Nevadans who knew enough to let the suckers win.

In February, there had been a meeting at the Nacional in Havana, a reunion for Lucky Luciano and a lot of his old friends. Sinatra sang at the hotel, and arrived with a loaded briefcase. The powers met and agreed that Siegel was history.

Meyer Lansky visited the Flamingo. He never gambled and hardly left his room. No one knows what he said to Siegel, though it is clear that Lansky was his last friend and defender in the organization. Maybe they just looked at the books: The bottom line for what the Flamingo had cost so far was $6 million. Surely Ben said it would all work out, and Lansky may have been sharp enough to guess the accuracy in that prediction. For the Flamingo was splendid. People liked being there. What did it need apart from fresh croupiers? It needed a touch of drama.

In June, Siegel was summoned to Los Angeles. He went to the North Linden Drive home of Virginia Hill—she was still in Europe, but she said he could use her place. On June 20, he dined out with a few friends and then went back to the house. It was a little after nine in the evening. He went into the living room and smelled flowers, but there were no flowers in the house. It was the smell of jasmine from outside drifting through an open window. He sat on the sofa, in line with the window, and he was shot to pieces by carbine fire from the flower beds. One eye was knocked across the room, with a few eyelashes still attached. There were nine bullets, and he was a mess, as well as dead, pretty no longer. Within the hour, in Nevada, three men, one of them Moe Sedway, went into the Flamingo and took over. In the next year, it made a profit of $4 million. Why? House rules, for one thing, but the fatal fascination of Bugsy's eye, too. It was 1947, after all, the era of film noir, when more Americans were disposed to see sinister shadows in the desert light.

38. Firings

At Mercury, for a moment, the tour bus pauses before we go deep into the Test Site. The vehicle is struck broadside by a wind coming up from the southwest—a swirl of dust is driven across the road in front of us. At most times of year on the high desert, there is a wind moving the top surface of the land along, and most of the time, that wind comes from the same, habitual quarter. It is a prevailing wind. The bus rocks and sways as the wind bends around it. You can imagine a hot wind that might pick up even a loaded bus and drop it down on the other side of the road.

At Alamogordo, in July 1945, there was great concern over the weather. Monday, July 16, was the scheduled date for the test firing of the atom bomb, the first time such an event had been attempted. There were winds and even thunderstorms up to a few hours before the 5:30 a.m. detonation. No one was entirely confident what those conditions might do to the fireball, and the thing called "fallout"—the scattering of detritus from the explosion. There were observation trenches already dug, twenty miles to the northwest and ten miles to the southwest. They would be full of scientists, observers, and sightseers, who had a right, they felt, to trust the prevailing wind. Yet no one could tell for sure whether the explosion might not alter and rearrange such normal things as wind.

They went ahead because General Groves had been given reports by his meteorologist, Jack Hubbard, that the weather would abate not long before 5:30. So it proved, and so word was able to be sent to President Truman in Potsdam—the conference there began on July 17—that the device had worked. But there had been other winds steadily in motion, from west to east, too, so Stalin was not surprised.

There were several uncertainties among those watching and responsible for Trinity. The scientists wagered over the explosive yield, and guesses went from 300 to 45,000 tons. Some reckoned the device might not work, or might perform in ways not foreseen. General Groves had been told that strong winds from the south could carry radioactive fallout to Albuquerque or Santa Fe, even back to the scientific base at Los Alamos; winds from the north could threaten Las Cruces, New Mexico, and El Paso, Texas. Whereas the prevailing southwest wind had nothing very much in its path except a small town named Roswell, and then a lot of nothing all the way to Amarillo (unless you lived in the nothing).

There was one more uncertainty: In the weeks before the Trinity firing, several of the scientists focused their fears on the use of the device (it was called "the device" to assist security and dispel the bad dreams), the thing they had been working toward for at least two years. For it was quite evident to all of them now that the military was in charge of the program.

Early on, the scientists had been spurred by the reports that Hitler's Germany might be working toward the same kind of device. Those reports were deliberately exaggerated by the military authorities; real intelligence (obtained in 1944) that the Germans were far behind in the "race" and were not seriously engaged in it was withheld. When the war in Europe ended, there was temporary relief among the scientists that their secret would not be needed now. But then their schedules were not altered, and the drastic scenarios for invading Japan became the new imperative. Some of the scientists were deeply alarmed at what seemed like the inevitability built into the process, that making the device could only lead, logically, to using it, and that no specific decision seemed necessary. In that way were consciences protected.

They knew that radiation was dangerous. There had even been talk among the scientists—who could be bloodthirsty in their inquisitive way—about taking radioactive waste, scattering it on the enemy, and introducing it into the German food supply. Oppenheimer himself reckoned on a plan, using strontium, sufficient to kill half a million Germans. But that was 1943, and it was nearly abstract thinking.

In the movie *Fat Man and Little Boy*, accurate in most other respects, a character is introduced, a young scientist (played by John Cusack), who is in love with a nurse (Laura Dern). They are an ideal couple for the future, but in work leading up to Trinity, Cusack's character becomes so seriously contaminated by radiation that he dies—horribly: His brain swells, his gastrointestinal tract is erased, and his lungs fill with fluid. The details of such a death are scientifically sound: That is what radiation can do. But the character and his death are fabrications. We need martyrs for a story to work, don't we? Yet Richard Rhodes's book *The Making of the*

Atomic Bomb recounts a real death: A cat at Los Alamos became contaminated—its jaw was infected, its tongue swelled, and its hair fell out. Not
quite enough for a movie.

So, at 5:30 a.m. on July 16, 1945, the Trinity firing took place. The blast
was later estimated as yielding 18,600 tons. In the trenches, some scientists
had put on suntan lotion in the dark beforehand. Most of them wore protective goggles, too, and gloves. I. I. Rabi felt a light not just like daylight
but the brightest light anyone had ever seen: "It bored its way right
through you." One man thought the entire atmosphere was going to catch
fire. Another noted the heat: "It was like opening a hot oven with the sun
coming out like a sunrise."

That's when Oppenheimer remembered words from the Bhagavad-
Gita—"Now I am become Death, the destroyer of worlds"—and Rabi felt
the elation pass and give way to chill: "It was a chill that came to one
when one thought, as for instance when I thought of my wooden house in
Cambridge, and my laboratory in New York, and of the millions of people
living around there, and this power of nature which we had first understood it to be—well, there it was."

The tour bus goes due north from Mercury, and in about eight miles it
crosses a ridge of hills and comes into the area of Frenchman Flat. This is
a dry lake—might a Frenchman have mined there once?—that was the
site of the first tests on the Test Site in January 1951. Eventually, there
would be five underground and fourteen atmospheric tests in the Frenchman Flat area, and our bus is now driving over the crackling playa. There
is a good deal of wild growth—scrub, sage, creosote, things that have
grown back after years of nothing. For Frenchman Flat was used throughout the 1950s. Then and now, the prevailing winds went from southwest to
the northeast; such a line would reach Caliente and Pioche, cross the
Utah border in the region of the Escalante Desert, and head on toward
Provo, nearly three hundred miles away.

There were bleachers put up in the safe quarter, from which important visitors could observe the blasts, and there were trenches dug a good
deal closer to ground zero. In 1953, a bomb yielding 15,000 tons was shot a
distance of seven miles into Frenchman Flat, with soldiers in trenches
only 4,500 yards from ground zero. There are photographs and films that
show these troops advancing toward the explosion—they probably had
sunblock and goggles. Rick shakes his head in a fatalistic way when he
tells us that, as if to say that the past is a weird thing, wrapped in its own
ignorance. But of course the past is always its own present. He does add

that on certain days in the fifties, tests were postponed if the wind force was so great as to propel the fallout farther than usual. This raises a question from someone in the back of the bus about the "downwinders," those people who found themselves living in the path of the prevailing wind. Rick admits that phenomenon, and says there is still litigation over the matter, such that he prefers not to comment.

The bus weaves over the playa, keeping to firm ground, and picking off several points of interest. We see low domes, some intact, some collapsed: These were shelters, some of two-inch-thick concrete, some of six-inch. There are also underground bunkers in the area, Rick tells us. Many of these tests at Frenchman Flat were conducted to measure the effect of atom bombs on military structures and personnel. We see a bank vault that was subjected to blasting and which seems to have survived. There are the remains of pens where animals were tethered. Pigs were favored, says Rick, in that the texture of their skin closely resembles that of humans. Some of the pigs were dressed in miniature uniforms, like those worn by human personnel.

In 1957, the Priscilla test involved a blast of 37,000 tons—in other words, over twice the force at Trinity—which was intended to test several different kinds of structure. Some motellike buildings were put up specially. A pine forest was organized, with the pine trees set in concrete footings. And a section of bridge was erected. This stands still, and it shows the huge contortion made by the blast in the I beam. This is now curved into something like an **S** shape.

Rick says that the general level of radiation in the Frenchman Flat area now is no more than the background levels in the rest of Nevada. But we do not go to ground zero, because that point still holds some risk of contamination forty years later.

As the scientists at Trinity settled their small wagers on the blast level, congratulated themselves on the extraordinary achievement, and began to worry, another bomb was loaded on board the *Indianapolis* at Hunter's Point in San Francisco. Four hours after the blast at Alamogordo, that ship set sail for Tinian, an island in the Marianas, just south of Saipan. That island had been captured from the Japanese in July 1944, and it was thereafter used as an air base for raids on the mainland. In time, Tinian was selected as the base from which atomic attacks on Japan would be conducted, using B-29 bombers.

In fact, the 509th Group had been based earlier at Wendover, just over the Nevada border, in Utah. That is where practice runs had been con-

ducted using the bomb. Then the 509th was moved to Tinian, which by
then was like "the largest airport in the world."

The *Enola Gay*, piloted by Paul Tibbetts, took off from Tinian at 2:45
a.m. on August 6, loaded with Little Boy, which weighed four tons. The
bomb was dropped from a height of 31,000 feet, and at 8:16 a.m. local
time, it exploded 1,900 feet above Hiroshima. That bomb had a yield of
12,500 tons. Birds ignited in midair. A temperature of 5,400 degrees was
achieved at the center. The writer Yoko Ota "could not understand why
our surroundings had changed so greatly in one instant. . . . I thought it
might be something which had nothing to do with the war, the collapse of
the Earth which it was said would take place at the end of the world."

There were 76,000 buildings in Hiroshima; 6,000 were not damaged,
but 48,000 were leveled. By the end of 1945, 140,000 people had died, 54
percent of the population of Hiroshima. It is reckoned that by 1950,
200,000 had died from the bomb and its effects.

Fat Man, another bomb, was dropped at Nagasaki, where it exploded
1,650 feet above the city at 11:02 a.m. on August 9. Its yield was 22,000 tons.
By the end of 1945, there were 70,000 dead; by 1950, 140,000—again, a
rate of 54 percent. Those bombs were reliable.

Of course, this is history, and the arguments over history cannot bring
it back or restore the innocence of a moment before such bombs were
exploded. Japan had seven thousand dedicated kamikaze pilots. It had a
strong army still, and its homeland to defend. It was estimated that a land
invasion might cost 2 million Japanese lives and 1 million American. One
man in the 11th Air Force felt sure he was destined to provide air cover in
such an invasion. He said, in 1998, that "the atom bomb canceled all that,
the war was over and all of us on both sides got to go home, except for the
210,000 killed at Hiroshima and Nagasaki. The bomb ended the war, and
its nuclear successors won the Cold War without firing a shot, on either
side. I call that a worthwhile achievement."

That's Charlton Heston, and he makes a sound point, even if his numbers are conservative, and even if one is disposed to argue that shots were
fired and lives lost in the Cold War—after all, Korea, Malaysia, Hungary,
Czechoslovakia, and Vietnam were all part of the Cold War. And, of
course, Fat Man and Little Boy were rather small bombs as such things
go—neither was as big as Priscilla, at Frenchman Flat in Nevada, in 1957.

People went home, but the very idea of home was altered, less safe,
just as dreams and the soundness of sleep were changed forever. But the
number of deaths and the winning of the Cold War are only early returns
in the game that was begun.

39. Gaming

NO ONE HAS EVER BEEN CHARGED FOR KILLING BUGSY Siegel,* and that forbearance encouraged the legend that "everyone" knew who had done it, or given the word. That's how the timing went off so well, with the nine shots hardly fired before new management went into the Flamingo to reclaim its own and put that place straight. If only Siegel had had such a knack for organization.

But he had played his vital role, not least as sacrificial victim. Sure, he had wasted mob money—but they would get that back soon enough, with interest. He had gotten out of line; he had let the vision thing go too far. Reason enough for rebuke. But putting him dead on the front pages was also free publicity; it was like, yet a lot less onerous than, dragging a how-itzer halfway across the West. A cute trick was spilling the blood far away, in one of the nicer parts of Los Angeles. Bugsy dead on the floor of the Flamingo would have been too gross, too pointed. But the idea that a Las Vegas casino was a game played in deadly earnest, by professionals, only added to the feeling that Vegas was shady, sinister, sophisticated, or a glamorous place to go. The public has never been put off by the notion that maybe hoods and crooks steer the place. It has been part of the appeal, so long as the atmosphere is tastefully managed. In its first era—its golden days, let's say—Las Vegas traded on being a dangerous place.

At the same time, for many of those invested in the Flamingo (and the casinos that followed it), once the fuss of Ben Siegel settled, it began to be evident that Las Vegas was an extraordinary opportunity, a game the house was bound to win.

So organized crime had nowhere to go but toward respectability. In the generation of "gangsters" that followed the rowdy era of Prohibition,

---

* The professional money was on Frankie Carbo.

that was an increasingly valuable insight. There was no need to remain outside the law in America when the laws were so flexible, so open, and so amenable. Indeed, it would have been nothing but a sentimental gesture to stay "outlaw." Gambling was a business acknowledged and catered to in Nevada, a business that, once you reflected upon it, offered an amazing accessibility to investment, development, and profit for people who had seemed cut off from such things.

Gangsters, criminals—whatever term one cares to use—were also businessmen in danger of being embarrassed by the inexplicable amounts of money—raw cash—that they had. All too many of them had run afoul of the police or the FBI, not for murder or brutality, not for running prostitution rings or gambling establishments, but for problems with the IRS. For all too often, they had—somewhere—far more cash than their ostensible corner-store businesses could support or explain. And cash kept under the mattress or behind the wall safe loses value because of the wicked inflation that corrupts every economy.

Hotel-casinos offered so many beguiling novelties to such victims of the system. To begin with, as Siegel had shown—and this is a great practical example in Nevada—you could spend, or say you had spent, between $4 million and $6 million to get your place right. It was not just a new business but also a new kind of architecture and construction, one in which luxury, opulence, and such things might become major attractions. For there may be couples in Ohio, New Jersey, or Pennsylvania who will be seduced by the idea of circumstances that defy the fixed grind of those hardworking states. The chance of transformation is part of the package.

In other words, a "hotel" operation works by laws alien to the hotel trade if your real purpose is to get people on the premises so they will gamble. And in Nevada, that was not just permitted but encouraged by a state that saw how far it might depend on the trade. According to the moral guardians of most of the rest of the country, gambling was a virus no sane place would admit. But Nevada was getting ready to see that it might be a sounder basis for existence than gold, silver, copper, or manganese in the ground. In the 1940s, Nevada put few obstacles in the way of the gambling business.

Beyond that, you had to be a Ben Siegel to fail. Gambling was not new. Enough criminals had experience of it to know that, granted the ability to understand and abide by the laws of odds making, gambling was a secure way of making a living. For instance, in the few years after World War II, gambling in Nevada produced gross revenues as follows (in millions):

1946	$21.5
1947	30.9
1948	35.8
1949	38.9
1950	39.4
1951	48.2
1952	55.2

Those figures covered the official business, and they had the charm of saying to the IRS, Look at us, we're getting better and richer every year, so of course we'll pay a higher tax bill. But they did not have to be regarded as the real or only figures for one simple reason: In 1945, 1946, and 1947, as now, gaming in Las Vegas has been that antique process, a cash business.

Check in at the hotel, and you will most likely give a credit-card imprint; your room, your meals at the hotels, and purchases in the hotel stores can all be kept on that charge account. You paid for your air ticket to Vegas in the same way. At home, you do much of your marketing on some kind of credit system that turns into paper records. Yet when you gamble, in the speed and excitement of the action at the tables, there is no accounting, no paper trail. Play the slots and you get no receipt. So there is no record of how the house has performed—the state of the art that permits skimming, just as it is open to money laundering. In other words, in the early days at least, before more stringent precautions were imposed on the count room (the hub where money is taken from the tables), it was easy to add or subtract substantial amounts of cash in the process, without leaving any record. And so, in a short-enough span of time to honor their basic acumen, those in organized crime discovered that the casino business might have been made for them.

You can skim if you're greedy—for decades, that was a steady practice that involved overweight middle-aged men going into the count room with an empty briefcase, coming out loaded, and going back to Cleveland or Chicago or Miami. You could dispose of stolen money, laundering it, as if it were clean already. But you did not have to do those things. For you could make a fortune on the regular, normal, business of gaming. You could pay your taxes and put your profits back into the large enterprise of the city, or whatever. You could make large donations to charity; you were likely to receive plaques, civic honors, and ringside seats at the big fights. You were another kind of made man, and your son did not even have to feel ashamed of the family history. You were no more crooked than most of the other people in American business. This is a transformation that has occurred in Las Vegas from one generation to the next. Just like the earlier shift, the one in which the frontier became "society," it needs no more than steady nerve, good lawyering, and a proper sense of publicity.

The state of Nevada steadfastly refused to be equivocal about gambling. Which doesn't mean that, over the years, it hadn't taken steps to be more intelligent. From 1931 onward, when gambling was legalized, gaming licenses were awarded by the counties of the state. They were passed out without much scrutiny, and the revenue produced was shared by the county (75 percent) and the state (25 percent).

But in 1945, sensing what was to come, and aware that some outsiders were looking at Nevada greedily, the state reassigned the licensing process to the Nevada Tax Commission. The state also introduced a 1 percent tax on the casinos' gross revenues. Then, in 1947, as if to reflect the potential and the notoriety of the Flamingo, the tax was raised to 2 percent (it would remain at that level for nearly forty years). The amount was modest, yet it was sufficient to transform the economy of the state. We have noted already, however, that the acceptance of Ben Siegel as an owner was characteristic of the Tax Commission's tolerance. The attitudes of the state were not just lax; they were supportive: Cliff Jones, lieutenant governor of Nevada, would be a part owner of the Thunderbird; and William Moore, who owned some of the Last Frontier, was actually a member of the Tax Commission itself.

The business developed in the late forties. In 1947, Milton Prell opened the Club Bingo, which a few years later became the Sahara. At much the same time, Wilbur Clark began construction on what would become the Desert Inn, but he faced many problems during the building and was rescued to such an extent by the Cleveland mob that he owned only 6 percent of his own place by the time it opened in 1950. Then there was the Thunderbird, which opened in 1948: Cliff Jones was a minority investor, but the real power was Marion Hicks, who had been loaned money by mob interests in order to finish the job. A $2 million investment, the Thunderbird was second in cost to the Flamingo—its name came from Navajo mythology, but Scandals on Ice (one of its big floor-show attractions) was strictly show business. It became the favorite lodging place of many well-known people, including Howard Hughes and Senator McCarran.

The modern Strip was beginning to take shape. From 1940 to 1950, the population of Las Vegas increased by 192.4 percent. As yet, the hotels were far smaller than is common today, and the crowd was generally well-to-do. Indeed, the chief rival to Vegas for the gaming fraternity at this time was

Havana. Nothing like the ordinary tourist or holidaymaker had yet been seen at the casinos, let alone the cut-rate bargain hunter of the sixties and thereafter. There were plenty of mobsters in Vegas, along with their women and sidekicks. It was a tough town, and there was candid talk about where the money came from, and where it went.

That talk reached the level of American society that had always been horrified by the threat of gambling to the country as a whole. There had been a few other fairly discreet killings beyond that of Siegel; there was evidently prostitution for those interested, and piles of cash. And so, in 1950, Estes Kefauver, a Democratic senator from Tennessee, became chairman of the Senate Select Committee on Organized Crime. The committee was in great part a publicity front meant to enhance Kefauver as a presidential candidate (he ran as vice presidential partner to Adlai Stevenson in 1956). But it had a real enough target, and Kefauver chose to hold hearings in Las Vegas.

Their proceedings were colorful. At one point, Virginia Hill told the committee that the only reason she could come up with for her uncommon influence among made men was that she was such a good cocksucker. Morris "Moe" Dalitz, once a gambler and bootlegger, but by then a leading force at the Desert Inn—a class joint—was asked just how he had gathered the nest egg that had helped him invest in Las Vegas. "Well, Senator," he said, "if you people wouldn't have drunk it, I wouldn't have bootlegged it." Cliff Jones summed up the robust Nevadan openmindedness to unsavory characters who thought to do business in Nevada:

> There were some people that you might say had police records and reputations of gambling in other places. But this seems to hold true, that people who came here when the state started to grow, they weren't particularly Sunday School teachers or preachers or anything like that. They were gamblers.

That was the honest experience of the frontier talking, not so ancient as to be forgotten, and so much more practical than the whimsy of Helldorado days. The desert had not had a good record at attracting homesteaders, ordinary families, or "decent" people. It had been a place for fierceness, lack of compromise, and the kind of record that could go nowhere else. Plus, the casino business was working.

Still, it was a crisis at a time when to be un-American could be stretched to cover many independent traits. There was a feeling that the federal authorities should take charge of gambling and impose as much as

a 10 percent tax on it. Many in the business said that such a measure
would kill the casinos in their tracks—a doubtful claim, as future numbers will indicate—but the threat was enough to rally Nevadans of all parties and classes. The new senator of 1954, Alan Bible, vowed to oppose the
measure, and he was assisted by the more experienced and more crafty
McCarran.

In fact, a bill calling for the 10 percent tax was introduced in the
House of Representatives in 1951, and challenged by McCarran in the
Senate Finance Committee. McCarran was not really a friend to gamblers, though in his time he had helped them get a footing. But at this
time of crisis, he wrote a letter to Joseph McDonald, spelling out the need
for pragmatism in casting the future of Nevada:

> It isn't a very laudable position for one to have to defend gambling.
> One doesn't feel very lofty when his feet are resting on the argu-
> ment that gambling must prevail in the State that he repre-
> sents. . . . I hope the time will come when we point with pride to
> industries of all kinds in the State of Nevada, with payrolls that will
> sustain the economy of Nevada. But that isn't today, Joe, and it
> won't be tomorrow.
>
> And it's going to take more than the building of housing proj-
> ects for rental, financed by the banks of the state, to accomplish
> that result. The City of Reno has grown immensely in the past 20
> years. The City of Las Vegas has come from a wide spot in the road
> to a community of 40,000 or more. That growth in neither instance
> was accomplished by industries with payrolls. It was accomplished
> by making the State of Nevada a playground to which the world
> was invited, and that playground has as its base gambling in all
> forms, and those who have been responsible for its growth upon
> this foundation cannot with propriety and good conscience take a
> long-haired attitude overnight.

40. Calculations

GOVERNMENTS COUNT THE CARDS AND PLAY THE ODDS LIKE anyone else. And so in 1950, when approval was given for the Nevada Proving Ground (the Test Site to be), it was of the highest relevance that the population of Nevada was only a little over 160,000, and 57,000 of that number (more or less) lived in Reno and Las Vegas. In other words, only another 100,000 were scattered across the enormous expanse of the state, which meant a little more than one person per square mile. Actually, the odds were much better, for the "rural population" of Nevada, then as now, was gathered around the northern towns of Elko, Ely, Winnemucca, and Battle Mountain, and south of Reno—Carson City and Minden. In the area of the state to the north and northeast of the Test Site, there were very few people—maybe one for every ten square miles. Those were viable odds.

But odds about what? About people getting hurt? Or, to be more precise, about important or difficult people getting hurt?

Suppose we recognize and concur with the case for dropping nuclear weapons on Hiroshima and Nagasaki, because the calculation of 100,000 or 200,000 lives against 2 or 3 million was proper and cogent, and because the deterrent effect of such weapons on future wars depended upon one or two actual, mortal examples. Still, suppose the war had taken a different turn. Imagine that peace came first in the Far East. Would America have dropped those bombs on a defiant Berlin? On European peoples, on Catholic and Protestant cathedrals, on art galleries that held part of the legacy of Western art? With fallout destined for Prague, Warsaw, and even the lines of the Red Army?

Or was it somehow "easier" for America to drop those bombs on an alien colored people whose culture was not understood? Was there even, in the deliberations, some streak of vengeance, the notion that Japan had asked for it, at Pearl Harbor? In so many ways, both geographical and cultural, Japan was far away, another place.

Apply the same kind of argument to the matter of bomb tests in Nevada. There were those in or close to the government who, by 1950, had a fairly accurate idea of the dangers. Robert Lifton's grim book *Death in Life* reported the fate of many immediate "survivors" of the blast and the fireball:

> [They] began to notice in themselves and others a strange form of illness. It consisted of nausea, vomiting, and loss of appetite; diarrhea with large amounts of blood in the stools; fever and weakness; purple spots on various parts of the body from bleeding into the skin. . . .

Of course, such knowledge did not always penetrate as surely as the radiation it described. "People don't want to hear that sort of thing," you sometimes hear. In 1950, as a child in London, every time I was bought new shoes, I put my feet in an X-ray machine and loved to see the bones of my wriggling feet. Those machines are banned now. And even by 1950, there were sane, responsible people who preferred not to know about the real dangers in radiation. Wallace White, the Nevada State Health Department person responsible for the Test Site, said, "Yes, there is radiation waste, but the only effect on you would be if you sat on the atomic waste long enough, you'd wear out the seat of your pants before you were ever affected with radiation exposure."

Just as the Los Alamos scientists came to see that use of their device was a given once it was constructed, and that the network of systems involved hardly offered the occasion for listening to their testimony and deliberating on decisions afterward, so the military-governmental attitude could easily separate actions and consequences. There was no defined place for anyone who had overall knowledge; even presidents told themselves that they were only as good as their advisers.

As such, decision makers looked at the odds: They sought isolation for a test site, which was advantageous on grounds of security as much as safety. But didn't they also dip into that traditional and still-active American mythology that the American West is relatively "empty," that it matters less, and that it is inhabited by reckless adventurers who deserve much of what is coming to them. Before dismissing that out of hand, consider that at the very same time Nevada was sinking deeper into a kind of damnation—that of gambling—and begging to be let off taxation for it.

Then recollect that the "downwinders" most aligned were Mormons— not exactly America's mainstream, but a people famous for their obedience to, and acceptance of, authority.

The Nevada Test Site received its authorization from President Truman the year after the first Soviet atomic bomb test, at a site near Semipalatinsk in Kazakhstan (about two thousand miles east of Moscow). The Soviets called their bomb First Lightning; America named it Joe 1. Then, only six months before the Test Site came into being, North Korean troops invaded South Korea. American and UN forces in that area risked being heavily outnumbered if Chinese troops entered the fray. Curtis LeMay advised atom bombing some North Korean cities—if there were such things—as an example.

So there was an obvious need for military testing. Indeed, the plans to build a bigger weapon, the super, or hydrogen bomb, were well under way. And testing in the South Seas was expensive and problematic. So much material had to be shipped out there. Bases had to be built. Sometimes, native populations had to be moved and relocated, and then brought back—with the embarrassing discovery that they had been brought back too soon. You play the odds and keep quiet about your losses.

Nevada was chosen. And it is still America's favorite dead ground.

The bus has moved on from Frenchman Flat, going north still, and comes to the Low-Level Radioactive Waste Management Site. This is a blue and white structure that involves a heavy white canvas awning raised over an asphalt pad that is meant to be thick enough to prevent any seepage. The canvas is intended to protect the waste materials from the sun. The waste materials kept there are trucked in by between five and ten trucks a day, from all over the United States. Much of it comes from the Lawrence Livermore Laboratory in California, and consists of contaminated soil and debris that has been exposed to radioactive isotopes or other materials. But some is of a more serious nature: transuranic waste, coming from materials with a higher atomic number than uranium 92.

The trucks must be brought here on public roads, and some come from nuclear facilities on the other side of the country. Some have been carried by rail. Eventually, it is planned that all of this waste will be sent to the Department of Energy's Waste Isolation Pilot Plant (WIPP) in the Carlsbad area of New Mexico. But there are problems with that facility,

*On the Nevada Test Site, a house that was built
to determine the effects of an atomic blast*
(Department of Energy)

not least the feelings of New Mexicans and discoveries that the caverns there may be more porous than was once thought. There is no realistic timetable for the transfer.

As a result, several large, shallow pits have been dug on the Test Site. They cover an area of nearly 800 acres and allow for the burial of four layers of large containers or drums of waste material. The pit now being used is 2 thousand feet long and has a capacity of 2 million cubic feet. It can take between two and five years to fill, and it is the fifth pit so far. As a pit is filled, earth is added to it, and when it is full, it is capped with a roof of rock, asphalt, and cement.

New building in what is now suburban Las Vegas

We see the containers, all with bar coding, for it is important to know what is there and how long it has been there. With the pits already covered, there is a system of sampling pipes to make sure the waste is not nearing a critical state. The groundwater table is a full eight hundred feet beneath the pits, and this is an area where there are only between four and six inches of rain a year.

Note, please, that none of this material is high-level waste, such as spent fuel rods or the materials used in the core of nuclear reactors.

It is a formality only, but the bus we are on is measured for radiation before it leaves this area. Of course, these pits are not ideal, but the problems of waste management have proved trickier than anyone anticipated. And as yet, neither the New Mexican solution nor the one in Nevada — Yucca Mountain — is available. Meanwhile, parts of the United States that do not permit the burial of low-level waste ship what they have to Nevada. It is a commercial arrangement. Our bus was fine.

Over the years, the Test Site has received strange cargoes. For, you see, the residue has to go somewhere. An aircraft carrying nuclear weapons crashed in Greenland once and all the affected soil was brought to Nevada. Then, in 1966, when a B-52 crashed near Palomares, Spain, carrying four bombs, the subsequent cleanup operation required 4,810 fifty-five-gallon drums of material being shipped to the Savannah River Site in South Carolina.

More recently, the need has arisen for a facility where entire bombs — sometimes not well maintained — might be dismantled and disposed of.

Thus, the construction on the Test Site of a device assembly facility (DAF). This is a very large and expensive construction, 100,000 square feet, much of it underground. It contains five chambers where the delicate work can be done, but built in such a way that in the event of a mishap, the roof would fall in, doing its best to bury and contain the radiation. This is a particularly secret installation that actually looks like a prison, with two watchtowers from which the surrounding countryside can be surveyed.

The DAF was finished three years ago, after contracting problems that ran it way over budget. But it has not yet been used. In large part, that is because it was originally seen as a place to which old Soviet bombs and missiles might be brought and rendered harmless. But that has not happened yet, because the various republics that once were Soviet cannot afford the service, and in some cases may be unable to lay their hands on all the hardware. For in winning the Cold War, the United States may have been a little overzealous. The trick could not be accomplished without the devastation of the Soviet economy. That left new nations not always in a position to pay for the upkeep of weapons or for the salaries of their minders. And so the rest of the world faces the dilemma of weapons that will not go away, and cannot be dismantled and forgotten, but could be the plunder of a fragmented society—and the coup d'état for terrorist movements.

41. Our Pack

WHEN GAETANO CROCETTI MARRIED ANGELINA BARRA IN 1914, they lived on South Sixth Street in Steubenville, Ohio. Gaetano was a barber, born and raised in the Abruzzi region, and he had been in the United States less than a year. But already he encouraged people to call him "Guy." In June 1917, the couple had a child, Dino Crocetti; two years later, Guy became an American citizen. As a teenager, Dino called himself "Kid Crochet" and boxed a little, but he was afraid of getting hit in the face. He had such a big nose. So he went into the local steel mill to work, and he thought of becoming a singer. In time, he got a job singing at the Mounds Club, outside Cleveland, which was owned by the Mayfield Road boys, Moe Dalitz for one. It was a fancy nightclub for outside Cleveland. There was a bandleader in Ohio, Ernie MacKay, who looked at Dino and thought of Nino Martini, a pretty successful fellow in light opera and lighter movies. "How about Dino Martini?" he said. Are we warm yet?

By 1940, he was Dean Martin, with a double hernia that left him 4-F. And no one, later, ever saw him hurry.

So he sang through the war years. He was nobody special, however, until the agent Lou Perry got hold of him and told him his nose was too big, and too long. But the surgery would cost $500, which was more than he had. So some of the old Mayfield Road boys put up the money for their Dino, and it was a terrific improvement. Things looked up. He got a job at the Havana-Madrid on Broadway between Fifty-second and Fifty-third streets. New York. 1946. And the warm-up comedian was this goof with a shark's quickness of attention and understanding; his name was Jerry Lewis. A few months later, they played Atlantic City together as a double act. "I knew it was happening," said Lewis. "The very first night, I knew."

They took off. They played Atlantic City, New York, Chicago, and Miami; they played the Copacabana; they opened a TV show for NBC; and Hal Wallis signed them up for Paramount, where their first picture was *My Friend Irma*, in 1949. A couple of months later, September 1949, they were in Las Vegas to play the Flamingo at $15,000 a week. By the early fifties, they were making $3 million a year—declared. God knows what the real figure was, because in Vegas they were getting thank-you packets of cash, a result of Jerry's gambling. That first time at the Flamingo, he ran up debts of $137,000, so he had to go in and see Dalitz. Jerry scolded Moe for letting his losses go so high when he was only splitting $15,000 a week. Jerry always handled the business, and it got worked out.

Their act had seized the country. No one was bigger. It was an act in which the sweet-voiced, very handsome, and relaxed stud would start to sing and the whole thing was messed up by the idiot. It was less an act than a dismantled act, a parody, a strange piece of postmodernism in which showbiz clichés and reckless improvs went hand in hand. It was dangerous, but it was cool, because Dean never let himself get flustered, and it had no more appreciative audience than it found in Las Vegas, a town that loved the way Jews and Italians did and didn't get along.

Here's the point: In the early 1950s, Dean Martin was bigger, cooler, and younger than Sinatra. If they had never met before, they were fellow singers at Capitol, where Dean had the hits. But much more than that, Dean was easy about being Italian, or "a wop," as he sometimes called it; he had boxed; he had more dames than Frank, and the more he had, the more he treated them like dandruff; and he had always been in with the mob. Whereas Frank in those years was in great fear of having lost his voice; he was crazed by the contemptuous way in which Ava Gardner treated him; he was as sorry for himself as Dean was cool—and so much of Sinatra came out of resentment, the good and the bad. He wanted to be on better terms with gangsters, for he admired them. But most of all, he wanted to be Dean Martin. None of this ever persuaded Dean to take himself one jot more seriously. And Dean had played Vegas first.

The growth of the casino business in the 1950s cannot be separated from the series of great entertainers who took the place on, or the way in which the ambience of a sophisticated nightclub was fostered and defined by them.

One of the great occasions in this story is Marlene Dietrich's opening on December 12, 1953, at the Congo Room of the Sahara. Dietrich was a few weeks short of her fifty-second birthday, and she was warned by many people she respected that Vegas was a rowdy, coarse audience, as well as at an altitude (2,033 feet) that was rough on the voice. So she studied. She saw the Vegas acts of Eddie Fisher and Tallulah Bankhead. She realized that her show was to last only somewhere between twenty and thirty minutes; the bosses feared the tables would go dead for too long. So, in effect, she was on and off, a few songs and the sensation of her appearance. She planned accordingly, and with Jean Louis from wardrobe at Columbia, she designed a gown that was skintight, with an exterior of black lace and a lining, below the waist, of flesh-colored silk. Above the waist, there were only carefully placed sequins that were like crescents beneath her still-remarkable breasts. She seemed superbly, yet tastefully, naked.

Tallulah Bankhead remarked, "Marlene told me she had nothing to wear—but I didn't know what she meant until I saw her." She sang, too.

Noël Coward was piqued, for he was one of those who had warned Marlene away. For $35,000 a week, in June 1955, he appeared at the Desert Inn. This was a perfect venue, for it was the most select place in town, a hotel of great luxury that aspired to be a country club, attracted the wealthiest clientele, and had a golf course good enough for major tournaments. Coward did two shows a night for four weeks—the dinner show at 8:30 p.m. and the midnight supper show. His act laid down a layer of London fog as Coward strode down the stairway, drawling "I'll See You Again." The audience was peppered with stars and celebrities, and Coward was a sensation. A best-selling album of the event was released with a cover that is one of the great images of Nevada's flux of reality and fantasy: Coward, in evening dress and an expanse of desert, drinking an English cup of tea.

Coward loved it, and it loved him. He wrote:

This is a fabulous madhouse. All around is desert sand with pink and purple mountains on the horizon. . . . There are lots of pretty women about but I think, on the whole, sex takes a comparatively back seat. Every instinct and desire is concentrated on money. I expected that this would exasperate me but oddly enough it didn't. The whole fantasia is on such a colossal scale that it is almost stimulating. I went from hotel to hotel and looked at the supper rooms. They are all much of a muchness: expert lighting and sound, and cheerful appreciative audiences who are obviously there to have a good time. I noticed little drunkenness and much better manners than in the New York nightclubs. The gangsters who run the place are all urbane and charming. I had a feeling that if I opened a rival casino I would be battered to death with the utmost efficiency, but if I remained on my own ground as a most highly paid entertainer, I could trust them all the way. Their morals are bizarre in the extreme. They are generous, mother-worshippers, sentimental and capable of much kindness. They are also ruthless, cruel, violent and devoid of scruples.

Then, in July 1956, at $55,000 a week, Judy Garland accepted a four-week engagement at the New Frontier. Seven thousand people were turned away the first weekend, so a fifth week was added. Garland sang all her great songs; she introduced her ten-year-old daughter, Liza; she was there, only a matter of feet away from the audience, doing her thing, and rising emotionally to the warmth of an audience. Maybe it was the desert air, or the air conditioning, but she did lose her voice for a few days. So she mimed the songs as a stand-in "sang" for her—Jerry Lewis, whose partnership with Dean Martin had just ended.

A balance was working out in the length of these shows. People were drawn to Las Vegas to see the great stars, and once there, they wanted a proper show. The gambling tables weren't badly affected, because not that many people could get into the nightclubs or the lounges for the acts. The casinos developed. The Sands opened in December 1952, beneath

The collapsed Sands, site of Sinatra's court, demolished so that fresh wonders could be built

the motto A PLACE IN THE SUN—a reference to the movie of the previous year, a mournful romance (loosely taken from Dreiser's *An American Tragedy*), in which poor boy Montgomery Clift yearned for Elizabeth Taylor and her rich lifestyle. The Tropicana would open in 1957, the Stardust in 1958.

The gross revenues from gambling reflected the surge (in millions):

1952	$55.2
1953	73.9
1954	84.3
1955	94.3
1956	115.6
1957	131.9
1958	145.0

Another way of conveying these figures is to say that, sometime in the early fifties, Las Vegas became larger than Reno. By 1960, Vegas had 64,400 people, while Reno had only 51,400. Equally, in the 1950s, the population of the state as a whole rose by 78.2 percent—from 160,083 to 285,278.

Those visitors may not have been as aware of gangsters as Noël Coward was. But it was evident throughout the fifties that criminal figures were not far away. The Kefauver hearings had made it plain that Nevada was willing to give a fresh start to people with dubious associations. Then, two years later, there began a prolonged inquiry into the building and operation of the Thunderbird. Stories in the *Las Vegas Sun* revealed that criminal money had gone into the hotel-casino, and it was suggested that there was a plot to remove Robbins Cahill, the diligent head of the Tax Commission. This shadow hung over the election for governor in 1954, and helped reelect Charles Russell over Vail Pittman. By 1955, the Tax Commission revoked the Thunderbird's license. That decision was taken to the courts, and in 1957 the license was restored, but only after the Tax Commission's right to take such actions was confirmed and strengthened. Indeed, the next governor, Grant Sawyer, introduced a Gaming Commission in 1959 with far greater power than the Tax Commission had ever had. Something else was happening: Federal authorities were beginning to take a more stringent view of the casinos. It was as if a pressure was beginning: If Las Vegas was content to run as a business, so be it, but egregious excesses were outlawed, just as a few sacrificial victims were required.

And so there were occasional killings, though invariably away from Nevada. In 1958, in Phoenix, Arizona, Gus Greenbaum, of the Flamingo, and his wife had their throats cut. Once again, no one was ever charged with those crimes.

There was a thrill of violence about Vegas, yet the violence was never allowed to interfere with business. Moe Dalitz remained closely tied to the Desert Inn and the Stardust, and in a few years he was instrumental in the plan to build the Las Vegas Convention Center. It was also Dalitz who forged the links that allowed money from the Teamsters to go in and out of the Bank of Las Vegas without any trouble.

But the most blatantly mob-run place of all was the Sands, led and inspired by Doc Stacher (a former ally to Longie Zwillman), Jake Freedman (with interests in Texas), and Jack Entratter, an agent of Frank Costello and Joe Adonis and the former manager of the Copacabana in New York. Entratter was an old friend of Sinatra; indeed, it was Entratter who had spoken to Columbia on Frank's behalf at the time of the casting of *From Here to Eternity*. In the end, Sinatra got the role of Maggio in that film because Eli Wallach honored a prior commitment to Tennessee Williams's *Camino Real* on the New York stage. There was no horse's head in the bed, but mob concern was offered in a friendly way.

That's how Frank's fortunes changed, and how the ideal of the gangster became so pressing in his insecure soul. For it was his way of getting even with the world. It was how Sinatra made the world give him respect. In turn, that led to his regular appearances at the Sands, from 1953 onward, his being approved for a gaming license in Nevada, and his purchase of 2 percent of the Sands (for $54,000). He was then given another 7 percent, making him second only to Doc Stacher among its shareholders. Dean Martin would later buy in for 1 percent.

"I can't tell you how happy this makes me," said Sinatra. "I've been trying for more than a year to get a foothold in Las Vegas because I believe it has a great future. . . . You know, an entertainer's life is somewhat uncertain. It all depends on the whim of the public. When I am finished as an entertainer, I want to have an investment that will ensure the education of my children and a sufficient income for me. I think the Sands investment will keep me very comfortably."

Sinatra had three children—Frank Junior, Nancy, and Tina—and together they put in three semesters in college. Kids!

Of course, very little in Frank's bearing suggested that college had anything to do with making it in the world. On the contrary, Sinatra's public persona—and this was developed in his many performances at the Sands—was based on innate talent, womanizing, drinking, and generally behaving like a little Caesar. Don't fuck with me—and don't get your hand caught in the cage.

The most famous of Las Vegas acts—that of the Rat Pack, developed at the Sands in the late fifties and the early sixties—was a kind of ritual enactment of would-be gangsters. The show itself owed a lot to the old Martin and Lewis routines, with interruption a motif, and mockery vital to the tone. But the increasingly forced air of middle-aged guys having a good time—of swinging, of ring-a-ding-ding—was accompanied by stories of Sinatra's arrogance and bad temper in and around the casino. Didn't he act as if he owned it, and as if powerful friends would always back him up? Wasn't this, in Sinatra's mind, the second coming and the belated triumph of Ben Siegel?

Professionally, Sinatra had outstripped Dean Martin—though Martin turned in several fine acting performances in the late fifties. Temperamentally, Frank was as needy for power and the leader's role as Martin preferred to be a bored bystander. But in the Rat Pack act, Martin was never derided or patronized in the way of Sammy Davis, Jr., Peter Lawford, or Joey Bishop. He was a brother figure, honored and forgiven if he sometimes teased Frank. He was also the one guy who could pull the rancorous, vicious Sinatra off journalists when the Maggio in him wanted to fight. And if Maggio was one of life's victims, Frank was the runt as bully.

So the crowds, and above all the guys in the crowds, came to the Sands to see and imagine being Frank—tender in song, rough in talk; a man's man and yet a maudlin wreck; the derided one who had become Chairman of the Board; the guy who could snap his fingers and have the world turn. And all Frank wanted was respect, an Ava who would obey him, and Dean's cool, his refusal to look worried. Frank still wanted to be like Dean. And the real gangsters kept Frank around for the trade he pulled in, for the allure, and because in his way he was such a terrific little wop hoodlum.

All of which could be just a sidelight to showbiz or Nevada history, but for the weird way in which it all got out of control, the way Sinatra's urge for respect meant he had to have the Kennedys for company, and the way Jack, at least, was drawn to the trashy women and movielike bravado that Frank offered (they were so close to being a reprise of Raft and Siegel, each wanting to be like the other). And there were women like Marilyn

Monroe used as bait in that awkward transaction, just as some close elections in 1960 were aided by mob influence. And it was as sordid and dangerous as the high officers of this country had ever dared be, and it came to a conclusion in a weekend orgy at the Cal-Neva—Frank's place by then—when a drugged-out Monroe was passed around sexually from Sinatra to Sam Giancana to just about anyone who was interested. And Dean Martin was there as a helpless onlooker; this may have been the moment when he really gave up the ghost.

Marilyn was dead in less than two weeks, under circumstances that only prove how hard it is to die simply once you have become an object of so much attention. Frank would have to give up the Cal-Neva because Giancana had been seen and taped there. The Kennedys pulled out in

A Lego city? The new nation-states of Las Vegas
fill the strip on a gray day.

time, and dropped Sinatra stone-cold. They betrayed old allies. Did that bitterness then assist the way in which Jack was taken out? Or is it all too easy to drop into the language and the superstitions of noir? You need not share other people's beliefs—that they were taken away for the weekend by aliens, or that the mob and other allies produced the events in Dallas in November 1963—but we need to recognize that such beliefs are firmly held. And in those early sixties, there were ordinary, levelheaded Americans who became paranoids and started to think the game was fixed. I can point to the moment; it was when Jack Ruby went up to Lee Harvey Oswald on police premises and put the gun into his body as if he were inserting a plug. Most of us saw that and felt the air of systemic corruption.

Who knows what Sinatra knew, or wondered about—but he was never the same again, never as loose or wild. He became middle-aged. Like any king of self-pity, he told himself that he had done it his way. But the legend of the swinging gangster has not died with him, just as American political life may never have recovered from the swoon of those few years. You don't have to cry for Marilyn, who was, at best, a cunning victim, one who engineered a lot of what happened to her. But America is another matter, and the terrible intimacy of Jack Kennedy and Frank Sinatra and the suspicion it fostered are cultural fallout, of which we are all downwinders now.

42. The Soil

THE BUS TOUR MAKES ITS LUNCH STOP AT THE CONTROL Point, at the southern end of Yucca Flat. We are now at the center of the area where the most tests were conducted—eighty-six above the ground and more than four hundred below it in this valley alone. The Control Point is a large room with curved walls, in which two rows of technicians could watch another wall of screens and metering devices. This is where the various tests were fired and monitored, and the roof of the building bristles with antennae that transmit information back to the Department of Energy offices in Las Vegas and signal radiation levels to those inside the Control Point.

The tourists fill the seats that once were occupied by masters of these arts, and we take out our packed lunches, careful not to spill mayo or mustard on the expensive machinery. Then to carry us through the meal, Rick loads a VCR with a tape that narrates the role of the Control Point and shows a number of underground test firings of bombs buried in the ground. They are very beautiful in their way, for on every firing, the high overhead cameras notice a kind of orgasmic, uniform shuddering in the land itself, like a blush or a ripple, or like the passage of some thought, before the ground itself caves in under cover of a great dust cloud.

It is clear from all of this that the Test Site is not just a world above the ground. There must be a network of tunnels—not just places where explosions were conducted but a labyrinth of recording sites, storage places, and even shelter in the event of mishaps. Those are not part of the tour. Nor do we go near Plutonium Valley, an area on the eastern edge of the Test Site. Tests were conducted there in 1955 and 1956, apparently to investigate the potential of accidents during the transportation of weapons, and the contamination was so serious that no one can now enter this section without full protective clothing. Yet the site is still used, to train those workers who might be called upon in the event of a nuclear emergency, like a core meltdown at a power station or a serious crash involving vehicles carrying nuclear materials, or anything else you or the most ingenious terrorists could think of.

Now, here is one of the great and terrible stories of the area. In the spring of 1954, diverse human enterprises were at work in the deserts of the Southwest. In the general area of the Escalante Desert, in southwest Utah, one great overlord was making the story of another. For, at the behest of Howard Hughes, who then owned the RKO film company, a group of men and women were striving to make Utah resemble the Mongolian steppes of the twelfth century. What that meant, in practice, was

John Wayne in The Conqueror, *on location in Snow Canyon*
(Museum of Modern Art, Film Stills Archive)

nothing more than the securing of properly pictorial angles and vistas, for no one knew or cared how Mongolia looked at any time in its history—not when John Wayne was set to play Genghis Khan while Susan Hayward was the high-spirited Tartar princess Bortai, on whom his sad and lustful eyes had fallen.

This picture, *The Conqueror*, is not a masterpiece (except in that perilous genre, inadvertent comedy), but why should every movie be good or lofty or even respectable? We have hard lives, and we deserve diversion (when *The Conqueror* was released in 1956, the world had such things as the 1955 signing of the Warsaw Pact to overlook). So let's admit that *The Conqueror* is a silliness, with grave and stilted dialogue by Oscar Millard intended to represent the epic figure of Genghis Khan and the wanton feeling of Bortai, who says, "I am consumed with want of him." All of this in the armor, leather, silks, and veils with which Hollywood is bound to imagine Mongol daily life.

The unit—sometimes as many as 220 people, including cast, crew, and straight-faced onlookers—was based in the town of St. George, Utah. A year before, about 150 miles to the southwest, on Yucca Flat, two bombs, named Dirty Harry and Dirty Simon, were exploded, and apparently the names were merited, for the bombs produced unusual amounts of radiation. A good deal of this dust, it is said, fell and was trapped in Snow Canyon, where much of *The Conqueror* was filmed. The movie involved horses as well as people, and there were stories from the location of problems with dust. There were powerful blowers brought in to get rid of the dust, and the actors were always having to have their faces and costumes swabbed clean.

Then, in the way of such nonsense, as the unit went back to Los Angeles to film interiors—tent scenes for the most part—director Dick Powell gave orders for sixty tons of the local earth (it had a pretty pinkish color) to be shipped back to match the exteriors.

Later research calculated that 91 of the 220 people on the picture developed some form of cancer. And 46 of them died at what might be considered premature ages. Dick Powell died of lung cancer in 1963, at the age of fifty-eight; Pedro Armendariz killed himself in 1963 on discovering that he had cancer (he was fifty-one); Agnes Moorehead died in 1974 of uterine cancer (at the age of sixty-seven); Susan Hayward died of multiple cancers at the age of fifty-seven in 1975; and John Wayne himself succumbed to cancer in 1979, when he was seventy-two. Fifty more fell ill.

The risibility of *The Conqueror* becomes immaterial. The novice in us begins to search for actuarial tables and medical textbooks. The skeptic argues that you can't measure anything about ordinary life by what happens to film stars. The rationalist asks for social analysis and detailed medical histories. Someone recollects that he hardly ever saw a photograph of Wayne when the actor didn't have a cigarette in his hand. People who worked on *The Conqueror* cannot forget the ordeal of being in the Escalante Desert or the consequences over the next twenty-five years. And it is in the nature of stars that, even if many of their films are as absurd as *The Conqueror*, we remember their stories, and ask the question.

In that same spring of 1954, the U.S. government continued hydrogen bomb testing in the Pacific. The first-ever hydrogen test, Mike, had obliterated the small island of Elugelab, part of the Eniwetok Atoll, in November 1952 with a yield of 10.4 megatons. That was nearly one thousand times more powerful than the Hiroshima bomb.

But, in March 1954, in the Castle Bravo test, something went "wrong." This test took place at Bikini Atoll, and it was expected to produce about five megatons. But the scientists had misunderstood the complex series of explosions and failed to recognize an important fusion reaction in lithium 7. The explosion produced a fireball that was four miles in diameter, with a yield of fifteen megatons. Some bunkers measuring the impact were destroyed. On a ship thirty miles away, a theoretical physicist, Marshall Rosenbluth, who had been driven to keep on with the work out of fear that Klaus Fuchs's espionage might have endangered the United States, was in a rain of fallout. The fireball "was glowing. It looked to me like a diseased brain up in the sky." Our language is very like the system of stardom in that it reaches out for signs that may convey the nature of complex experience to others. There was a crater left in the atoll, 250 feet deep and 6,500 feet in diameter.

Eighty miles away, a Japanese fishing boat had been affected by fallout. One man died. Many others were ill. The American communiqué, designed to withhold crucial information from the Soviets, stated that the test was large, but never out of control.

But can a test really be a test if it is under control? If the results are certain, what need is there for a test? If the game is really fixed, really under control, then there is no gambling.

Not all the work on the Test Site has been destructive. There are places where small communities were built and polished in order to see how well they would withstand blast and fire. At such times, the scientists and the workers became like designers and decorators on a film. Why not? All of these events were filmed.

In May 1955 (so many tests then were carried out in the spring, before the labor, the retrieval, and the checking became unbearable because of the heat), the Apple 2 tests involved the building of a small town—there were stores that were supplied with real food, hospitals that were fully equipped. Otherwise, how could you be sure that the food had become poisoned and the hospital made useless? There were also hundreds of mannequins set up to determine the impact on people. And as if the Test Site workers were modest or conservative, they dressed the mannequins, too, just in the way some of the pigs in the Frenchman Flat tests were fitted with special jackets and sweaters.

Some of these wrecks remain. There is what is called "a typical American home," two stories, with a chimney stack and wooden walls on which scorching or stains have weathered into the hard color of rust. The doors and windows are all gone and you can see into the empty rooms. A device yielding 29,000 tons was exploded on a 500-foot tower, only 6,600 feet away from the house, and it serves as a nostalgic reminder of those days when a structure could be left standing while all the life was sucked out by the hot wind.

There are films of these tests, in which you can see the anxious faces of the mannequins tossed around like fruit, and in which pressure itself seems to register on film as a brush stroke smoothing the air. Once upon a time, these little films were part of the Civil Defense Program, advising on the best ways to get through an attack. There is an oddly wholesome suggestion that "it," the shock, is all over in a few seconds. Nothing hints at the way time then erodes and strips away the body itself.

We drive past this house, going farther north still, until we are in the far northeast quarter of the Test Site, almost twenty miles away from Mercury. We are coming to what I take as the climax of the tour. It is set in rolling country, so that you have no hint of what you are about to see. The bus stops and the ground rises to a wooden observation site. You go forward, climbing slightly, and you find yourself on the brink of the Sedan Crater.

Here, on July 6, 1962, only months before the Cuban missile crisis, they exploded a device yielding 104,000 tons, buried 635 feet under the ground. The crater is like a geometric form, by which I mean to say that there is no apparent irregularity. All the sides descend and slope inward at the same angle. These walls seem raked. The lip of the crater is tidily round. But I have not conveyed the scale. It is 320 feet deep, and 1,282 feet

The crater called Sedan
(Department of Energy)

across. As much as 12 million tons of earth were vaporized or moved. It is, I think, next to Hoover Dam, the most beautiful man-made thing in the state of Nevada. Indeed, it is already on the National Register of Historic Places, which means, I suppose, that even if the Test Site came to be abandoned one day, no one could spoil this bleak wonder.

As you look at Sedan, you may realize that only a few miles farther on, to the east and the north, lie those notional places of Area 51, the bases that are not acknowledged. Who knows what beauties lie there, or how long it will be before we are deemed ready to comprehend them?

Someone in the party asks Rick if we are safe on the brink of Sedan.

Sure, he says, the radiation is only noticeable in the bottom of the pit.

In fact, the worst soil was removed in the early 1960s. It was taken to a remote part of Alaska to see what effect it would have on virgin soil. Then all of that dirty stuff was brought back and put in containers that were in turn put in pits, and which are covered and domed now and which are therefore reckoned to be safe.

43. Mr. Hughes

No doubt about it: In the 1950s, Las Vegas was a place where people could go to indulge some of those tastes not normally allowed in the United States. They tested themselves with naughtiness and danger. Guys, businessmen, golfing foursomes went there without their wives and reckoned in the streamlined anonymity of smart hotels to get arranged with some young woman for a night or two. There were single women in town, too: They might be showgirls, flight attendants, croupiers, hookers, or even the young hopefuls who had realized that Las Vegas was the new hot place to be discovered. So there was a meat market going on. And sometimes osteopaths went home to Pontiac, Michigan, with this yarn that one night they'd gotten very nicely interactive with this beautiful young thing, and *God*, if next day it hadn't turned out that she was Moe Dalitz's favorite squeeze. That Vegas!

Well, here's another story: You could often see this tall, dark, by no means unattractive guy prowling around the floor at the casinos. He wasn't more than fifty, and he looked thoughtful, or like someone who'd been around. He would be studying women, strangers, quite coolly, as if they were pictures on the wall at a gallery. And he would take several ruminative looks from different directions. Then he would walk away and go up to this suit who was very deferential to the tall man. And they would be discussing something. Then the suit would approach one of the women, and he would say something like "My friend over there noticed you, and he thought you seemed like the most attractive and interesting woman in the room. So he'd like to invite you upstairs to his suite."

And the woman would look to see which guy the suit meant, and she'd say, "Oh yeah, that one," and there might be a little negotiation, or there might not. But say the woman was ready to go on up and see the view. Then the suit took out a pen and a typed sheet of paper, a legal form allowing that the woman would have no claim, ever, against her partner, identified as Howard Robard Hughes.

Perhaps the strangest chapter in Las Vegas history grew out of the honest appreciation of a guy with a hobby. Not women. No, early in the 1940s, when he was getting into the whole art of flying boats, Hughes realized that the new Lake Mead, the splendid surface brought about by Hoover Dam, was an inviting landing place for the Sikorsky S-43.

More than that, Hughes liked the dusty frontier moods of old Las Vegas. His father's great wealth had come from oil drilling, and Hughes liked to think he was a miner's man, as well as a flyboy and the lofty squire to many Hollywood actresses. Go further still, and it's possible to believe that even that early there were enough hints of the faraway soul in Hughes to have him look out on the desert space and say to himself, This must be the place. Though he became, for a few years, the master of Las Vegas, he was hardly ever seen. Rather, he was in the air—like strontium 90 or the chance of a big bonanza—a pioneer of loneliness. Maybe no one has ever explored that inner frontier more than Howard Hughes.

That he liked the isolation is evident in the way, one day in January 1957, he ordered up a Constellation and a TWA pilot and, with a few male business associates, he and Jean Peters flew from Los Angeles to Tonopah. He had been courting the actress for a few years, but he had wooed other actresses before (Jean Harlow, Ida Lupino, Katharine Hepburn, Terry Moore, Ava Gardner, Jean Simmons—and then there was Jane Russell, the girl he had made famous in *The Outlaw* and for whom he had designed a properly revealing brassiere, just as if she had been a bomb site for the war). The plane landed at an airstrip outside Tonopah (what is now one of those half-secret experimental places, specializing in rocketry), and the party were then driven into town to the Hotel Mizpah where, in an upper room, Hughes and Peters were married under the names G. A. Johnson and Marion Evans. There was no party at the Mizpah. Instead, the party flew straight back to Los Angeles.

A few years earlier, in 1953–1954, Hughes had actually lived for a time in a bungalow on Desert Inn Road. It was called the Green House. He sometimes thought of moving his base of operations to Las Vegas, but his closest aides said it was impractical. Hughes was tempted by the lack of inheritance tax in Nevada, as well as the freedom from state income tax and corporation tax. According to Joan Didion, he was also touched by Vegas because it was a place where you could get a sandwich at any time of night or day. And if you wanted peanut butter and anchovy—coming up.

The idea of Las Vegas would not go away, and it was, in fact, more tempting because of the evident success of the hotel-casino business. The state gambling revenues continued to climb (in millions):

1955	$94.3
1956	115.6
1957	131.9
1958	145.0
1959	172.1
1960	197.3
1961	209.3
1962	229.6
1963	252.0

The business doubled in about six years, and yet by 1960, the population of the state was still only 285,278, when the population of Las Vegas stood at just over 64,000. The crowd coming to Vegas, especially in the boom years of the late fifties, was increasingly middle- and working-class. The Rat Pack shows might have been expensive and exclusive, but their aura was dragging in a broader-based audience. Plans were afoot for new hotels built on a more lavish scale than the first ones.

In the early sixties, the developer and motel pioneer Jay Sarno turned his eyes from Atlanta to Las Vegas. In 1966, he opened Caesars Palace — in most key respects, the crucial event in Las Vegas moving from first to second generation — and a few years later, he followed it with Circus Circus. These were not simply places at which to stay and gamble; they were attractions in themselves — the one strenuously based on the empire and pomp of Rome, the other so constructed that circus acts would play above the casino floor. At both places, a lot of the staff wore costumes, and there were sights and diversions intended to make the ordinary tourist and holidaymaker marvel. Of course, at the same time, Caesars Palace was open to charges of being a vulgar travesty of Roman culture, a shameless pandering to uneducated sensation seekers. But for the first time, a hotel-casino had a theme and a deliberate plan to create a fantasy atmosphere. Just as Hollywood was dying, or retreating, so a Vegas casino had sprung into life looking like the setting for a camp movie.

Caesars, as it happened, was built by a partnership that relied on Teamsters' money. Yet, in those same early sixties, through the aegis of Robert Kennedy, the Justice Department, and the FBI, Las Vegas was coming under increasing scrutiny for its underworld connections and for the extensive practice of skimming. Wiretaps and more courageous journalistic reporting built up a portrait of the town and its business as still dominated by mob interests. The criminal investigations started in the sixties would lead to many indictments and convictions: not least, against Meyer Lansky himself, though Lansky contrived to live out his days in Miami, too "sick" to face any charges.

The public has never been put off by the revelation of outlawry. Gamblers do not necessarily expect a fair shake or an honest game; they need to pursue their own psychodrama, and such things are only enhanced by paranoia or insane optimism. But Las Vegas and Nevada were anxious again, and so they looked with awe and gratitude on the astonishing performance of Howard Hughes in the late 1960s.

In the fall of 1966, Hughes seemed confused about where he should live. He had been in Boston a few months, at the Ritz-Carlton, and he had many other options. Suddenly, he settled on sandwich heaven, Las Vegas. But he wanted complete secrecy, with an arrival in the small hours of the morning. He went by train as far as Ogden, Utah, and then took a privately rented train to Las Vegas, arriving at 4:00 a.m. on November 27. From a crossing north of the city, a car drove him to the Desert Inn, his preferred place, where he and his entourage took sole possession of the top floor, the ninth. Then they asked for the eighth, too, to dispel any chance of spying or surveillance.

Hughes was paying for the rooms, of course. But he never left his own suite, and most of his aides were Mormons, not inclined to gamble. As the Christmas and New Year season approached, the Desert Inn saw its best rooms—many of which were kept for heavy players—being monopolized by the straight and narrow. On behalf of the hotel, Moe Dalitz protested; he asked Mr. Hughes to leave. In return, Hughes offered to buy the Desert Inn. It all took a few months to work out, but in the end, Hughes paid $6.2 million in cash and took on $7 million in outstanding liabilities. In return, he leased the 450-room Desert Inn until the year 2022.

Hughes was sixty-one, and a shadow of his former self. He had lost weight; he ate little and slept badly; he took far too much codeine and Valium; and it is fairly certain that he did not leave his suite for months at a time. In hindsight, there is some reason to ask whether he was sane, or even in control of his own life. We do not know how to regard or judge Howard Hughes: Was he a real man, torn between shyness and arrogance, the urge to withdraw and the desire to control? Or was he a mythic or fictional being? Is it even possible that he was taken to Las Vegas by others to help alter the reputation of the town? To that end, we know that there were old ties between Robert Maheu (one of Hughes's most trusted aides) and Johnny Rosselli, one of the top mob men in Las Vegas.

The scenario is more tempting in that the old bad habits of Vegas did not change under Hughes. At the Desert Inn, for instance, the mob continued to make key appointments. And in the Hughes years, skimming went on without abatement—nowhere more so than at the places Hughes himself owned.

Still, I think that Hughes, even if he was in bed most of the time, in bad health, endlessly watching movies as dire as *Ice Station Zebra* (made in 1968), was a Monopoly player who regarded Las Vegas as a board game he had to cover with hotels—his. The Desert Inn was only the beginning. He bought the Sands, the Frontier, the Castaways, and the Landmark in Vegas. "This is a business that appeals to me," he wrote in one of his memos. He seriously considered moving his medical school in Miami to Vegas. He took a relentless interest in the affairs of the city and the state, trying to make Paul Laxalt* his instrument. He even went so far as to try to persuade or bribe the American government into ceasing underground bomb tests at the Test Site.

There is no clinching evidence that Hughes ever went mad—if we know what we mean by that. He was a wretched manager. His mishandling of the casinos and his suspicions about his own aides were all too debilitating. He had worsening physical conditions, for which he took very little good professional advice or treatment. But is that mad, or just melancholy, forlorn, self-destructive, or the act of someone who believes in nothing? It is in wondering about the answers to those questions, I suppose, that we have made Hughes into a spook or a spirit hovering over modern times, with a little bit of Charles Foster Kane and a little bit of the madman. It's too intriguing a portrait to forget, and too muddled to explain. In the end, you can make of Hughes what you want to; his power left him historically vulnerable. But if ever the desert deserved a hermit king, Hughes is that man.

Nor was he crazy in his anxiety over nuclear testing. Atmospheric tests ended with the Limited Test Ban Treaty of August 1963. But the Test Site only went underground, and in April 1968 came the Boxcar test, the biggest ever conducted there, with a yield of 1.3 megatons. Hughes heard

---

* The Laxalts are the most famous Basque family in Nevada. Robert was a novelist and writer—*Sweet Promised Land* (1957) and *Man in a Wheatfield* (1964). Paul was lieutenant governor, then governor (1967–1970) and senator (1975–1987).

of the plans for it and wrote repeatedly to the government, and to Lyndon
Johnson, to have it stopped. These letters are genuine and personal, and
they are lucid, if not eloquent:

> It just does not seem to me that the citizens of southern Nevada
> should be forced to swallow something that the citizens of central
> Nevada would not tolerate and something that was removed from
> the Aleutian Islands because the Russians objected. I think Nevada
> has become a fully accredited state now and should no longer be
> treated like a barren wasteland that is only useful as a dumping
> place for poisonous, contaminated nuclear waste material, such as
> normally is carefully sealed up and dumped in the deepest part of
> the ocean.

Hughes even sent Maheu to see LBJ, with money to buy him off. But
Maheu was too ashamed to make the proposition. Boxcar went off.

In 1968, Hughes lost $3.2 million in Las Vegas; for 1969, the figure was
$8.4 million; in the first half of 1970, he lost another $6.8 million. Some
aides told him other aides were stealing. It was also clear that skimming
was going on. So he changed his mind and signed a proxy that assigned
his rights to three of his attorneys. Sick with pneumonia, Hughes was put
on a stretcher, taken in a van to Nellis Air Force Base and then by Lockheed JetStar to Paradise Island in the Bahamas. He next took up residence
at the Britannia Beach Hotel. He had done four years in Vegas, nearly to
the day, just like a president or a prisoner. Less than six years later, he
died, in the air, on a plane carrying him from Acapulco to Houston —
where he had been born — leaving us to decide whether he was the sad-
dest of all the rich men or the teller of a unique, austere tale.

Not that he and Nevada were finished with each other. Not long after
he died, an alleged will was found, on the desk of a public-relations officer
at the office building headquarters of the Mormon Church in Salt Lake
City. This will was not long, and not really remarkable except for leaving
one-sixteenth of the estate to Melvin DuMar of Gabbs, Nevada.

"What, me?" said Dummar when they found him (the spelling of his
name was one of many errors in the will). Then Dummar thought and
recalled a night in oh, January 1968, it must have been, when he was driving from Gabbs to Las Vegas, and he found a man off the road, somewhere between Tonopah and Beatty. He wore baggy pants and tennis
shoes; he looked like a bum; he was bleeding from one ear, and he said he
was Howard Hughes.

Melvin drove the man to Vegas, dropped him at the Sands, and gave him a quarter. That was that.

Well, you know this story. There was a thumbprint on the envelope the will was in, and Melvin Dummar recanted in time. The estate went to the proper heirs. But it was a great story and one that both Nevada and the curious Howard Hughes deserve. For everyone driving those roads at night, listening to Art Bell's radio show out of Pahrump, half expects something wondrous or ruinous is going to happen. It's a way of keeping awake, looking for the tattered half-life that only needs discovery.

44. Downwind

HOWARD HUGHES HAD HIS OWN MEDICAL INSTITUTE, IN Miami, but while resident at the Desert Inn in Las Vegas, he had stored his urine in jars, in dread that it had some dark tale to tell, yet refusing to trust it to medical analysis. He was obsessed over his own health, but he didn't trust doctors, with some reason: Doctors who saw his corpse in Houston told the press that it was "an ordinary death." They kept back the information that the tall man weighed only ninety-three pounds, that bits of broken hypodermic needles were in both his arms, that there were sores all over his back, a recently made tumor wound on his head, and that he had a separated shoulder. The autopsy report was buried in the same air of secrecy, and, in fact, the pathologist who did the autopsy said that he had misinterpreted the word *milligrams* for *micrograms*. So actually there was one thousand times more codeine in the dead body than he had said at first. Somehow, such things had been hushed up. After all, there were so many reasons not to let the idea gather that this was the estate of a madman. Despite all the inroads of paranoia, fear and loathing of good advice, mismanagement, and the ways of self-destruction, Howard Hughes was worth somewhere between $600 and $900 million when he died. Yet he feared so much—and fears are the greatest beliefs. Not that Hughes was the kind of paranoid crank who lived in some small shack in the desert. He had spent much of his life in high business affairs, and he had had plenty of intricate dealings with the government. All the more reason for him to be suspicious? Or a persuasive training for the view that it is easier for governments to make a mess than build a decent conspiracy? In the end, perhaps, the greatest paranoid respect for governments comes out of a deep fear of disorder. For God's sake, we say to ourselves, *someone* has to be in charge; otherwise, we might begin to do an inventory of the Soviet

Union's old hydrogen bombs, and wonder where the missing ones are, or
who has them.

Hughes never knew—because the government never let the argument
out into the light of day—that in 1948 the Atomic Energy Commission
pressed for the Proving Ground (now the Test Site) to be not in Nevada
but on the Outer Banks of North Carolina. More or less, that means Cape
Hatteras, where the gusting wind (except in hurricane season) goes
steadily from west to east, and would have carried fallout over the Atlantic
Ocean. Bermuda might have been vexed, and Western Europe might
have realized that nothing separated it from the Carolinas except the
centuries-old loyalty and perseverance of the Gulf Stream. But American
authorities at the time were given the incontestable proof that a test site at
Cape Hatteras would mean fewer American citizens exposed to what was
recognized as dangerous material. Nevada won only because the site
required was already owned by the government.

Yet the people of Nevada lost, too, along with Utahans and anyone
else with a case to be made as a "downwinder." And it has only added to
the misery of most of these people that the "authorities" have contested
the diagnosis that they fell ill and then died because of exposure to the
fallout from bomb tests. Over the years, there have been official responses
to expressions of fear that range from "fear itself" being the greatest stimu-
lant to cancer to the idea that we would all be healthier with just a little
radiation. Of course, those responses are often part of a legal strategy, as
well as the piety that "our" government is always intent on doing the best
thing for us. So it is valuable to remember that as early as 1948—with the
example of Japan to go on, as well as the established theory of radiation
and its properties—"they" knew that a test site in Nevada would incur
more danger.

Danger? Darlene Phillips was a teenager in the 1950s, and she sometimes worked during the summers at Bryce Canyon, a great tourist attraction and camping ground in Utah, about eighty miles northeast of St.
George. She was a test groupie, if you like:

> Everybody in the dorm in Bryce Canyon would get up early, before
> dawn, and get on the catwalk which faced west. It would be kind of
> chilly, and we would count down with it because we knew what
> time it was to go off. Then you would see the whole sky light up as
> if the sun were coming up backwards, and even the shadows of the
> trees would be wrong, casting their shadows in the other direction.

And I should have known then that the world was upside down, that it was wrong, but I didn't.

Later on, she became anemic; some of her hair fell out; and she realized that her immune system had collapsed. Her intellectual response to this came slowly. She was a Utah Mormon, and she moved away from the Church only gradually, because her feeling of having been a victim cut so violently against the official wisdom. Then her husband's two uncles died, both of them from leukemia, after they had been prospecting in Nevada and were caught in a dust storm. Some soldiers stopped them, told them to wash the car and take a shower. But they were dead in five years.

Of course, this is anecdotal material, which hardly counts as proof. But Darlene Phillips is one among many in a book entitled *American Ground Zero: The Secret Nuclear War*, written and photographed by Carole Gallagher, who spent years in and around southwest Utah, meeting and talking to people who had been "downwinders." For the most part, these are people who were generally unknown before the book in which they appear was published. They are cowboys, people who had worked at the Test Site, people from the military, farmers, shopkeepers, many of them Mormons, many of them constitutionally obedient to government, anti-Communist, and ready enough to support the Cold War need for testing weapons. But they are people who developed cancer, heart disease, sterility, and birth defects in the years after the tests. Roughly spoken, they are people who, like the sheep of Nevada and Utah, from the early fifties onward, lost their wool, delivered stillborn lambs, or just died in great numbers. The body of testimony in Carole Gallagher's book is that of steadfast country people, devout and conservative, who felt not just physically ravaged but also betrayed by authorities they had trusted.

In June 1957, Robert Carter was a seventeen-year-old U.S. Air Force man from Utah, part of a group of servicemen deliberately exposed to the Hood shot, 74,000 tons, the biggest atmospheric test ever done in Nevada:

The explosion went off, and I remember feeling the confusion that just blew me, it just blew me 40 feet into the mountainside and all those men with me. I felt elbows, I felt knees, I felt heads banging, I felt my head hit the ground. I felt dirt in my ears, my nose, it went down my throat. I had a bloody nose. I felt all those terrible things that you don't want to go through in your whole life. I remember

the ground so hot that I couldn't stand on it, and I was just burning
alive. I felt like I was being cooked. After the shot my coveralls were
cracked and burned, there was so much heat.

That language seems . . . well, colorful, doesn't it? And years later,
Carter was alive to talk to Carole Gallagher, even if he was in a wheel-
chair a lot of the time because of his back, even if he had clinical paranoia
by then. There you are, the official attitude responds: The guy was disturbed. That's why you're not to trust Carter's other story—that, during
the Hood shot, he saw not just pens of animals burned "beyond recogni-
tion" but also chain-link cages with men handcuffed to the fences. You'd
have to be mad to believe that, wouldn't you? Yet others testify to seeing
the same thing, and when they spoke, they were taken away to a hospital
and told they had imagined it, and they were given drugs and instructed
never to mention it again.

Carole Gallagher's is not the only book. *Justice Downwind*, by Howard
Ball, told a similar story several years earlier. That contains such stories as
Gloria Gregerson's. She was from Bunkerville, Nevada, and she remem-
bers playing under the oleander trees as a child, and shaking them, so
fragments of fallout as big as blossoms fell down. She wrote her name in
the dust that gathered on the family car. She died in 1983, aged forty-two,
having had ovarian cancer, stomach cancer, and leukemia. The same
book recounts government handouts in the 1950s warning that "from time
to time, locals with Geiger counters of their own might be spreading word
about readings off the chart. But not to worry, not to panic; such things
were temporary, and would adjust."

The anecdotes are fearsome. But there are experts who challenge
them. They point out that we hardly know enough about cancer yet to be
able to trace its origins exactly. There are millions of types of cancer that
cannot claim radiation as a cause. Again, "fallout" affects the imagination
deeply, but is hard to track. Many bombs raise their own local winds and
weather; explosions at different heights can have radically different
results; rain after a bomb may bring down fallout that otherwise would
have floated. Indeed, some claim that the Soviet Union suffered as much
from Test Site fallout as Nevada or Utah! It's so hard to be sure.

The few legal cases in this area have proved that point. In 1982, Judge
Sherman Christensen handed down a decision to the effect not just that
the dangers were real, and proven, but that the Atomic Energy Commission had acted fraudulently. A year later, the United States Court of

Appeals in the Tenth Circuit reversed that decision. In 1984, Judge Bruce Jenkins found that tests had caused cancer, and that the government had concealed information about the tests. Again, that decision was reversed by the U.S. Court of Appeals—same circuit. Four years later, the Supreme Court declined to take up the matter.

You can argue this both ways: that the cases were not properly proved, or that the authorities are terrified of precedents that might expose them to so many other actions. For the potential damage here is far from merely local. There is now a Radiation Exposure Compensation Act, introduced by Senator Orrin Hatch and Representative Wayne Owens, both of Utah, in 1990, but it covers only a narrow strip of the United States: southern Nevada, southern Utah, and northern Arizona, and only a few, specified types of cancer.

Carole Gallagher responded to that legislation with the words of a U.S. Air Force colonel: "There isn't anyone in the United States [or anywhere else] who isn't a down-winder." Gallagher goes on to note that there are scientific estimates that our atmosphere now contains five metric tons of plutonium, whereas five pounds could kill everyone on the planet. Equally, while it has been admitted that plutonium, dangerous for 250,000 years, in some cases, threatens the area around the Savannah River bomb factory in South Carolina, four times that amount of plutonium is in the land of Nevada.

Nothing is as ominous in Gallagher's book as the interview with Dr. John Gofman. Gofman was once a part of the Manhattan Project: He helped discover uranium 233; he is the author of *Radiation and Human Health*; and he worked at the Livermore Laboratory. He has strenuously maintained the danger of small amounts of radiation and has linked it to the increase in types of cancer. But, most striking of all, as an ex-insider, he no longer feels able to trust government statements on the matter because of their proven falsehoods in the past. His own warning reports incurred efforts at refutation and withdrawal of research funds:

> I consider the whole idea of subjecting people to a toxic influence without their consent is an outrage whether it's done for weapons testing or nuclear power, nuclear medicine. You have no right to do that to people. . . . It's about one in three people in the United States now that will have a brush with cancer. The latest figures that I have worked out were about 16 percent to 18 percent that would die of it. . . . I don't consider the Department of Energy a

credible agency. I don't see how you could, for example, for the lies
you know they told back in the time when they were called the
Atomic Energy Commission.

Of course, the tests have stopped. People will die of their cancers.
Reversals of judgment spin time out further. And, today, as if to demonstrate how harmless such things were, the Department of Energy brings in
tourists to stand at the lip of Sedan Crater, with guides who tell you that
the radiation is all at the bottom of the pit.

Don't put your hand in the cage. And don't misunderstand the complex and even infinite nature of cages. Gen. George Lee Butler, now
retired, was once in charge of the U.S. strategy for a nuclear war. In
December 1993, he entertained Russia's defense minister, Pavel Grachev,
at the Omaha headquarters of U.S. Strategic Command. By then, the
Soviet Union was no more; Americans could feel satisfied that the Cold
War had been won. Butler talked to Grachev about the possible total
elimination of nuclear weapons one day soon:

"General Butler," said Grachev. "I cannot agree with you. Nuclear
weapons are what make us a great power."

"With all due respect," said Butler, "nuclear weapons are what make
you a feared power. What will make you a great power is the fact that you
are becoming a democracy."

It is fine rhetoric, and finer still for a man in that position. Since then,
Russia has dwindled in power and authority. It has mislaid some of its
bombs, and the United States has hardly begun to examine the difficult
counterexamples to the proposition that it has always been a democracy.
For in Nevada, the government launched a large, irreversible gamble
with the fate of many people, without even telling the people that they
were players.

45. Steve Wynn

STEVE WYNN WAS ELEVEN WHEN HE FIRST SAW LAS VEGAS IN 1953, and the boy was wide-eyed. He saw cowboy clothes, with people on horseback riding sometimes from one casino to another. But "the place was a spectacle with a strange kind of exotic energy." What does a kid actually remember? Just the fact that he was enthralled and that he saw it through the eyes of his father, a chronic loser who was always looking for some big break. Wynn is still wide-eyed, though his rapturous stare now barely masks the blindness that is coming with incurable retinitis pigmentosa. So let's say that he is wide-voiced, too, nearly always breathless, exuberant, and so pleased with himself, it takes you aback. If you're staying at his Mirage, for instance, you begin to realize that the friendly voice doing the narration on the in-room promo for the hotel—the first thing you get when you turn on your TV—and the voice on the hotel PA encouraging you to try this and that is that of Steve himself. And that's not because he was too cheap to pay an actor, or because he reckons he's as good as any actor. It's just because he *wanted* to do it, and because why shouldn't the kid be barker, too, if he owns the place? And maybe the thing that made him want to own it is because he always dreamed of the thrill, the power, and the theater of being the guy who stilled the noise with "Ladies and gentlemen, Mr. Las Vegas . . . Steve Wynn!"

Mike and Zelma Wynn, his parents, based the family in Utica, New York, but Mike was often away. He was in the bingo business, managing and sometimes calling games along the East Coast. He had been Michael Weinberg once, and his father had been away so much—following a vaudeville career—that Mike had foster parents. Mike's fortunes went up and down, but he always managed a high style, even when he was in debt because of his own uncontrollable gambling. The trip to Vegas, in 1953, had been because Mike was looking into opening a bingo parlor above the Silver Slipper. But he got edged out. Steve recalls "a man-child, an insecure, lovely man with his heart on his sleeve and a kid's attitude. He was good at promoting bingo, but he had a gambling problem. He believed in not worrying."

Or not letting the worry show. Despite the father's debts, Steve was sent to the Manlius Military Academy, a prep school for West Point. But when Steve was a senior in high school, the family moved to Miami for Mike's health, and they lived in the Fontainebleau Hotel, Ben Novak's grand hotel of the Eisenhower era.

"It was so glamorous," says Wynn, "that it had no sign out front, and all the Europeans with money were there. We lived next door to Harry Mufson, who had built the Eden Roc, and went from one hotel to the other for coffee at night.

"[Mufson] and Novak dressed nicely and walked around like they were kings; [everyone bowed down to them] then talked about them behind their backs. All the Jews and Italians and Frenchmen, all they did

Steve Wynn
(Mirage Enterprises)

was talk about the guys who owned the joints. I was seventeen, eighteen, sitting there and thinking that it wasn't a bad life."

That's where he first met his wife-to-be, Elaine, also the child of a disastrous gambler. Steve went to the University of Pennsylvania, from which he would graduate with a degree in English. But then, in 1963, at the age of forty-six, Mike Wynn died during open-heart surgery. "Nothing worse can ever happen in my life," says Wynn. But the loss was a directing factor. Steve was intending to study law at Georgetown when he discovered the terrible debts left by his father. So, with Elaine, he took over the bingo business—he called the numbers; she did the books—and paid off the debt. Law was by then a thing of the past, if it ever stood a chance.

Once he was in the clear, Wynn moved to Las Vegas and bought into the Frontier for 3 percent. This is the one awkward moment in the narrative, and the one place at which the kid could have been helped by acquaintances met at the Fontainebleau, and by veterans who wanted to help Mike Wynn's boy, for the Frontier had a shady reputation. Years earlier, Ben Siegel and Meyer Lansky had had an interest in the place, and it had a steady reputation as an unsuccessful joint, enough to make some people believe that it was more deeply and regularly skimmed than other places.

Steve ran the slots at the Frontier when some of the owners were convicted of cheating at cards in Los Angeles. Another was tied to the Zerilli mob in Detroit. Wynn did all he could to separate himself from those types. He sold out his 3 percent and then watched the mysterious cleansing operation of Howard Hughes, who moved in and bought the Frontier for $14 million. In fact, the Los Angeles cheating had been at the Friars Club (a show-business place), where the players included Tony Martin, Zeppo Marx, and Harry Karl (married to Debbie Reynolds).* Those convicted included Johnny Rosselli. The sale of the Frontier involved the lawyer E. Parry Thomas, a man who had become as close to Hughes as he had been with the Teamsters. Indeed, Thomas was a key figure in the evolutionary process that allowed Las Vegas to assume that the funding of the hotel-casino business had turned respectable. Thomas was by then chairman of the Bank of Las Vegas.

Thomas took a liking to Wynn, and maybe saw a success in the making. He advised and then helped fund Wynn in a liquor-distribution busi-

---

* Later on, Debbie moved to Las Vegas and opened her own hotel-casino out on Convention Center Drive, incorporating her Movie Museum, with an eighty-seat theater. It folded in 1998.

ness, Best Brands, that operated in Reno and Las Vegas. This gave Wynn a modest capital basis, and the urge to start developing. He saw—or did Thomas alert him to?—a small wedge of land, 160 feet wide and 1,300 feet deep, next to Caesars Palace and leased to them as parking ground by Howard Hughes. The Hughes empire in Las Vegas was beginning to crack apart, largely because his lieutenants were fighting one another. It's not clear how much Hughes knew, or consented to. But Thomas floated the sale for $1.1 million. Less than a year later, Wynn sold the land outright to Caesars Palace for $2.25 million. This was only after he had threatened to build a new, small casino on the site.

Wynn used his profit to acquire 5 percent of the Golden Nugget, one of the older establishments in town, in the Fremont Street area, but losing money by then, archaic in its feel, and a place being swindled by some employees. On a campaign to clean the place up, Parry Thomas helped persuade Buck Blair, president, to appoint Wynn as director. Adding to his shareholding, Wynn was voted president and chairman of the Golden Nugget in August 1973. Then he reformed the place, rehired a staff, and in two years moved its profits from $1 million to $7 million. This was the first demonstration of his liking for a classy place as an inducement to gamblers. Indeed, his transformation of the Golden Nugget was the first step in the recovery of the entire Fremont Street area, which had become very much the shabby end of town.*

Then in the early 1980s, Wynn moved his base to Atlantic City. He purchased the Strand Motel, a dump, for $8.5 million, gave the place a dramatic fix, and reopened in December 1980 as the Atlantic City Golden Nugget. He had revenue of over $180 million in his first year. This operation was enormously aided by Wynn's friendship with Michael Milken, who helped raise the money.

Atlantic City had a real impact on Las Vegas. Although gambling revenue built in Nevada in the early eighties, the rate of increase was slowing. There were so many other ways and places for Americans to gamble. Las Vegas was having to compete with theme parks, foreign travel, and the extensive American leisure industry. Moreover, as the town had become safer and more earnest, there were those who said it was duller. The great entertainers of the fifties and sixties were less and less evident. Instead, Las Vegas had become the home or refuge of entertainers like Wayne New-

---

* Years later, Wynn was a leading light in developing the "Fremont Street Experience," a cunning bit of urban renewal.

ton, Paul Anka, and Don Rickles, who seemed to play few places outside Nevada. So the figures were not as buoyant as they seemed (in billions):

1979	$1.9
1980	2.2
1981	2.4
1982	2.5
1983	2.6
1984	2.9
1985	3.2

Since the building of Caesars Palace, there had been only two significant additions to Las Vegas: the fifteen-hundred-room Intercontinental (in 1969), which became the Las Vegas Hilton; and, in 1973, the two-thousand-room M-G-M Grand. Both of these enterprises were led by Kirk Kerkorian, born in 1917, the son of a San Joaquin Valley farmer, and not just a hotelier but also the owner of both the M-G-M and United Artists film companies. But the Grand in Las Vegas was also to be the site of one of the city's greatest disasters. In 1980, a fire there killed eighty-seven people and was later ascribed to inadequate alarms. All of a sudden, the enormous new structures seemed very vulnerable. Kerkorian was not discouraged—he would come again—but the fire surely had an effect on the general public (and it involved damage claims of at least $1 million per life lost).

It was in these doldrums that Steve Wynn reckoned on his own destiny as the man fit to restore Las Vegas. He sold out his several interests in Atlantic City to Bally's for $450 million, and he used the capital to prompt Milken to go on the market for him with junk bonds. He felt that the hotel-casino had to change, that it could no longer be the casino floor with rooms piled on top. The hotel had to be an attraction; it had to take on some of the qualities of a theme park and the fantasy-driven movies of the 1980s. Inherent in this idea was the notion that gambling might not be the sole reason for going to Vegas, and that families might be induced to make the trip.

For something very close to $1 billion, with architect John Jerde, Wynn built the Mirage. Not since Caesars Palace had there been a hotel-casino with such atmosphere or glamour. In so many ways, Wynn reckoned that the city had never properly learned from Jay Sarno's example of the 1960s.

The Mirage Hotel, with volcano

The Mirage opened in 1989 with three thousand rooms. It has a volcano in the forecourt outside that (depending on wind and weather—
fallout is always considered in Nevada) goes into spectacular eruption
every fifteen minutes. Inside the main entrance, the visitors have to walk
through a tropical rain forest to get to the registration desk—and the forest
isn't just kitsch; it's well-done, and it's matched by the huge aquarium
behind the registration desks. Over the years, the Mirage has acquired
Siegfried and Roy and their tigers, some dolphins, a very handsome pool
that includes islands, nine restaurants, and an unbeatable reputation for
service. Nearly ten years old, the Mirage still feels fresh and alive, and it
justifies its habit of charging more for rooms.

For it was part of Wynn's philosophy that he wanted to attract people
used to going to the best hotels in the world, so there was no need to offer
them a room for $30 a night. Indeed, the Mirage has superb suites for
celebrities and high rollers, and in Shadow Creek, it has a magnificent
eighteen-hole golf course kept just for Steve's guests.

In the depressed or somnolent mood of the eighties, there were many
experts who doubted the viability of the Mirage. But on opening day, it
attracted twice the anticipated number of people. Year after year, it has
more than 2 million guests. In its first quarter, the casino had $44 million
in profits. Mirage Resorts—a public company of which Wynn is the major
shareholder—has had an average annual return on investment of 22 percent since the Mirage opened.

A part of that is Treasure Island, next door to the Mirage, which opened in 1993 and which features a sea battle with eighteenth-century ships in a small lake (Buccaneer Bay) on the Strip. That's right, you have only to walk by to watch the show for free. Inside, Treasure Island has 2,900 rooms and an overall presentation aimed one class below that of the Mirage, but with Wynn's characteristic sense of perfectionism. At the very moment Treasure Island opened, Wynn demolished—with zest and showmanship—the old Dunes so that he could build the greatest of them all (so far), the Bellagio.

The Bellagio opened on October 15, 1998, and it was a far more successful media event than the first opening of the Flamingo. Virtually every national magazine ran splashy stories about the hotel, its rarer attributes, and the opening-night party, which drew stars from every walk of American celebrity.

The hotel-casino, designed by John Jerde again, has a clunkier wingspan than the Mirage, in a style that can remind very few guests of Lake Como. But inside, everything is on a grander scale: With three thousand rooms, the Bellagio cost $1.6 billion to build and decorate (maybe a quarter of the funding came from Wynn himself). There is an 8-acre replica of Lake Como between the hotel and the Strip, a place where illuminated fountains are like Busby Berkeley chorines after dark. It is not remotely like Lake Como—despite Italian trees transplanted, how could it be?—but it is a bold new stroke for Las Vegas.

Nearly everything is more sophisticated. The rooms are larger, the bathrooms, especially, are spacious enough for a pasha's dream. The walkways on the casino floor that separate the tables, allowing visitors to pass by, are twice as wide as those at the Mirage. There is room for carpet and marble flooring. There are tasteful canopies over every gambling table. The lake—a view of which is part of the treat at many of the hotel restaurants—is an authentic body of water, with Wynn's antique speedboat at its mooring. The several swimming pools have a Roman air, as if rivaling Caesars or San Simeon. This is a Vegas hotel that verges on a dress code. There are no hard rules, but at many of the restaurants and the theater where the Cirque du Soleil's O plays, it is customary for people to dress up. This is no small gesture in Las Vegas—it could even spell doom for the Bellagio. For this is a hotel where you feel the old barriers, the gulf, between them and us, and wonder which you are. Early announcements put room rates at $200 and over per night.

For which you get the extra space, a range of over a dozen restaurants, including Le Cirque from New York, Olive's from Boston, Aqua from San

Francisco, and Julien Serrano's Picasso. At all those places, a reasonable dinner works out at $100 a head, and if you want a good seat for O, that's another $100. O is one of the great Cirque du Soleil fantasias, and—true to Wynn's trademark—it involves a stage that frequently serves as a pool. O is a pun on the French word for water, and part of Wynn's brilliant yet simple instinct that nothing's more luxurious in the desert than water.

There is also Steve's art gallery, an inner chamber where he has his paintings on the wall: $300 million worth or more, including Monet, Picasso, Cézanne, and van Gogh. He had bad advice with the purchasing, but he loves pictures the way he loves water. And he had a little assist from Nevada, too.

In 1997, a state law was passed that permitted a tax exemption on paintings purchased for over $25,000. That sort of benevolence was not unusual, and Wynn had added significantly to the treasury of good art in Nevada. But there was a catch. The legislation required that the pictures be on show for at least seven hundred hours a year. No problem. And free. There, the Bellagio required clarification on the law, for Wynn had required that even residents of the hotel pay $12, and even $22, a head to inspect the art. Eventually, in May 1999, the Nevada Assembly gave final approval to Wynn's tax break, but it insisted that Nevadans could enter the art gallery for only $6 a head.

The Bellagio is sumptuous, and it is a departure. But it is a gamble. In advance of its opening, there were analysts in the gaming business who were uncertain how well it would do, and how it might affect the other Mirage operations. By November 1998, in fact, the Bellagio was offering bargain midweek rooms at $89 a night. In February, during Valentine's Day week, you could get a room for $159. But the prices at O and the restaurants hadn't begun to falter—and they were full. The Bellagio in its first year is a striking popular success, and the talk of Las Vegas—but I'd wonder about its margins and its fate if some other hotel becomes the hottest place in town.

That could happen. Dining at Prime, a very good steak restaurant within the Bellagio, my family could see the fountain show and a version of the Eiffel Tower going up on the other side of the Strip. If we had craned our necks, we might have seen the Venetian getting ready, right opposite the Mirage (on the site of the old Sands). And way down at the end of the Strip (in what you'd have to call the worst location), there was Mandalay Bay, scheduled to open in March 1999.

The Paris is going up, with its own Eiffel Tower.

With numbers like these:

Mandalay Bay	3,700 rooms	cost $1 billion	March 1999
The Venetian	3,000 rooms	cost $1.2 billion	summer 1999
Paris	2,900 rooms	cost $760 million	fall 1999

The city is to have 127,000 rooms by 2000. Can it fill them? Are the novelties in theme and atmosphere sufficient? Or are we close to a point of saturation, where the "sets" on the Strip are little more than all the worlds possible on a studio back lot?

The real life of a casino doesn't alter much. Only a few games are played, and they're played everywhere. The slot machines are not Venetian in spirit or redolent of the rain forest. I wonder about a future of new kinds of gambling (closer to life's plays, say) and a new kind of place—call it Bugsy's, a noir casino, where people are encouraged to live or behave like gangsters, or where the big bonanza every night is a kind of tontine, one person who is actually rubbed out, offed, in the open—gangland-style—all wrapped up in legalese beforehand, all winnings going to the victim's estate. Free from inheritance tax, of course. Crazy? Maybe. But there's something staid in gambling as it now stands. The spirit of the wicked needs new life.

46. Yucca?

IT WILL BE SAID THAT WE APPROACHED THE NEW MILLENNIUM in such a stew of pride and anxiety, as if these things had not been negotiated before, more or less. In the year 2000, the events of the First Dynasty in what is popularly known as "ancient Egypt" will have occurred five thousand years earlier. Yet there are radioactive isotopes that remain busy and dangerous—so that one embrace could kill you—for, say, 250,000 years. By now, moreover, this progressive world has accumulated a good deal of that vibrant matter, more sometimes than it knows how to count or keep track of. So where should we put it while we are waiting?

It is not as if those charged with that decision can wish the problem away, or write it off against the past. No one can go back that one step and make the quite reasonable suggestion that nowhere should have to have this stuff, let alone assume that it will be safe for what is an unimaginable period. In other words, we are making a defiant gamble with the future, and looking to see which places have the most meager claim for being spared. An underground cavern beneath Central Park? Not likely, though it might be argued that that location would give the site an army of constituents, many of them vocal, if not eloquent, and enough of them lawyers to see that the burden would be paid attention to. No, you know where "we" decided to put it—in a place that, one has to admit, has been so tainted already, it might as well be Nevada.

In their turn, Nevadan politicians—notably, Senators Harry Reid and Richard Bryan, and Representatives John Ensign and Jim Gibbons—contested the proposition. Look, they have said, Nevada has done enough already for the United States; Nevada is a state dependent on tourism; and it is also the fastest-growing state in the union. No matter, the majority of Congress know only that they don't want the dump in their states; and that practical politics ensure that it must go to one of the "deserted" states;

and since Nevada has so much experience already . . . case closed. Bring on the rhetoric that asks woeful Nevadans to remember the job opportunities that such a dump will bring with it.

The Nuclear Waste Policy Act of 1982 established the responsibility of the federal government for finding repositories for high-level waste—the most dangerous—from nuclear weapons plants and civilian power plants. The uneasy process of finding candidate sites settled on two places: the Waste Isolation Pilot Plant, carved out of salt beds, 2,150 feet deep, near Carlsbad, New Mexico—the smaller of the two, for less toxic materials; and for everything else, the major site, a cavern 800 feet within Yucca Mountain, Nevada, immediately to the west of the Test Site, about one hundred miles northwest of Las Vegas, and about twenty-five miles east of the California border.

There are different estimates, but we can probably count on somewhere between twenty and thirty local dumps of radioactive waste throughout the United States. They vary enormously in size and inherent problems, but they are all hazards that this state or that would rather not have. Take the case of Hanford, arguably the most potent.

Hanford Engineer Works, on the Columbia River, near Richland, Washington, is the place where most of the plutonium enrichment was done for the American nuclear program. That business stopped in 1987, but in the years since 1943, there had been more exposure to contamination for the local population than was desirable. That was bad enough. But what was left at Hanford was more confounding.

The 560-square-mile site (including the banks and waters of the Columbia) now includes nine spent nuclear reactors; the reactor units from more than twenty nuclear submarines; several cubic miles of contaminated soil; over 2,000 metric tons of irradiated fuel; 700,000 cubic yards of solid waste; and 177 underground tanks, ranging in size from 55,476 gallons to 1.13 million gallons—containing plutonium, other radioactive elements, and unknown chemicals. Most of those tanks are a single steel shell surrounded by concrete. It is known that the cocktail in some of those tanks has made for gases that could explode. Some have argued that there is a possibility of a chain reaction at Hanford that could turn into a mighty and disastrous explosion. And all that material has, somehow, to be delivered to Yucca Mountain.

You may remember the careful labeling employed at the waste pits on the Nevada Test Site, a place that deals with far less toxic materials. That comes from the bitter lesson of Hanford, where waste materials had been mixed together, without record or forethought. No one knows exactly what all those tanks contain, or how the elements could interact. Equally, it is clear that many of the tanks have leakage problems, just as the Hanford Site as a whole passes materials into the Columbia River. It is one thing to quarantine an immense amount of soil, but rivers do not wait for such a gathering process.

There are other scary things going on over the brow of some hill—and while they are not exactly covered up, there is no great urge at the Department of Energy to report them. In July 1998, the *San Francisco Chronicle* told how a ship from South Korea was about to dock with three twenty-six-ton casks containing spent nuclear fuel rods from power stations in Asia (standing next to those rods for an hour would be fatal). The ship was to pass under the Golden Gate Bridge, then under the Benicia Bridge, to dock at the U.S. Naval Weapons Station at Concord. The rods would then be put on a train that would go back to Martinez, over the Benicia Bridge, and then by way of Sacramento to the rail line that goes through Gerlach, Winnemucca, and so to Ogden and then north to Atomic City, at the Idaho National Engineering & Environmental Laboratory. The dates of arrival and transportation were kept secret, but the admission was made that there have been over 150 such deliveries in the past forty years.

The stuff has to go somewhere. The United States traded fuel rods to developing countries in Asia in the fifties and sixties, and it is part of the deal that we take the refuse back. Or would you want it to remain in those countries? That's only a microcosm of the bigger question: Should America take on the old weapons (and waste) of the Soviet Union, or leave it to the vagaries of that part of the world? Remember the building on the Nevada Test Site for the dismantling of old weapons—unused as yet, but poised to carry out the burdensome responsibility of victory in the Cold War.

It was also revealed that the train to Atomic City, which passes through such rugged country as the Black Rock Desert, would be tracked along the road by a van full of radiation experts from the Lawrence Livermore Laboratory. Yet all of the material headed for Atomic City—the great wreck of Hanford, as well as stuff at Aiken, South Carolina (close to the Savannah River Site)—must still get to Yucca Mountain, along with debris from maybe another twenty locations.

But not quite yet. According to the 1982 act, Yucca Mountain should have opened in 1998. In the campaign on behalf of Yucca Mountain, the tiny amount of rainfall in the area was held very important. That part of Nevada reckons on about six inches a year. Early estimates were that the moisture would then take "hundreds of thousands" of years to reach the caverns where the waste was to be stored. That tiny amount, it was thought, over such a lengthy period, would do the minimum amount of damage to the casks and containers. The biggest risk in any storage scheme is degradation of the containers, which could allow radioactive material to seep back into the water supply of the area. However, in June 1997, it was revealed that new tests had found that rainwater had found cracks that would carry it into the cavern in only forty years.

That rain is a problem that must be dealt with. There's an answer in the Carlsbad experience, where magnesium oxide has been used to fill empty spaces and absorb the moisture. We are a society that believes in its ability to find answers, and we have to be, given our capacity for generating problems. But Carlsbad has cost $2 billion to build, it has an annual budget of $185 million, and it will be full in thirty-five years. Research at Yucca Mountain, with major excavation still to come, has already cost $2.4 billion. Fifty or so years ago, when the Manhattan Project was launched, it was far easier to carry out such sweeping secret plans. Today, government is open to so many forms of protest and litigation. Yucca Mountain may be inevitable, or the only possible resort, but it will not come cheap.

Even then, it involves so many kinds of gambling—that the weather in southern Nevada may not alter; that the gases in some casks will not explode; that the transportation of every last load of poison will not make for contamination; that the dumps will never be raided by terrorists; that Las Vegas—the nation's gaming resort—may not be deterred by the thought of that mountain of toxicity so close at hand.

Yet we are probably correct in assuming that the nuclear arsenal of this country is better accounted for than that of our potential enemy in the Cold War. That prolonged trial is said to have cost this country—in terms of making arms, rockets, bombs, and keeping men in the services—$4 trillion. And it must have cost the Soviet Union about the same. We won— didn't we?—but doesn't that mean, sooner or later, that we are obliged (out of self-interest) to tidy up the wreckage on the loser's land and start to pay for his defeat? Didn't we enter into that sort of deal with Japan, and aren't the stakes much higher, now, with the remains of the Soviet Union?

In other words, we can no more let Russia founder economically than we can trust that no Soviet bomb or packet of waste or deposit of nerve gas falls into the wrong hands. After all, terrorism does not actually need to deliver locally if its weapon is dirty enough. When Yucca Mountain was tested, for instance, the survey found chlorine 36 that came not from the Nevada Test Site but from Russian tests carried out so far, and so many decades, away. Fallout is like music or the word of God: It goes everywhere. A terrorist could blow up his own backyard and eventually endanger most of the rest of the globe. Meanwhile, we hear stories of former Soviet soldiers or scientists—often the keepers of bombs—who have not been paid properly. We have only to recollect human nature, that urge to take your life to the tables, to see the dangers that victory has exposed us to.

Some gamblers sit at a table enclosed in the cell of *now* and the next few seconds: If they win, they think, they are changed. They are like a government that waits for problems to arise and then tries to solve them. There are other gamblers who work in a larger space: They reckon on their lifetime; they see the arc of relationships, of children, of careers or callings, of great things to do, and they hope it will all prove worthwhile. As a government, they would take a longer view, think in larger terms, and take every bit of advice before coming to decisions.

In that way, we may come to regret having won the Cold War, not just because we spent $4 trillion on hardware instead of health, education, and racial unrest (though those things have warped us already) but because a fairly small strategic decision—to make the bomb—and the seemingly modest trial of concealing the knowledge that it was not necessary have had such profound and irreversible effects. We needed, in those

Palm-tree farming: a small business south of Las Vegas, where fully grown palms can be purchased for immediate atmosphere

early 1940s, to have a form of government that did not separate scientists and generals and the president, and which did not let events overpower us. We need it still, yet we are left with the vivid, interminable half-lives of elements in the ground and in the air—natural, knowable things, things without a will or mind of their own—that could make a mockery of safety, of victory, and continuity.

In far more ways than gaming could ever express, Nevada is the providential testing place for our recklessness. So we should study the volatile mixture of its danger and beauty, then wonder which we deserve.

THEN, ON ONE DAY, QUIETLY (THERE WAS AN AMERICAN AIR-lines crash in Arkansas that killed nine on the same day), the *New York Times* ran two front-page stories:

In the first, it disclosed that long-term plans for storing nuclear waste at the Savannah River Site, near Aiken, South Carolina (second in importance to Hanford), had been aborted. The containers of waste had been generating a dangerously explosive gas, benzene. In 1998, the Department of Energy had decided to abandon the program and seek alternatives. Representative John Dingell said in a General Accounting Office report that "mismanagement" had led to an "extraordinary, and pathetic, waste of taxpayer money. All we have to show for $500 million is a 20-year delay and the opportunity to risk another $1 billion to make a problematic process work."

In fact, the GAO admitted that new plans might run as high as $3.5 billion—if they worked properly. The reaction from Hanford—where the problem is more grave—was one of "huge concern."

But, of course, the problem within the United States is one that confronts the richest economy and the most powerful nation in the world. Other places have fewer resources. The second report concerned Vozrozhdeniye, or "Renaissance," an island in the Aral Sea on the borders of Kazakhstan and Uzbekistan. It was there in 1988 that Soviet scientists and soldiers buried hundreds of tons of anthrax bacteria—enough to kill everyone on Earth several times—to avoid U.S. inspection. They added bleach, which was supposed to destroy the anthrax.

Eleven years later, two things are apparent: Not all the anthrax was neutralized, and the island is growing—misguided irrigation schemes by the Soviets have had the effect of shrinking the Aral Sea. The island has grown from 77 square miles to 770 in a decade. Very soon now, it will join the mainland.

PART THREE

Collects

His smile disappeared. Did he understand? I couldn't be sure.
But that hardly mattered now. I was going back to Las Vegas. I
had no choice.

—Hunter S. Thompson, *Fear and Loathing in Las Vegas*, 1971

Nevada is ten thousand tales of ugliness and beauty, vicious-
ness and virtue.

—Richard G. Lillard, *Desert Challenge: An Interpretation of
Nevada*, 1942

A pretty view of one of many ground zeros, Dirty Harry, May 19, 1953
(Department of Energy)

THOUGH NEVADA HAS NEVER YET BEEN A CROWDED STATE, still it has its throng, and there are so many Nevadan lives and stories not named or wondered over so far. So we offer collects or prayers for the unknown members of the crowd.

At about 1:00 a.m. on September 4, 1998, two HH-60G Pave Hawk helicopters crashed about twenty-five miles north of Indian Springs, a desert area known as the "Fallout Hills," base level well over three thousand feet, with peaks at six thousand feet or more. They were on a night exercise, and all twelve men aboard the Hawks were killed.

The helicopters, it seemed, were part of a squadron based at Nellis Air Force Base, but it is possible that night that they were operating out of another base, at Groom Lake or Papoose Lake. The air force needed more than twelve hours to issue a statement on the accident. Even then, they were vague: The two helicopters might have collided; they might have crashed separately. Brig. Gen. Theodore Lay said, "It's a fairly remote area. That's why we took so much time."

The "remote" area is actually within a web of amazingly sophisticated military installations, a place where tiny human movements on the ground are easily monitored. So there is another possible reason for delay: The estimated site of the crash could have been a little off—twenty-five miles north of Indian Springs, and say twelve miles or so to the west, would have put the helicopters over Plutonium Valley, one of the most radioactive parts of the Nevada Test Site, a place so toxic that no one can go in there without elaborate protective clothing. That could have taken a little time.

. . .

There are shapes in the desert that could be the past or the future.

AS SOUTHERN NEVADA HAS BEEN TRANSFORMED IN THE LAST sixty years, so Las Vegas has gone from being a city of about 8,400 residents in 1940 to a place that has over a million by now and is growing. Go twenty minutes or so down the Strip from the Mirage, turn off the main road, and the blacktop reaches out into the desert with lines and loops of new houses. They are going up as fast as sets, and sometimes they don't seem much more solid or durable. But they are estates and avenues with pretty gilded names, and there are flags to guide you to the show houses. And still the bright new properties are more spacious, and yet so much cheaper than refugees from California are accustomed to that they are vexed to find they can't just roll over their sale price from San Jose, Oxnard, or Riverside. They're going to have to pay some damn capital-gains tax!

And the malls come in behind the new estates, like canteens, commissariats, and cemeteries backing up the front-line troops. The desert is buffed away, and turf is put in to surround the new houses with harsh lawn. Sprinklers saturate the turf until it grips and holds. From your new property, you can gaze out at desert, but look quickly, because there are plans to fill that view with yet more estates. There seems no slackening in the number who want to come to Vegas to live, to retire, to grow golden in the dark air, to get away from as many taxes as possible, and to see just how much they can do with their golf handicap before they die. These aren't necessarily people coming for the casinos—though maybe they'll take their birthday dinners at the Bellagio or at Caesars, why not?—but if the kids come to stay from the East, sure, they can go to the casinos.

The population of Nevada has increased with startling enthusiasm.

1940	110,247
1950	160,083
1960	285,278
1970	488,738
1980	800,493
1990	1,201,833

The increase from 1980 to 1990 was about 50 percent. At least as big a spurt is expected for 2000, which would mean a population of about 1,870,000. Allow the same percentage increase for each decade in the twenty-first century, and the population would be over 6 million by 2030. Two-thirds of that would probably be in the Clark County area—Las Vegas, Henderson, Boulder, Laughlin. But by then, the Reno-Sparks area might also be getting on toward a million. For the same kind of building ventures are pushing back the desert north of those cities. Las Vegas now has over five hundred churches, seven major hospitals, the largest convention center in the United States (2.5 million conventioneers a year), two daily papers—the *Sun* and the *Review Journal*—the eighth-busiest airport in the nation, almost 100,000 hotel rooms, nine cab companies, nearly three hundred days of sunshine a year, a university campus, a symphony orchestra, a dance theater, the Chamber Players, an opera theater, and the Rainbow Company children's theater group. It has some of the most daring and innovative approaches to architecture in the world—and the Liberace Museum. At the same time, Las Vegas has the highest suicide rate in the nation, a rising problem of teenage gangs involved in drugs, a Yellow Page telephone directory in which nearly one hundred pages are given over to the "Adult Entertainment" section ("Blonde, Beautiful & Barely Legal," "Your Fantasy Is My Relief," "Nasty College Girls—Direct to Your Room"), and the unhindered success of a business that can destroy lives and families. It has parking and traffic problems, the onset of air pollution, a constant worry about where the water will come from. It has some of the more grotesque and depressed architecture ever seen in the world (your nightmare in concrete)—and the Liberace Museum.

There are still "old-timers" around who remember Helldorado Days, the Rat Pack's sardonic attitude, and the sultry glamour of the old hotel-casinos. They recall the small, manageable town where everyone knew everyone else, and where the adventure of Las Vegas was fresh and pungent. Today, they say, it's turned automatic, bureaucratic, mass-market, perfumed, and anonymous. Such people cannot believe they live in a city that has major traffic jams as well as the indifference of suburban sprawl. They lament the way the hotel-casino business has shifted its attention to families—and children, for God's sake! There was a time—wasn't there?—when Nevada was meant for grown-ups, for men who'd quite likely left their families behind, and who were prepared to stand or fall at the tables and live by the code of the desert. Gambling then was akin to fine old whiskey; today it's like Coca-Cola. Once upon a time, Nevada was a place for outcasts, adventurers, and tough godless men who believed in the whim of chance. Now, it's another kind of Disneyland, too damn slick and organized for its own good.

"I'd move on," some of these old-timers mutter—they couldn't really: They are mortgaged in and they have their HMO in town taking care of them—they aren't what they were, or what they dreamed they might be still. They are pensioners in Las Vegas, old men with one-bedroom apartments on the north side of I-15, an old sedan that still runs, and a regular place for lunch at Denny's. "I'd move on," they say, and the complaint trails away, as sad, watery eyes realize there is nowhere else much to go. Not unless they drove into the desert and walked away from the car—just as cocky as Noël Coward—or took a powder tonight. You don't have to believe that all the suicides in Las Vegas are broken gamblers. There are other kinds of dismay that no symphony orchestra is going to stop. Las Vegas has a lot of elders who came for the sunshine, the dry air, the lack of taxes, and the old days. But they have lived to have doctors tell them the sun will kill them, that the dry air and the air conditioning play havoc with old lungs, and don't talk to me about taxes. Oh sure, there's no state income tax and no estate tax, but Nevada is loaded up with every bit of excise tax and consumption tax it can think of. Why, I heard that Ralph Heller on the radio the other day—writes for the *Daily Sparks Tribune*. They're still Nevadan up there, I guess. And he said that Nevada has the twelfth-highest per capita tax burden in the nation. Around $1,500 a month, he said. What I say is, Spare me some of that, and tax those damn casinos more.

In fact, in Nevada in 1998, a politician made the same case. Aaron Russo was a movie producer—he did *The Rose* and *Trading Places*—and he was running against Kenny Guinn, the favorite, to be the Republican candidate in the November election for governor. Well, Russo's big pitch was, Don't listen to the propaganda that Nevada is "tax-free" for ordinary folks, and pay attention to the fact that the tax on the casino industry is still only 6.25 percent, which it has been for eighteen years. Of course, nowhere near enough listened. Guinn beat Russo easily and went on to become governor. It has gotten so bad that there's an establishment in Nevada now—the casinos and the government—and no amount of hard common sense is ever going to break it. It's all part of today's America.

OCCASIONALLY, THE NATIONAL PRESS WILL POUNCE UPON gambling and bring back the news that its profits are faltering, as if gambling were just a matter of money or business. The feeling lingers that we should not need gambling, and that one day somehow it will get the better of us. And so, on January 2, 1992, the *New York Times* ran the story "Long Seen As Safe from Slumps, Las Vegas Finally Feels Recession." Gambling revenue for October 1991—October is a key month—was down 12 percent from the previous October. Well, yes, but October 1990 had been the greatest month in the history of the business, with revenue of over $450 million—revenue meaning the difference between the money wagered and that paid out. And that difference is somewhere in the region of 8 to 15 percent of the money wagered. Apart from October 1990, October 1991 was the best October Las Vegas had had yet. The craze wasn't quite over. After all, on October 31, 1991, the Dow stood at 3069.10; and in January 1991, George Bush had directed the invasion of Iraq.

In hindsight, the eighties are looked at as a bad time in Las Vegas history, but annual gambling revenues in Clark County rose from $2.3 billion in 1986 to $4.04 billion in that "gloomy" 1991. The seven leading public casino companies showed average profits for the years 1986–1990 as follows:

Circus Circus	24.9%
Hilton	21.4
Caesars	16.3
Showboat	11.7
Aztar	11.2
Bally's	10.4
Mirage	7.5

And in 1990, Mirage Resorts was just about to take off, to the extent that by 1996, *Fortune* magazine was rating it one of the best-run businesses in the country.

But America as a whole has been spreading gambling across the country in the eighties and nineties. By 1994, twenty-three states had legal casinos, to say nothing of the number of states that had adopted lottery schemes. In 1993, Americans gambled $394 billion; by 1996, the figure was $500 billion. In 1996, 6 percent of gross national product went for gambling and 8 percent for groceries.

In 1982, the U.S. gambling revenue was $10.4 billion; by 1994, that sum had climbed to $40 billion. Of that $40 billion, $6.6 billion was attributed to Nevada and New Jersey slot machines, $3.6 billion to table play in those two states, $3.4 billion to Indian-run casinos, $5.2 billion to other casinos, and $13.7 billion to lotteries.

Of course, by the summer of 1998, the Dow was over 8,000 — that business had done even better — and a president had gambled not just his reputation and future but maybe the chance to help Russia (among other things) on the gamble of telling a lie in public and under oath. Bill Clinton's face is as good a portrait as we will ever find of the American smile watching the ball about to drop or the card in the act of turning.

Nevada had every reason for feeling good. It had increased its business and its profits, despite bold new investment. When New York, New York opened on New Year's Eve 1996, it began to make profits at the rate of $31,000 an hour. The competition from so many other states and forms of gambling has only made Vegas feel more important. There had been changes, and the casualties of competition: the Riviera went bust; Steve Wynn sacrificed the Dunes to make the Bellagio; and even the great and famous Sands was demolished in November 1996 to make way eventually for the Venetian (set for three thousand rooms at a cost of $1.2 billion).

Maybe the Sands stood for classic Las Vegas. Maybe in some cultures it would have been bought by the city or the state and made into a museum. But the land on the Strip is far too valuable for such sentiment — remember that in one hundred years or so, Hollywood has not yet made a proper museum to itself. No, this culture is too greedy for reverence, too eager to move forward, and too uninterested in the past. The logic of such progress is not to build the Bellagio or the Venetian out of rock, for they will have to come down one day, too.

Nevada changed in other ways. The new theme casinos clearly brought more people (and more families with kids) to Las Vegas. In surveys, people reported that they were coming to Las Vegas for a family holiday, for the entertainment, for the shopping! In 1993, gambling revenue in Las Vegas was 31 percent of total receipts. By 1996, that figure had fallen to just over 25 percent. In a report released in July 1998, it was discovered by the Las Vegas Convention and Visitors Authority that, for the first time, some of the annual 30 million visitors regarded Las Vegas as an "entertainment" destination as opposed to one for "gambling." The Forum at Caesars Palace announced that it would be expanding when the same report claimed that 67 percent of visitors put shopping as their first priority, and only 18 percent gambling.

All of which may suggest the shrewdness of Steve Wynn in having a swanky art gallery at the Bellagio, a place for people not accustomed to, and maybe intimidated by, art galleries. While gambling revenues remain so buoyant, there may be no cause for alarm. Even if gambling rates modestly in surveys, most people do get to the tables, or the slots.

For the new dominance of the one-armed bandits is very striking. More and more floor space is being given over to them. More and more clients at the casinos, the elderly especially, head for those machines and stay there hour upon hour, as if they offered dialysis. The house has no objection; it does very well on the machines, it can calculate the odds precisely, and it has learned the strategy of putting the frequent jackpot machines at the most crowded spots on the floor to draw people in. And if the slots seem working-class, then note that in September 1998, in Reno, for $30 wagered, a San Francisco man won $30 million—the biggest slots win ever, so far. Two months later, in Vegas, a woman won $27.5 million.

But the slots habit bespeaks a clientele that feels ignorant of table etiquette or alarmed at the risk of making fools of themselves in front of more expert players. As a result, most casinos run training sessions where a croupier as good as a stand-up comic will take the crowd through the rules of the game while coaching them in the best ways to play. Incidentally, that education is a more or less tacit admission to the suckers that the house is going to win, and it reaffirms that excellent new wisdom in Las Vegas, that the house has no need to cheat. We, the public, are being trained in a graceful way of losing.

It is also evident that as table play is in decline, so stakes at some tables are going up—another thing to keep the timid, cautious player away. The ultimate outcome of that trend is the increased provision being made for high rollers, otherwise known as "premium players" or even "whales." According to another *New York Times* story, premium players may wager up to $250,000 per visit, and there are several thousand of them. "Whales" are people ready to bet $1 million or more, and there are only about 250 of them in the world. The casinos lust after these players and are ever more inventive about ways to secure and hold them. There are free luxury suites that are enormous, garish, and ornate; somehow, the test of true taste or style is always avoided at Las Vegas, lest any other cultural trends or imperatives intrude on gambling.

Is it possible, one day, that some casino will be a place for just premium prospects—Bruce Willis, Dennis Rodman, Larry Flynt, Kerry Packer, Adnan Khashoggi, some unknown Japanese, and the sultan of Brunei—and the row upon row of little old ladies who sit from one meal to the next at "their" machine, lulled by the ceaseless tintinnabulation of their little bells? It's not the Vegas of popular iconography, with a cowboy and a duchess at the same table, a thin-lipped mastermind, a wily Oriental, and just our hero, with a beauty blowing on his dice for good luck. No, there are times when a roomful of slot machines resembles some photograph of early industrialization—with slaves at the machines, obsessed, deluded, and, above all, lonely.

Most people go to Vegas in groups large enough to ward off such fears. They are old folks' clubs, or bowling teams, honeymoon parties, family reunions, company outings, and so on. The loners are taken most often for hard-core professional gamblers. Or are they just people who are constitutionally alone?

Alone in Las Vegas, you can get the feeling that for all the King Arthur ambience, the Egyptian front, the rain forest, and the pirates' picnic atmosphere, one hotel-casino inside is like all the others—it's a gaming floor where you can't find your way to anywhere, with no windows and no sense of direction, with floors of hotel stacked on top of it, with the rooms always the same, always fine, frosty, and fresh-linened, but dead, if you know what I mean. And the food is terrific, but just a little impersonal— which is how Steve's voice is beginning to strike you whenever you turn on the TV. And altogether, you're worn out by watching the idiots and the stooges and the old folks "having fun," and you've run out of the wicked mischief that likes to study married couples at the next table in the dining room wondering whether to murder or divorce; either way, they're into legal bills. You are struck by the monotony of the setup, the architecture or whatever they call it, and you marvel that there are some architectural books written over the years that get excited about the look and feel and spaceyness of Las Vegas, as if they couldn't tell a depression home when they saw it. And you are through watching the table life, where so many moments are crucial, and exciting, and desperate, and wonderful—after all, they're all so uninteresting. Who cares if it's a 6 or the 7? Who cares whether or not Nicklaus, say, can sink the thirty-footer, or the next girl will smile at you, or if you'll be okay if you drive a solid mile on I-15 with your eyes shut?

In 1997, Professor David Phillips, a sociologist at the University of California, San Diego, reported that suicide rates were as much as four times higher in cities that had gambling as in those that did not. These are anecdotal details — the guy whose small business is on the skids, who has two children in college, and then the market slumps; the woman with breast cancer, divorced, who reckons she'd just as soon take her shot at having a good time for a few months as do the radiation and the chemo; and then there's the drunk (played by Nicolas Cage) in *Leaving Las Vegas* who goes there to die, as if the place could deliver no truer, deeper function.

It isn't just residents, either; visitors to Las Vegas kill themselves more often than visitors to San Diego or New Orleans, or wherever. Frank Fahrenkopf, the spokesman for the American Gaming Association — a lobbying group for hotels and casinos — argued that gambling had very little to do with suicide. People in the West, he said, had always killed themselves more often, because they were "without personal support systems." Can't someone tell him how up-to-date the West has become, and what a modest, thriving city Las Vegas is? Also, if gambling is three-quarters as important as groceries, isn't it in the bloodstream by now, like cigarette smoke?

How long will it be in a society of free-enterprise litigation before someone has the wit to sue a casino for encouraging gambling in her father, her husband, or even herself?

Gambling has not spread in America without such anxieties. President Clinton at one time talked about a federal tax on gaming revenues as a way of paying for Social Security, or whatever. The gaming industry was stunned to the quick at any suggestion that their privileged tax status might be endangered. In response, they backed Bob Dole. Steve Wynn hosted a lunch for Dole at his Shadow Creek golf course that raised $478,000. Clinton dropped the tax idea, but he then proposed a national commission on gambling.*

More to the point, and more ironic, in 1998 California voters faced an election proposition that would permit Indian casinos in the state to do

---

* That commission reported in June 1999 and recommended that political contributions from gaming interests be restricted, that betting on college sports be banned, and that the minimum age for players be held at twenty-one.

openly what they had been doing furtively for some time—to gamble. California was too close to home for the Nevadan gaming interests to allow this. They paid for a massive advertising campaign on California television against the Indian casinos. One commercial had a pretty young married couple wheeling a stroller of kids in their choice neighborhood, when suddenly a casino reared up out of the ground like Godzilla. The casino didn't look like anything precisely famous in the modern Vegas skyline, but still it was just the kind of thing Nevada deals in. Many Indians regret their own gaming institutions, but they have found no other way to lift their people out of American poverty. After all, a wrecked family can at least attempt to pay for their damage if they have shares in a flourishing casino.

Is it so strange that the casino business should grasp the dark image of their churches? Not really. Steve Wynn's father was a victim of chronic gambling, and Steve himself has been heard to say that people shouldn't gamble. But, if they do . . . he could be called as prosecution witness in a suit against himself, which is the height of Americanness.

THERE ARE PLENTY OF PEOPLE WHO ARE IN NO DANGER OF adding to Las Vegas's suicide statistics: The people who don't, and won't, go there. I have been surprised at how many people I encounter—and plenty of them Californians—who have never been to Las Vegas and who have no intention of going. I say they should try; I make the case that it is unlike anywhere else on Earth; I go deep into my own feelings and say that it is so beautiful and so terrible (or so spectacular and so daunting) that they owe it to themselves as Americans to test it out. Doesn't the ultimate metropolitan experiment deserve that much from us? On December 31, 1999, and January 1, 2000, with tickets for Streisand, there will be nowhere more appropriate to be (even if, especially if, you reckon that on that night there will be some ceremonial for slipping from bad to worse) than in Las Vegas, the most complete embodiment of a time without history, structure, humanism, or discourse.

Hell, you mean? say the skeptics. Or maybe Heaven? I wonder. Think of the damage done by history, structure, humanism, and discourse.

Over the years, I've made a small collection of the world's worst opinions of Las Vegas. Of course, it includes all that early scorn that Nevada was no more than a colony of California, a scratching ground for a crazy few, and an idea that gave up the ghost when it took on gambling and divorce in order to survive. But there are so many other, more recent gloomy warnings:

- In *City of Nets*, Otto Friedrich's enjoyable yet not very searching history of Hollywood in the 1940s, published in 1986, he says:

> Las Vegas today is what Hell might be like if Hell had been planned and built by New York gangsters. It is the kingdom of pleasure, where everything is permitted, then perverted and parodied. Where pleasure is defined (as in *Mahagonny*) in terms of indulgences for sale, gambling, whiskey, prostitution. Where thousands of tourists are loaded into a row of garish hotels and encouraged to squander their money in joyous revelry until it is all gone. Pleasure grimly organized and sold, around the clock, mass-produced and mass-consumed—what could be more Hellish than a gangster vision of Paradise?

- Something close to that spirit can be found in Hunter Thompson's *Fear and Loathing in Las Vegas* (of which a good deal belongs to the illustrator, Ralph Steadman), published in 1971. Thompson has the reputation of a wild, libertine egalitarian—drugs for all—but there is a puritan and a social critic in there, a lash to others' depravity, and he had this to say about one of Vegas's most profitable and crowded places:

> The Circus-Circus is what the hole hep world would be doing on Saturday night if the Nazis had won the war. This is the Sixth Reich. The ground floor is full of gambling tables, like all the other casinos . . . but the place is about four stories high, in the style of a circus tent, and all manner of strange Country-Fair/Polish Carnival madness is going on up in this space. Right above the gambling tables the Forty Flying Carazito Brothers are doing a high-wire trapeze act, along with four muzzled Wolverines and the Six Nymphet Sisters from San Diego. . . . So you're down on the main floor playing blackjack, and the stakes are getting high when suddenly you chance to look up, and there, right smack above your head is a half-naked fourteen-year old girl being chased through the air by a snarling wolverine. . . .

- And then, in September 1998, in the *New York Times Book Review*, Timothy Foote, reviewing Timothy Egan's *Lasso the Wind*, wrote:

Head on up to that water-guzzling urban monstrosity, Las Vegas,
and the Sands Hotel (the iniquitous landmark of many a Sinatra-
struck youth) is blown sky-high by ambitious developers.

This all sounds too awful and fulminating for response, but let me try.
And let me say first that small errors can be crucial. The Sands was not
blown "sky-high" in the way bombs were; it was elegantly collapsed by
explosive techniques refined in the America that is always making anew. I
have argued elsewhere that buildings go up and down in Las Vegas without a sense of the monumental. They are plays upon the imagination, as
much setlike as solid (of course, they are solid, in the sense of safe). It is as
if the desert base and background inspired building with a sense of imper-
manence or potential makeover. You may not admire that, but as an
approach, it is modern, intriguing, and suggestive of many truths in our
culture. It is also an attitude pioneered in Los Angeles, and in the set making of Hollywood.

Then again, there are things about Circus Circus that would horrify
Nazis, not least the number of Jews in the casino organization, and in the
audience, to say nothing of Chicanos, blacks, Orientals, or whatever else.
There is a certain amount of anonymity and uniformity palpable in Las
Vegas, but one cannot deny the condition that helps supply this—the lack
of discrimination and the welcome offered to common people. Nor do I
see any hint in Reich culture of the cheek, the insolence, the experimen-
tation that would put gambling and the circus, propriety, and sex side by
side. America has real potential dangers in its well-fed drabness, its bland
homogeneity, its mindless consistency. Yet it is also a country in which
surreal outrages of juxtaposition arise all the time, like the way in Carson
City, say, that the U.S. Mint building (the state museum) confronts the
city's most gaudy casino.

And in Otto Friedrich, we find fewer errors of fact than mistakes of
observation or insight. If he felt the revelry in Vegas was joyless, then I
wonder how often he was there. Indeed, one of the great perils in being
alone there is having to see what a terrific time other people are having.
That melancholy may develop a philosophy meant to confound the bases
of others' pleasure (much of depression rests in this doleful superiority),
but no one can deny the fact of pleasure. And if there are pleasures that
have emerged in this century—collecting plastic handbags, pop music,
the movies, being in Las Vegas—that do not match collecting Russian
icons, Mahler, Donne, or being at the Canyon de Chelly, what is confirmed in the argument that some things are *real* pleasures or *real* beauty,

while others are just the bogus things that can deceive uneducated or classless people?

People do have fun in Las Vegas. You know that because they keep going back there, despite the knowledge that they will lose their money. Hope springs eternal and delusional, you say. Yes, that's so, but don't forget how close the abandonment of monetary stock comes to an ideal in the educated creed. Great gamblers have seen through the grim absurdities in capital and its accumulation. They know money is merely a game (like 10,000 on the Dow), and they insist on being playful with it. There is ease and even transcendence in that feeling. You may disapprove of gambling, or drugs, or fucking other people's wives and husbands, but don't let those habits off so lightly that you ignore their intense pleasure. You will only reform them out of the human soul if you can replace or match the pleasure.

But Friedrich's foreboding has gone astray earlier, in the notion that Las Vegas is Hell as designed by New York gangsters. Again, there's such an assumption there that gangsters are without education or class, humanity even, and that they are single-mindedly wicked fellows cackling with glee to see Hell in practice. Whereas, gangsters, I suspect, are as mixed-up as Friedrich or you or me. Many of them have devout faiths, but even those who do not are aspiring toward good and better things—more fun, more order, more business, more status. They're every bit as alarmed by Hell as you are; they were seeking Heaven in Las Vegas. Aha, says Friedrich, but that sort of Paradise *is* Hell.

No, it's not. Hell is rebuke, torture, and eternal punishment for those who have sinned. Las Vegas may be founded on a paradox, or a trick, but the idea that you will play and strive and then lose is not hellish. For many of us, it's a profound and absorbing metaphor for life. Gangsters want to be legitimate, and nowhere better than in Las Vegas have they made it. If that alerts you to the irony (shall we say?) that American society and business are dependent on strains of criminality, so be it. Gangsters believe in family, getting yours, having a good time, a lovely house—and giving to charity. They want to be model citizens according to the American way. In which case, why despise their taste?

Caesars Palace is a gruesome parody of Rome; the Luxor is camp Egypt; there are no real snakes at the Mirage. All true. The structure and atmosphere of Vegas are only as accurate to life as the formulas of Hollywood genre films—wasn't *Casablanca*, years ago, a kind of junky theme casino, ludicrously distant from the real North African city and its Nazi guests?

The case can certainly be made that Las Vegas would be a sad model for twentieth-century America. I suspect that most visitors to the city feel that from time to time. That does not dispel or cancel out the pleasure available there. It may help us realize that the pleasure is closely allied to a kind of danger. I have tried to show, in that respect, how Las Vegas resembles the other great Nevadan theme park up the road—the Test Site—where the world may have been saved, yet tainted at the same time.

For myself, I came to this book for two main reasons—an intense feeling for the desert beauty of Nevada and an unsettled fascination with Las Vegas. But I have spent much of my life in love with (and at war with) another uniquely American way of offering fantasy in preference to reality—the movies. And I feel about the movies, as I do about Las Vegas, that while we might have been better off without them entirely, how can you take your eyes away from the sight? Las Vegas teaches us the very startling lesson that Hell and Heaven may be the same place, and so the old class war will go on forever there.

ONE POINT AROSE IN THAT SERIES OF ATTACKS ON LAS VEGAS that needs comment—its water guzzling. In the same book review, Egan is quoted as arguing that in the long run Las Vegas itself is "unsustainable, in terms of water use."

That may be so. But look at how much has been accomplished so far. Recollect that Las Vegas was only developed in the first place because there were springs there, and because the area proved so rich in artesian wells. More than that, note that modern Nevada could never have come to be without the building of Hoover Dam and Lake Mead.

At the end of this century, Las Vegas takes about 80 percent of its water from Lake Mead—and yes, it uses water the way a casino uses neon. When you stay in Vegas, the water is the ornamental lake outside the hotel, the pool within, the playground of the dolphins, the twenty-four-hour-a-day shower, and the glasses of iced water on your table as soon as you sit down. It's there in the lawns and the sprinkler systems—it's an attitude about water that the rest of Nevada regards as wasteful or indulgent. In 1991, Pat Mulroy, general manager of the Las Vegas Valley Water District, estimated that she had water needs covered until the year 2006. Today, the city feels confident about going as far as 2030. But that's only because, in the early nineties, it went about sinking a lot of wells all over the state that reached down to the aquifer level. Farmers and ranchers were very concerned at that, and they made the case that they were so few, while their product served so many. Agriculture can easily seem more basic and noble than tourism. Thus northern Nevada had one more reason for disdaining the south in the southerners who could bring about drought in a state and kill off the farmers to the north.

But the truth is more complex, what Mulroy called "a colliding of the new and old West." She argued that agriculture (in 1991) was using 90.3 percent of the available water, was producing 6,010 jobs, and annual revenue of $168 million. Steve Wynn looked up at that and said he employed more people at the Mirage than the whole farming industry. Tourism and gaming use only 9.3 percent of the water, employ 547,100 people, and bring in $19.4 billion in revenue a year.

No wonder all the political thrust for the state comes from Las Vegas; no wonder the rest of the state feels numbing anger and frustration.

Of course, there are dangers. With the great new suck on the aquifer, there are ranches that might lose their water. With other sources drawn off, there are forms of wildlife—the rare desert pupfish, for one—that could be wiped out. There's another kind of danger: Suppose gambling suddenly waned (because of government intrusion or because America's ingenuity found some other pastime); then Las Vegas and Nevada would be ruined. Granted, and add this: In the new attention to the aquifer, it was found that in southern Nevada the water table had amounts of plutonium—leached in from the Test Site—that were moving far more quickly than had been thought possible before. Pat Mulroy said, "The plutonium doesn't concern me because the flow pattern is not toward Las Vegas." It was going toward Death Valley. Water knows. Meanwhile, the true voice of the gambler runs the show in Las Vegas.

And gamblers tend to worry in the short term. They fear that 7 may not come up. They forget that the asteroid may hit the Strip. So are you more alarmed about the dangers you know, or the ones you don't know? Las Vegas might be wreckage in a hundred years, or five hundred; it might be a ghost town in a hundred and Crazy Jane again in five hundred. You had better learn to trust the patience of the desert, and know that if you play long enough, it gets back its money. But Las Vegas is that rare thing: a city built in the spirit that knows its days are numbered. That's the eerie spirit of its profound casualness. The house itself knows that it is only there by the grace of God. And the whole show can boast that it is what would have happened if God had had the money.

Or the nerve.

· · ·

A DOZEN OR SO MILES WEST OF AUSTIN, IN ONE OF THE WIDE, flat valleys that form the deep-sleep rhythm of Highway 50, there are signs on either side of the road. They are barn red wood, the letters cut in white; they are the sort of signs that history puts down for us to marvel at. Nevada is often generous with such things—they help to keep the spaceyness in place, maybe—and many of them are not exactly exciting. These two are different, for someone has had the simple yet bold idea to set them at angles. They make a diagonal that slants across the road, and they proclaim PONY EXPRESS TRAIL, 1861–68. You follow the line in either direction, and in that sweep, you cannot fail to entertain the notion of heroism.

Even now, this *is* called the Loneliest Road in America. Go back 130 years, strip out the road, allow that every now and then Shoshones might take a fancy to one of the valleys, and then hear the deliberate, undeterred rhythm of a lone Pony Express rider coming and going. Of course, they never used ponies, and I wonder at the gallop, even with the ideal set of relay stations where a rider stumbled off one exhausted mount and took over a fresh, patient horse amazed at its brother's fatigue.

Let us just say the Pony Express rode this way, and let us suppose that being alone was each rider's greatest hazard. Still, one could hardly suppose and digest that flourish of diagonal trail now without awe— the medium was once more extraordinary than messages—for all except those who trusted love letters to gallant men who could ride through such emptiness without opening up the letters and reading them for themselves.

I WAS DRIVING PAST WHEELER PEAK ONE APRIL DAY, GOING south on Route 93 toward Pioche. Wheeler then, all 13,063 feet of it, is on one's left. But that day, I could discern only the dark, suggestive lower slopes, so far apart that it was possible to surmise Wheeler's full reach. Everything about those first hints of incline was concealed in a dense jumble of brilliant clouds.

It was a cold day, with an unkind wind blowing. I stopped the car to see if I could make out any further details of mountain within the cloud. Nothing. But the parked car was swaying as I sat there, as if there were people in the back making strenuous love.

Something of the same metaphor could be applied to the clouds. A first take might have called them leaden or mercurial. But as I studied them more, I could see so many subtle hues in this huge bag of cumulus all over Wheeler—steel—the color of Persian cats, pewter and mauve. Like bruising. And these clouds were roiling and wrestling; one could see them move and maneuver.

And then, from within them, there appeared a vertical shaft of light that stood against the sideways lunging of the clouds. The shaft seemed to be running with liquid honey or gold. I felt I could see movement in its air. Was it rain there, rain lit up by a sun that had poked a hole in the darker cloud?

It did occur to me that, for some people, just as likely an explanation would be that some spacecraft or alien intervention was occurring there; after all, this is Wheeler Peak, a classically, momentously large mountain, the upthrust of soul—yet abrupt on that flat range all around—where a thing of significance might be expected to happen, if it had any self-respect.

I never gave this interpretation a glimmer of serious attention. Still, I sat there for several minutes, watching what was not just a lovely, provocative spectacle but one I had never seen before. Some kind of marvel was transpiring, even if it involved nothing more or less than light and weather on that uncommon day.

All I am saying is that in Nevada—and other wild places—the weather can be so strange as to verge on the wondrous, the supernatural, and the edge of fiction.

I HAD SEEN A TURN TO THE SOUTH INDICATING RAWHIDE, A departure from Highway 50, that loneliest road. Highway 50 that day was never free of traffic—there was always something jockeying behind me, waiting to overtake, so impatient or so anxious to be done with the loneliness. You have to guess that traffic on that road must have quadrupled or more since someone had the impudence, the big-city hubris, to put up those LONELIEST signs.

But a road *off* Highway 50, even a blacktop one—that is getting beyond loneliness and into the dull ache of philosophy. This spur headed off southward, a little uphill. It passed a farm on the left, and then there was nothing until the blacktop after twenty miles or so gave way to a well-maintained dirt road, which was wide, smooth, and free from awkward rocks.

There was an expanse of valley floor or playa ahead until the road swung to the right and I could see mining in the far distance. There was an escarpment tidily terraced with the levels of thrown-up earth. There were buildings. This was still Rawhide.

You can't say that name without wincing. It was a movie once (with Tyrone Power), set in the back of nowhere, with Rawhide a stage station. There was Clint Eastwood's TV series, with the "Raw-*hide!*" of Frankie Laine's song. Rawhide is so fake a name now, so camp, it might be set in neon above a gay bar on the outskirts of some military base. You can hardly say Rawhide without innuendo smothering the meaning.

Yet Rawhide is a mine still, people still toiling away in a place far from anywhere. And as I looked around at desolation and the spills of rubble that might be so valuable, an aircraft came directly over my head. My hair whipped up in the rush. I felt my parting bite deeper.

The aircraft was at perhaps one hundred feet, or two hundred, the height of a big building. But in the desert, if there are hills around like those near Rawhide, then those Fallon jets—just practicing—can come out of nowhere, ripping the air apart, and let you waver in the change of pressure. Fallon is only ten minutes away at their speed, and the flyboys test out their skill at hugging the ground. The plane dipped and rose on the turn and then vanished into a fold of hills, its shadow like a crazed kite dragged behind, trying to keep up.

PRAY FOR THE COWBOYS, LEST THEY TURN INTO POETS. Cowboys are like Rawhide these days; they hardly know whether they're wearing their own clothes or are dressed in costume. There are ranches in Nevada, near Elko, especially, working ranches still, though most of them are owned by rich men who live elsewhere and go to Nevada two or three times a year to "kick back." The cowboys have cell phones and the office is computerized, but the horses and the cattle are the real thing, and there are guys doing the job who want to be left alone with it. But nowadays they are pursued by magazine photographers and cigarette campaigns; they are asked if they have any poetry; and they get invitations to leave the ranch and be part of some dude cattle drive for guys from Marin and Malibu—twelve days on the range, under the stars, with USDA steaks, for $3,400. So the real cowboys, the last of them, get their boots and their hats to "look right." And the better they look, the worse they feel. And sometimes they think of getting work as truck drivers going over the long range at night, listening to Art Bell on the radio, alone in the big cab with all those wheels under them. And they grow a little more tight-lipped, in case they find themselves talking that poetry stuff.

Rodeo, Fallon

THERE ARE THOSE FOR WHOM ART BELL IS ALREADY A PRAYER against the night. And he may be the world's best-known living Nevadan (Andre Agassi is a possible rival, but he goes all over the place). "Coast-to-Coast A.M. with Art Bell" is a radio show that plays for five hours every night, a live call-in talk show, conducted by Bell from his modest studio in Pahrump, Nevada, that small town over the Spring Mountains from Las Vegas.* It is a show that plays on 390 American stations, and it has an

---

* People in Pahrump are vague about where Bell is—he likes to stay private. But it is somewhere up Homestead Road, beyond the two dainty brothels. In October 1998, Bell stopped doing his show for two weeks, for reasons never given. For a moment, his faithful suspected anything and everything. In fact, his sixteen-year-old son had been sexually solicited by a teacher.

audience of around 15 million. As it happens, the show fills out the daily menu from Jacor Communications, the company that also plays Rush Limbaugh and Dr. Laura Schlessinger—the one in the mornings, the other in the afternoons.

I have listened to both of them, driving across Nevada, and noted the rapport between Dr. Laura's serene yet fierce dismissal of feeble call-ins and the craggy upheaval of the Nevadan landscape. She does not pander to the pain people nurse; she seeks only to stop the damage their self-indulgence may cause. She is conservative, if you like, old-fashioned— she is also a very rapid, intuitive listener, who can gauge the mind and the life that is calling her and crunch its excuses, its second-guessing, its self-ishness. And her unequivocal commentary on taking responsibility accords with the innate violence and beauty of Nevada.

Art Bell may be as conservative as Dr. Laura. He says he is, and he has a tough, abrasive voice, the voice of a man who says he likes to keep to himself, to be a loner, despite the millions listening. But he broadcasts by night, when you can no longer see or feel the epic audience of the mountains or the emptiness. And Bell specializes in a mysteriousness permitted by the dark. He speaks increasingly of "a quickening," by which he means a kind of spiraling toward disaster in both world economy and terrestrial weather and a condition of readiness in which more and more of his listeners report having seen lights in the night sky, UFOs and aliens, spiritual manifestations, and the ultimate openness of "all we glorify really is the possibility that we as humans are more than we appear to be."

More or less, throughout the night and over the years, Bell's tough voice—it comes in amid the static like a pilot who has brought his plane over the Pacific—hints at an end to the world, some great whirling of economic disaster and meteorological outrage in which "they" emerge as our new shining masters. Yet I'm never quite sure whether Bell believes in this or has just cottoned to the great mounting but unending theme for night-time and Nevadan radio. He does play all over America, and to that extent he broadcasts a Nevadan attitude, a readiness, a state of mind, which—it seems to me—has had a real impact on America in the last ten years or so.

Whereas Dr. Laura knows we are exactly the wrecks that radio's imprint reveals: She is the fierce mistress of our sighs, our hesitations, and all the small, striking ways in which we lie to ourselves. Maybe she suits America better than Bell, but they are both important, and great voices, and extraordinary radio, if you want to negotiate the long roads of the state without passing into dream.

. . .

NEVADA DAY! DON'T BE TOO CAST DOWN IF YOU HAVE FOR-
gotten that October 31 is the date of Nevada's birth. I was able to be in
Carson City on that day in 1997, the 133rd anniversary of the state's admission to the union. It wasn't until 1891 that the idea arose of celebrating
Admission Day, and making an official state holiday out of it. The habit
set in, in Reno, until 1937, but in the following years, the Grand Birthday
Party was relocated to Carson City, the state capital.

I have not found the opportunity before to say much about Carson
City, which must be one of the smallest state capitals in the United States,
and most charming. Nevada Day in 1997 was a fine, clear fall day, with the
trees on Carson Street turning and little pockets of snow in the clefts of
the mountains that separate the town from Lake Tahoe. That main street,
a part of Highway 395, is still the spine of Carson City, a long, straight drag
with all the handsome state buildings, the Nugget Casino, the shops, and
the fast-food places mixed in together. There are lawns and an open
square outside the Nevada Supreme Court, and there is a fine equestrian
statue there of Kit Carson, looking up at the mountain with the white letter C there.

For three full and leisurely hours, a parade came down the main street,
a parade, for the most part, of ordinary, humdrum things and people,
yet done out of fondness and duty. After the overflight of four F/A-18s
from Fallon, there were three hours of high school marching bands, the
Nevada Highway Patrol, Governor Bob Miller and his wife in an open
car, Miss Nevada (Amanda Gunderson), many state officials, dogs for the
blind, mounted posses, agricultural machinery, the Sons and Daughters
of Erin, clowns, fire departments, an infant Miss Nevada (Dyllan Skye
Sapp), bike clubs, Girl Scouts, Boy Scouts, Kenny Guinn (who would be
running for governor the following year), rodeo associations, senior citizens, rottweiler owners, and tae kwan do students. Did I say marching
bands from high schools—all in their uniforms, passed down from one
generation to the next?

There were 241 entries in the parade, and the crowd lined the main
street all morning long, taking it all in, the ordinariness of northern
Nevada. I believe there is no such parade in Las Vegas. Yet here, everyone
had their Nevada Day lunch. And all the while the sun shone on the uniforms, the polished saxophones, the barbecue sauce in the roadside stalls,
and the lifelong tan of maybe forty thousand people who had come into

Carson City to watch, like the people of Wessex come into Casterbridge for the summer fair in a Hardy novel.

JOE WILLIAMS HAD SCHOOLED HIMSELF TO STAND THERE, upright and tall, without so much as a flicker of gesture or vanity, singing the blues. He believed above all in the purity and directness of his own voice, and he liked to turn it on so that it simply filled the hall and the imagination of those listening. He stood still so that his breathing might go as straight as possible to us. It is a way of singing that has to assume some treasury of song, out there, up there, in there, somewhere, that simply passes through the singer and is donated to the world. "Every day," he sang, "every day I have the blues." And the stress lay not just on the steadiness of the pain, but the loyalty with which he promised to sing.

And Joe Williams had elected to live in Las Vegas, though he still led the traveling life of a singer on the road. But in Seattle, a year earlier, he had been taken ill with asthma, or what was called a respiratory ailment. He thought it was the dampness in the northwestern air that might have brought it on. That's why he loved the dry of the desert.

But he was ill again, and he was eighty years old. And he had gone into the Sunrise Hospital on the Maryland Parkway, south of McCarran Airport, for treatment. Now Williams lived, with his wife, Jillean, about three miles away on the east side of Las Vegas. He had been a professional singer for decades with the Basie band and as a solo act. He had made records and many appearances on the *Tonight Show*. I say that just to stress that he lived on the east side, which is not necessarily the part of town where successes live.

On the Sunday, the last Sunday of March 1999, he told a friend who visited him at Sunrise that he was seeing spirits in his room—it was a private room. The next morning, early, his wife talked to him on the phone and he told her he wanted to get out of the hospital. She told him to be patient and said she would be by later.

No one knows exactly what happened, except that, quietly, without alerting or disturbing anyone, Joe Williams got up, got dressed, and walked out of the Sunrise Hospital. This was some time before noon. He was not well; he could not have made rapid progress. But he walked, in a northeastward direction, toward his home. It was a pleasant day, not too hot. There was the usual traffic, but no one stopped or noticed or reported an elderly black man, tall, with white hair, in evident distress. Perhaps Joe

Williams showed no distress but just looked toward the hills east of Las Vegas—Frenchman Mountain and Sunrise Mountain, modest peaks—and enjoyed the day and did his best to take deep breaths.

His body was reported around 3 p.m. by a resident. He had died just a few blocks from where he lived, and I see no reason why anyone should assume that anything with Joe Williams was less than under control and for the best. He liked the dry air. Don't we all?

I AM GOING NORTH AGAIN—THE WAY I BEGAN THIS BOOK. But farther this time, past Gerlach, all the way to the straight line of Nevada's northern border. It is the part of the state I love the most, the part I see when anyone says "Nevada." Yet time and again as I worked on this book, saying "Nevada" made most people answer "Las Vegas," as if that's all there was to it.

For myself, I am quite content to abide by southern Nevada, the spike driven into the Southwest, and the gathering of Las Vegas, Hoover Dam, Henderson, and even Laughlin. That is where the people and the power are, that is where the affairs of state are determined, and that is where business and progress test their flimsy hold on the ground. I like to be in Las Vegas—for a few days at a time; I see no point in disapproving of its gambling, when our world is caught up in so many larger games of hazard and chance.

Driving near Las Vegas

But I insist on the north—and not only Reno, Winnemucca, and Elko, smaller places that seem more secure than Las Vegas and which are as old and plain as the small cities to be found all over the West, places that have dug in and learned to put up with the hardship, the severity, the isolation, and the eternity of provincialism. No, I mean the north beyond those towns, the north that has only itself to offer, the land that has so few people, no power, and not even the long-shot chance of being "discovered." For even as I extol the place, and may tempt you, it is a long way to go to get within striking reach of it. And there are next to no comforts there, no facilities. Yet all the rest of the state, from Boundary Peak to Wheeler, all the way along Highway 50, all the way along I-80, and all there is north of that—from Jackpot to Jarbidge to McDermitt to Denio to the last bit of the northwest quarter, where there is not even one small place to name—is Nevada, too. And the emptiness is vital, even if it exists only as a warning or a signal to the bustling, expanding south.

I know: You can step out of the Luxor, say, and feel the closeness of the desert; that is part of the advertised Egyptian experience. But more than that, I relish the way in which some of the most fabulous, outrageous, and moderne gestures of Americana are loomed over by the silent emptiness of the sustaining state. Nevada is the north and the south; it is the greatest concentration of hotel rooms in the world and the expanses in which there is no bed to be found. And, in the end, the corridors of the Mirage, say, make an unexpected rhyming with those stretches of waiting highway in the north.

Not that the north of Nevada is, as they say, "staggeringly beautiful," so demandingly spectacular that tourists make a journey there for its own sake. There is nothing as exquisite as the Canyon de Chelly or as epic as the Grand Canyon. I have driven the Burr Trail in southern Utah, and that and many other places in that state are like savage stage sets or the perfect places for Western drama. Yellowstone is more awesome. The chocolate mesas of Wyoming and the greasy grass rolling prairies of Montana are more picturesque. California itself, as one might expect of the ideal catalog of narrative locations, has Carmel, Death Valley, Shasta, Yosemite, and the Sierra, which are all more gorgeous, more extreme, more more than northern Nevada.

I love all those places, but in hardly any of them is it possible to be alone. I was born and raised in England, where, sometimes, you feel the island is one traffic jam fidgeting its way here and there beneath overcast skies. I had not seen anything like desert until I came to live in California and a friend, Tom Luddy, offered to drive me from Las Vegas to Telluride,

Colorado. We went for the film festival there, and it was a good festival, but the landscape and its light meant more to me than being in the dark.

What I am about to say comes with very little scientific explanation, and I am shy about offering it as a therapeutic easing for others—after all, I do not want to find northern Nevada crowded. But I believe, for myself, that there is something beneficial, uplifting, and calming in being out and about in the sunlight and emptiness of that place. I know there are such things as "light therapy," and I know there is an odd tradition of depressed, or repressed, Englishmen—"mad dogs and Englishmen," remember?— finding themselves, or feeling better in the desert and its glowing silence. That's maybe why I prefer to be there alone, or with someone I can show the wonder to, a novice. And the being alone is a kind of modest gamble, too: You make sure your car is serviced; you have some water in the trunk; you never quite lose the thoughts of what you would do—once you had gone thirty or forty miles up the dirt road—if the car died. Would the light protect you, or burn away the very calm it had instilled?

So I am driving north, out of Winnemucca—you'd have to get there, or Boise, Idaho, really, before you could begin this journey by road.

I take Route 95 north out of Winnemucca, for I want to go to McDermitt first, on the Oregon border. It's a long, curving road north, seventy miles or so, with Paradise Valley—a farming enclave—off to the east, and Orovada the only town on the way, poised beneath Sawtooth Mountain in the Santa Rosa Range. McDermitt is not much more than a dot on the ground. In 1940, the district population was around 560; it can't be more today, even if there's the "Say When" Casino, its neon faded in the sunlight.

McDermitt is named after a Col. Charles McDermit, commander of the military outpost there, which was intended to guard settlers and travelers. But those buildings were turned over to the local Indians— Paiutes—in 1886, once a state of peace had been established. There's a supermarket, a filling station, and a few old "Western" buildings, but you can go through the town without changing gears or finishing a sentence. Then you're in Oregon, and it's another hundred miles or so to Boise. But as Boiseans I've known will admit, Boise ain't much.

I stop in McDermitt for coffee and a break, and read the local paper— the *Humboldt*; no other papers get here, it seems, and the TV reception out of Boise is pretty shaky, unless you've got a dish.

So I go back down Route 95 until I reach the Route 140 turnoff to the west. You wonder why such a road exists, for it goes a mighty long way from nowhere to nowhere. And if on the map it seems like the way to

Fountain statuary, The Forum, Caesars Palace—is this

Denio, when you get to Denio, there seems to have been no reason for coming.

But Route 140 is near enough ninety miles, looping west and then northwest to Denio. Before you come to the turnoff, you see the road like a ruler through the scrub and the sage, monotonously straight ahead, a place to test your car's power. And it's a well-made road, all the way, with dirt roads off it to the west, one of which could take you to Summit Lake and the ruins of Camp McGarry—a fort that lasted from 1867 to 1871. Summit Lake is not just lovely; it's surreal and haunting—Why a lake

Heaven or Hell, if you have the gangster turn of mind?

with nothing else? you wonder. More than fifty years ago, an old Paiute or Shoshone told the writer of a guidebook, "Summit Lake much better to sit. There can sit long time, can see very far." And the idea has lasted that the Indians went there sometimes just because of the desolation.

It turns out to be a special day, I mean in terms of light, and as the afternoon sun drops—it is mid-September, and ninety degrees—I see the secret color in the Nevada landscape. Here and there, I'm sure, I have called it gray, purple, slate, and mauve. And all those colors, and more, are there. But there is another color that appears only in certain light, and seems to be drawn up to the surface by a low sun, as if it were moisture, feeling, or the kind of primer wash that painters use.

You could call it grass, khaki, gold, or dun, but this day I see, without question, that it is the color of a lion's skin—not the mane, but that skin drawn tight over the ribs and the stomach. It is a dry color, ocher and sage and dunglike, yet glowing, as if you could feel the heart pulsing within the lion's body. It is a color that holds back until the end of the day, and I have never seen it elsewhere.

Route 140 heads due north nearly, but just a few miles short of Denio it turns off to the west again. You can go on and see Denio, on the Oregon line again, with one bar—the Diamond—that has a few slot machines and a low ceiling papered with money. Then it's back on Route 140, going west and seeming to climb.

But first you pass one of those small, wondrous Nevada lakes—Continental Lake—maybe three miles long and a mile and a half across. It has a pink, pearly sheen to it—why not? opal is sometimes mined in the area—and it is large enough to hold the full mountain range nearby upside down on its smooth surface.

The road climbs, and you begin to see the mountains flatten off into buttes or mesas, browner than that lion's color. We are in the Sheldon National Wildlife Refuge by now, a place where you may see antelope, wild mules, and even wild horses sometimes. The next town down the road is Lakeview, Oregon, and that is another sixty miles away.

There is no one on the road as I pass Big Spring Butte to the north, and I can see the sliver of the small reservoir beneath it. We are in the Sage Hen Hills, and the actual border with Oregon comes next at around six thousand feet. But I will go on a little farther, just a few miles, keeping the spirit of Nevada until I reach the place where the land suddenly drops off. I do admit this is a place in Oregon, but you cannot resist the natural boundary, the sense of the great plateau, with the lowlands beyond.

It is still warm at five o'clock, still bright, and the road is so good, you could think that the emptiness was abandonment, that everything else is over—for the day at least. I use binoculars to look down on the parchment of Oregon spread out below, and I can see no life or movement. There are no places there, and if there are a few farms, there is no sign of life or work on them.

This is the only major road coming across Nevada's border without a casino of some sort within three or four miles. The state tries to make its big gift available as soon as possible. Here, there would be no point. There are no people who live here who need to keep in touch with luck. Sometimes gliders use the place to launch out into the spirals, but there is no one here this day.

In Oregon, I am on the edge of Nevada, the most natural, precipitate brink, with a view that is as close to primeval as any you will find in America. But the wind and the air are modern, as well as the tawny hue in the ground. The wind eases and the prickly silence of Nevada comes in on me like an embrace. I can hear myself breathing, hear my heart.

And then from out there, over the crumpled plain of Oregon, looking north, there comes the gong and thud of a sonic boom as some aircraft breaks the sound barrier. The plane is too fast to see. But the sound is slow, grand, and sad, like a tree falling, or a cello string bursting—sound unheard by anyone else, maybe. But I am here to hear it and I cannot tell whether—as an omen—it means beginning or end.

But things change. Between hardcover and paperback, Steve Wynn found himself overextended. All the new rooms, all at once, did not sell, and in March 2000 Mirage Enterprises was bought out by Kirk Kerkorian and MGM. At about the same time, Art Bell announced his retirement. I doubt that Wynn and Bell can stay quiet for long, but one spring showed again the short distance between empire and ghost town.

Postscript

The entire history of Nevada is one of plant life, animal life, and human life adapting to very difficult conditions. People here are the most individualistic you can find. . . . They want to live free from government interference. They don't fit into a structured way of life. This area was settled by people who shun progress. Their way of life would be totally unattractive to most, but they chose it. They have chosen conditions that would be considered intolerable elsewhere.

—quoted in John McPhee, *Basin and Range*, 1980

Vision is the art of seeing things invisible.

—motto on the desk of Steve Wynn

NOTES AND
RECOMMENDED READING

P. vii "People living east": quoted in *Snowshoe Thompson* (Carson City, Nevada: Carson Valley Historical Society, 1991), p. 5.

vii "Insert key": part of check-in package, Bellagio Hotel, Las Vegas, February 1999.

1 "It reads like": Mark Twain, *Roughing It* (New York: Penguin, 1981), pp. 298–299.

7 "a sheet of green water": Captain J. C. Frémont, *Report of the Exploring Expedition to the Rocky Mountains in the Year 1842, and to Oregon and North California in the Years 1843–44* (Washington D.C., 1845); see also, George Wharton James, *Lake of the Sky: Lake Tahoe* (Silverton, Colorado: Vista Books, 1996).

11 "Frémont's habits and impulses": Allan Nevins, *Frémont: Pathmaker of the West* (Lincoln: University of Nebraska Press, 1939), p. 613.

11 "sweet as a perfumed breeze": ibid., p. 16.

12 "to overspread the continent": *The Trailblazers* (Alexandria, Va.: Time-Life, 1973), p. 158.

12 "Whither thou goest": ibid., p. 70.

14 "In the sight of": Frémont, *Report of the Exploring Expedition*, p. 21.

15 "Only trust me": Jessie Frémont, "The Origin of the Frémont Exploration," *Century Magazine*, vol. XIX, 1890–1891, p. 768.

20 census figures: see Russell R. Elliott (with the assistance of William D. Rowley), *History of Nevada*, 2d ed. (Lincoln: University of Nebraska Press, 1987), pp. 404–405.

21 "if He'd had the money": Steve Wynn, on *The Charlie Rose Show*, May 20, 1997.

28 Spirit Cave Man: see *Nevada Historical Society Quarterly*, Spring 1997, including S. M. Wheeler, "Cave Burials Near Fallon, Nevada," and Donald R. Tuohy and Amy Dansie, "Papers on Holocene Burial Localities Presented at the Twenty-fifth Great Basin Anthropological Conference, October 10–12, 1996."

30 "They don't need": Maurice Eben quoted in David Brown, "The Secrets of Spirit Cave," *Washington Post Weekly*, May 13–19, 1996; see also Carey Goldberg, "Oldest Mummy in North America 'Found,' " *New York Times*, April 27, 1996.

33 voting figures: *Reno Gazette-Journal*, November 7, 1996, and Electoral Division, Clark County.

34 prisons: information from the Nevada Department of Prisons, Administrative Office, Carson City, January 15, 1999.

35 "We found the state": Twain, *Roughing It*, p. 180.

35 "So everybody said": ibid., p. 346.

35 "it captivates and": James Nye, address to First Territorial Legislature, October 2, 1861; see Elliott, *History of Nevada*, 2d ed., p. 72.

36   "the jury system": Twain, *Roughing It*, p. 349.
39   "I did the best": Greg Logan, "Boxing Gets Another Black Eye," *San Francisco Examiner*, July 13, 1997.
40   Marc Ratner: conversation with the author, August 11, 1998.
41   boxing: see *The Gamblers* (Alexandria, Virginia: Time-Life, 1978), pp. 217–231.
44   "Welcome to Nowhere": *Black Rock Gazette*, September 3, 1993; also see Raymond M. Smith, *Nevada's Northwest Corner* (Minden, Nevada: Silver State Printing 1996), p. 82.
45   "Anything lacking meaning": Kevin Kelly, "Bonfire of the Techies," *Time*, April 25, 1997, p. 62.
46   "The Festival represents": Tim Hill, letter, *San Francisco Chronicle*, September 9, 1997.
46   "Burning Man is a boil": *Time*, September 15, 1997.
47   "Some may try": Smith, *Nevada's Northwest Corner*, p. 138.
50   "Good-bye, God": see David W. Toll, *The Complete Nevada Traveler* (Virginia City, Nevada: Gold Hill Publishing, 1996), p. 163.
54   "So the hills are": Walter Van Tilburg Clark, *City of Trembling Leaves* (New York: Random House, 1945), p. 552.
54   "On both sides": Arthur Miller, *The Misfits* (New York: Viking, 1961), p. 28.
57   *USA Today*: March 31, 1997.
61   education: see *Reno Gazette-Journal*, September 15 and 16, 1998.
65   "Sure, he's the most fascinating": Tommy Dorsey quoted in Kitty Kelley, *His Way*, (New York: Bantam, 1986), p. 64.
66   "To say that": Nancy Sinatra, *Frank Sinatra, My Father* (New York: Doubleday, 1985), pp. 164–166.
68   "You just try and": Kelley, *His Way*, p. 322.
70   anthrax bacteria: see Todd S. Purdom, "2 Men Accused of Possessing a Biological Toxin in Nevada," *New York Times*, February 20, 1998, and "Tests Indicate Seized Material Is Nonlethal Form of Anthrax," *New York Times*, February 22, 1998.
76   land-speed record: see Warren E. Leary, "Teams Duel in Nevada Desert Over Land Speed Record," *New York Times*, September 9, 1997; October 14, 1997; October 29, 1997.
79   "Amy wrote this": Donald R. Tuohy and Amy Dansie, "A Modern-Day Inquisition by the Pyramid Lake Paiutes," *Nevada State Museum Newsletter*, March–April 1998, p. 4.
83   deal: Alan Truscott, "Bridge," *New York Times*, May 10, 1998.
86   Manly Party: see Leroy and Jean Johnson, *Escape from Death Valley* (Reno: University of Nevada Press, 1987).
87   Rachel: see Glenn Campbell, *Area 51 Viewer's Guide*, ed. 4.01 (Rachel, Nevada: Glenn Campbell, 1995); David Darlington, *Area 51: The Dreamland Chronicles* (New York: Henry Holt, 1997); and Phil Patton, *Dreamland* (New York: Villard, 1998).
89   "not an alien, but": Tessa Souter, "A Town Like Rachel," *Independent on Sunday*, June 2, 1996.
89   Extra-Terrestrial Highway: see Darlington, *Area 51*, pp. 242–253.
92   Little A'Le'Inn: see Campbell, *Area 51 Viewer's Guide*, pp. 47–48, and Chuck Clark, *The Area 51 & S-4 Handbook* (Rachel, Nevada: Chuck Clark, 1997).
95   "I'm not into": Darlington, *Area 51*, p. 20.
96   "Because I hate you": Campbell, *Area 51 Viewer's Guide*, p. 48.
96   "If anyone knows": ibid., p. 35.
97   "UFOs may originate": Clark, *The Area 51 & S-4 Handbook*, p. 63.

102 Caliente hearing: see Darlington, *Area 51*, p. 113.

103 Cashman Field Center hearing: see ibid., p. 114.

106 "Manhattan Public Library": author's conversation with Linda Hansen, July 14, 1998.

109 Sherrice Iverson case: see Cathy Scott, "Teen Charged in Slaying," *Las Vegas Sun*, May 29, 1997, and Cathy Booth, "The Bad Samaritan," *Time*, September 7, 1998.

109 "whether or not to bring": Barney Vinson, *Casino Secrets* (Las Vegas: Huntington Press, 1997), p. 134.

115 Tahoe depth: see Glen Martin, "Virtual Flight Under Lake Tahoe," *San Francisco Chronicle*, August 13, 1998.

116 "often as we lay": Twain, *Roughing It*, pp. 192–193.

121 "three months of": ibid., p. 188.

122 *Rose Marie*: see David Stollery, Jr., *Tales of Tahoe: Lake Tahoe History, Legend and Description* (1969).

122 "Tahoe is a lake": *The WPA Guide to 1930s Nevada* (Reno: University of Nevada Press, 1940), p. 195.

123 George Wingfield: see C. Elizabeth Raymond, *George Wingfield: Owner and Operator of Nevada* (Reno: University of Nevada Press, 1992).

128 mineral production: see Elliott, *History of Nevada*, 2d ed., pp. 406–407.

128 "I can prove": Raymond, *George Wingfield*, p. 91, and *San Francisco Call*, February 5, 1909.

131 Tahoe residents and visitors: See *Sunset*, June 1978; Carla Marinucci, "Clinton to Tahoe's Aid," *San Francisco Examiner*, June 27, 1997; and information from Tahoe Regional Planning Agency, June 15, 1998.

131 "There cannot be . . .": Marinucci, "Clinton to Tahoe's Aid."

133 "You can see": *Sunset*, June 1978.

134 "exactly what we need": Marinucci, "Clinton to Tahoe's Aid."

136 Donner Party: see George B. Stewart, *Ordeal by Hunger: The Story of the Donner Party* (Boston: Houghton Mifflin, 1936).

139 "Most fortunately": Elliott, *History of Nevada*, 2d ed., p. 274.

145 "Women with money": *The WPA Guide to 1930s Nevada*, p. 145.

150 Wardell Gray: see Bill Moody, *Death of a Tenor Man* (New York: Walker, 1995); and Earnest N. Bracey, "The Moulin Rouge Mystique: Blacks and Equal Rights in Las Vegas," *Nevada Historical Society Quarterly*, Winter 1996, pp. 272–288.

153 "A piece of wilderness": Richard Misrach, with Myriam Weisang Misrach, *Bravo 20: The Bombing of the American West* (Baltimore: Johns Hopkins University Press, 1990), p. 47.

154 "The landscape boasted": ibid., p. xiv.

157 "The end of night": Miller, *The Misfits*, p. 43.

161 Gass: see Stanley W. Paher, *Las Vegas: As It Began—As It Grew* (Las Vegas: Nevada Publications, 1971), pp. 37–43.

165 Brenda (the name may vary): Department of Energy, Nevada Operations Office, PO Box 98518, Las Vegas, NV 89193 (tel: 702-295-0944).

168 atom bombs: see Richard Rhodes, *The Making of the Atomic Bomb* (New York: Simon and Schuster, 1986).

172 auction: see Paher, *Las Vegas*, pp. 65–104 (with exceptional archival photographs).

174 "The promoters": ibid., p. 77.

179 "What regrets": Luis Alvarez, *Alvarez* (New York: Basic Books, 1987), p. 8.

180 "Killing Japanese": Curtis LeMay Papers, Library of Congress, Box 200 (quoted in Richard Rhodes, *Dark Sun: The Making of the Hydrogen Bomb* [New York: Simon and Schuster, 1995], pp. 21–22).

182 conference: see Elliott, *History of Nevada*, 2d ed., pp. 275–276.

182 "a steep, narrow gap": Edmund Wilson, *The American Earthquake* (New York: Farrar, Straus and Giroux, 1958), p. 368.

184 ". . . the men at the river": ibid., p. 370.

184 Hoover Dam: U.S. Department of the Interior, "Hoover Dam," leaflet for tourists (1993).

193 Eniwetok and Bikini: see Rhodes, *Dark Sun*, passim.

193 USS *Nevada:* see Brig. Gen. David C. Henley, *Battleship Nevada* (Fallon, Nevada: Western Military History Association, 1988).

195 "Boulder Dam is to": Richard G. Lillard, *Desert Challenge: An Interpretation of Nevada* (Lincoln: University of Nebraska Press, 1942), p. 120.

196 "I see no elements": ibid., pp. 42–43.

197 "Nevada, 'tis of thee": ibid., p. 40.

198 Tony Cornero: see Bruce Henstell, *Sunshine and Wealth: Los Angeles in the Twenties and Thirties* (San Francisco: Chronicle Books, 1984), pp. 60–62, 66–71.

204 "(1) To periodically proof-test": U.S. Department of Energy, handout, June 1991.

207 Ben Siegel: see John L. Smith, "The Ghost of Ben Siegel," in *The Players*, ed. Jack Sheehan (Reno: University of Nevada Press, 1997), pp. 81–91; Dean Jennings, *We Only Kill Each Other* (Greenwich, Connecticut: Fawcett, 1967); *Bugsy* (1991), the movie directed by Barry Levinson and written by James Toback.

216 cat at Los Alamos: see Rhodes, *The Making of the Atomic Bomb*, p. 569.

216 "It bored its way": I. I. Rabi, *Science: The Centre of Culture* (New York: World, 1970), p. 138.

216 "It was like opening": Philip Morrison, quoted in Studs Terkel, ed., *The Good War* (New York: Pantheon, 1984), p. 512.

216 "It was a chill": Rabi, *Science*, p. 138.

218 "the largest airport . . .": in Morrison, *The Good War*, p. 177.

218 *Enola Gay:* see Rhodes, *The Making of the Atomic Bomb*, pp. 705–709.

218 "could not understand": Yoka Ota, quoted in Robert Jay Lifton, *Death in Life* (New York: Random House, 1967), p. 23.

218 "The atom bomb . . .": Charlton Heston, letter, *Los Angeles Times Book Review*, August 16, 1998.

221 gambling statistics: see Elliott, *History of Nevada*, 2d ed., pp. 408–409.

223 Estes Kefauver: ibid., p. 329; Smith, "The Ghost of Ben Siegel," pp. 36–37.

223 cocksucking: see Smith, "The Ghost of Ben Siegel," p. 85.

223 "Well, Senator": ibid., p. 37.

223 "There were some people": ibid., p. 5.

224 "It isn't a very": Jerome F. Edwards, *Pat McCarran: Political Boss of Nevada* (Reno: University of Nevada Press, 1982), pp. 154–155.

226 "[They] began to notice": see Lifton, *Death in Life*, p. 57.

226 "Yes, there is radiation": William Wallace White, *Caring for the Environment: My Work with Public Health and Reclamation in Nevada* (Reno: University of Nevada Oral History Project), p. 212.

231 Dean Martin: see Nick Tosches, *Dino: Living High in the Dim Business of Dreams* (New York: Doubleday, 1992).

232 Dietrich: see Steven Bach, *Marlene Dietrich: Life and Legend* (New York: William Morrow, 1992), pp. 367–369; Maria Riva, *Marlene Dietrich* (New York: Knopf, 1993), pp. 634, 636–637.

233 "This is a fabulous madhouse": Cole Lesley, *Remembered Laughter: The Life of Noel Coward* (New York: Knopf, 1976), pp. 340–341.

235 gambling figures: see Elliott, *History of Nevada*, 2d ed., pp. 408–409.

236 "I can't tell you": Kelley, *His Way*, p. 219.

243 Castle Bravo test: see Rhodes, *Dark Sun*, pp. 541–543.

247 Howard Robard Hughes: see Sergio Lalli, "Howard Hughes in Vegas," in *The Players*; Donald L. Barlett and James B. Steele, *Empire: The Life, Legend and Madness of Howard Hughes* (New York: Norton, 1979).

248 gambling figures: see Elliott, *History of Nevada*, 2d ed., pp. 408–409.

251 "It just does not seem": Barlett and Steele, *Empire*, p. 344.

254 "Everybody in the dorm": "Darlene Phillips," in Carole Gallagher, *American Ground Zero: The Secret Nuclear War* (New York: Random House, 1993), p. 274.

255 "The explosion": "Robert Carter," in ibid., p. 57.

256 "From time to time": Howard Ball, "Downwind from the Bomb," *New York Times Magazine*, February 9, 1986.

257 "There isn't anyone": Gallagher, *American Ground Zero*, p. xxv.

257 "I consider": "John Gofman," in ibid., p. 302.

258 "General Butler": see R. Jeffrey Smith, "A Believer No More," *Washington Post Weekly*, December 22–29, 1997; see also David Hoffman, "Walking a Nuclear Tightrope," *Washington Post Weekly*, March 30, 1998.

259 Steve Wynn: *The Charlie Rose Show*, May 20, 1997; Jon Christensen, "The Greening of Gambling's Golden Boy," *New York Times*, July 6, 1997; Doreen Carvajal, "Defamation Suit Leaves Small Publisher Near Extinction," *New York Times*, October 8, 1997.

268 Yucca Mountain: Thomas W. Lippman, "At Hanford's Nuclear Graveyard, A Nightmare of Endless Potential," *Washington Post Weekly*, December 9–15, 1991; Michael Hythe and Bernadette Tansey, "Nuclear Rods Won't Sneak Past Public," *San Francisco Chronicle*, July 6, 1998; Matthew I. Wald, "New Mexico Site Is Approved for Storage of Nuclear Waste," *New York Times*, May 14, 1998; Wald, "Doubt Cast on Prime Site as Nuclear Waste Dump," *New York Times*, June 20, 1997; Wald, "Plan to Bury Waste in Nevada Moves Forward," *New York Times*, December 19, 1998.

273 two stories: Judith Miller, "At Bleak Asian Site, Killer Germs Survive," *New York Times*, June 2, 1999; Matthew L. Wald, "Step in Storage of Atom Waste Is Costly Error," *New York Times*, June 2, 1999.

275 "His smile disappeared": Hunter S. Thompson, *Fear and Loathing in Las Vegas* (New York: Random House, 1971), p. 96.

275 "Nevada is ten thousand": Lillard, *Desert Challenge*, p. 3.

277 "It's a fairly remote": Steven Lee Myers, "12 Airmen Die As Two Copters Crash in Dark While Training," *New York Times*, September 5, 1998.

279 population: see Elliott, *History of Nevada*, 2d ed., pp. 404–405; U.S. Census, 1990; Michael McCabe, "Rural Nevada Has Growing Pains," *San Francisco Chronicle*, February 19, 1991.

284 gambling: Brett Pulley, "Casinos Paying Top Dollar to Coddle Elite Gamblers," *New York Times*, January 12, 1998.

285 suicide: see Sandra Blakeslee, "Suicide Rate Is Higher in 3 Gambling Cities," *New York Times*, December 16, 1997.

287 "Las Vegas today": Otto Friedrich, *City of Nets* (New York: Harper & Row, 1986), p. 289.

287 "The Circus-Circus": Thompson, *Fear and Loathing in Las Vegas*, p. 46.

288 "Head on up": Timothy Foote, *New York Times Book Review*, September 6, 1988.

290 water: see Timothy Egan, "Where Water Is Power, the Balance Shifts," *New York Times*, November 30, 1997; Robert Reinhold, "Battle Lines Drawn in Sand: Las Vegas Seeks New Water," *New York Times*, April 23, 1991; Robert Macy, "Chemi-

cals May Prove Harmful to Vegas Water," *Reno Gazette-Journal*, November 1, 1997.

297 Nevada Day: *Reno Gazette-Journal*, October 31, 1997, and November 1, 1997.

298 Joe Williams: Ed Koch, "Jazz Great Williams Dies at 80," *Las Vegas Sun*, March 30, 1999.

307 John McPhee, *Basin and Range* (New York: Farrar, Straus and Giroux, 1981), p. 215.

INDEX